STUDIES IN NEO-ARAMAIC

HARVARD SEMITIC MUSEUM
HARVARD SEMITIC STUDIES

Frank Moore Cross, editor

STUDIES IN NEO-ARAMAIC

edited by
Wolfhart Heinrichs

Scholars Press
Atlanta, Georgia

PJ
5281
.S78
1989

STUDIES IN NEO-ARAMAIC

edited by
Wolfhart Heinrichs

Library of Congress Cataloging in Publication Data

Studies in Neo-Aramaic / edited by Wolfhart Heinrichs.
  p. cm. -- (Harvard Semitic studies)
    Includes bibliographical references.
    ISBN 1-55540-430-8 (alk. paper)
    1. Aramaic language. 2. Syriac language, Modern. I. Heinrichs,
Wolfhart. II. Series.
PJ5281.S78 1989
492'.29--dc20   89-24386
                                   CIP

Printed in the United States of America
on acid-free paper

Studies in Neo-Aramaic

Printed with the support of
the David B. Perley Assyrian Memorial Fund

Table of Contents

VI. Philological and Literary Studies

Foreword

The David B. Perley Assyrian Memorial Fund

The history and culture of minorities does not lend itself to study easily. This is particularly true when a minority has suffered persecution and dispersal away from its traditional geographic base. Such is the problem faced by Assyrians or those Middle Easterners whose liturgical or present-day language is Aramaic and who adhere to the tradition of a separate Assyrian identity.

Having been uprooted by war and persecution from villages and towns in Ottoman and Iranian areas, many Assyrians made their way to the United States where circumstances allowed for social and political security but where community maintenance proved difficult. The retrieval of history and culture emerged as a concern of the community after the initial period of readjustment. But scattered or lost resources have hampered efforts in the past by community members and outside scholars to fill the gap in knowledge, particularly in the medieval and pre-modern history of the community.

It is to this end that the David B. Perley Assyrian Memorial Fund was established in 1979. Specifically, the Fund is intended to help in the preservation of Assyrian culture and history by identifying and collecting archival materials for placement at Harvard University and by helping to finance the publication of scholarly works about the community.

The man for whom the Fund is named was born in Harput, Turkey, into an educated family of town priests belonging to the Syrian Orthodox Church (Jacobites). He left Turkey in 1918 and journeyed to the United States, where he studied, worked and lived in Massachusetts and New York. David Perley took much time from his law practice to serve the Assyrian organizatons that began to be established in this country. He also wrote widely on the Assyrians and had a particular interest in history. The Assyrian community worldwide has honored David B. Perley during his lifetime in many ways. At his death on July 14, 1979, his wife Elinor, his daughter Penna Redvanley, and friends and members of the community established this Fund.

The committee that administers the Fund at Harvard University and the Assyrian community are pleased to offer this volume as the first in a series devoted to furthering the goals of the David B. Perley Assyrian Memorial Fund.

Eden Naby

Introduction
Wolfhart Heinrichs

In recent years the study of the various Neo-Aramaic languages and dialects has gained an unmistakable momentum and moved towards defining itself as an autonomous field of study. In 1984 the first international panel exclusively devoted to this field was convened on the occasion of the Eighteenth Annual Meeting of the Middle East Studies Association (MESA) in San Francisco. This was followed by a similar panel in 1985 at the MESA meeting in New Orleans and a third such gathering at the 1988 MESA meeting in Los Angeles. At the first meeting it was decided that an annual newsletter with information about ongoing research in the field was a desideratum, and Otto Jastrow of the University of Erlangen-Nürnberg, West Germany, kindly volunteered to undertake the task of compiling, editing, and distributing such a newsletter. Four issues have been sent out since 1985. The mailing list is strictly limited to scholars working in the field. The present volume is another sign of this renewed spirit of collaboration among scholars in the field, and it is hoped that it will attract other scholars—whether they be Semitists, general linguists, or anthropologists with an interest in language— to do research in this fascinating area which still holds the promise of new discoveries of totally unknown and unexpected dialects, some dead, some alive and many unfortunately moribund.

There is no doubt that for many of the Neo-Aramaic languages and dialects the prognosis is rather bad. Some are clearly on the brink of extinction, others may vanish before coming to the attention of the scholarly world. Even some of those that can still boast of a fairly sizable number of speakers today are severely threatened. The main reason is an ever-increasing emigration of those who speak them from their traditional homelands to the large cities in the Middle East and beyond to Europe and America where a gradual assimilation to their host nations takes place. Extensive fieldwork—the sooner the better—is thus of the utmost urgency. The diaspora situation has some advantages in this respect because, due to the political difficulties of doing research on minorities in Turkey, Iran and the Arab countries, the researcher will find easier access to data on imperfectly known varieties of Neo-Aramaic in his backyard—provided his backyard is in Chicago,

Jerusalem, Södertälje (Sweden) or any other place where there is a high concentration of speakers of Neo-Aramaic.

An Overview of the Linguistic Situation

Since for many readers—even those who can claim expertise in some other area of Semitic studies—the world of Neo-Aramaic will be mostly terra incognita, it will not be deemed amiss to include here a general outline of the linguistic situation. The term "Neo-Aramaic," rather than denoting a homogeneous language, covers any and all of the contemporary offsprings of the ancient Aramaic language. To recapitulate briefly the well-known facts: Aramaic had started in the ninth century BC as the local language of small kingdoms in northern Syria and Mesopotamia, became a standardized administrative and international language in the Persian Empire of the Achaemenids (Imperial Aramaic), and gradually supplanted Akkadian and the Canaanite languages (Hebrew and Phoenician) as spoken languages, the Fertile Crescent thus becoming uniformly Aramaic. At the same time it had to yield to Greek as the language of high culture (though not completely), but it came back at the beginning of our era as the official language—with some dialectal variety—of a number of small short-lived pagan kingdoms (Palmyra, Hatra, Petra [Nabataeans], Edessa, the latter soon to become the first Christian state in the world). The Fertile Crescent, in the centuries up to the Islamic conquest, was mostly divided between the Roman, then Byzantine Empire in the west and the Parthian, then Sasanian Empire in the east. No longer an official state language, Aramaic became the medium in which the various religious groups in the area expressed themselves: the Jews (who had used Aramaic continuously since the days of Imperial Aramaic), the Samaritans, the Christians, the Mandaeans and presumably also the Harranians (Sabians) and the Manichaeans each developed their own variety of written Aramaic in a distinctive script. Due to the geographic and political situation two main varieties of Aramaic evolved, a western and an eastern one, each with a cluster of written dialects: Jewish-Palestinian, Christian-Palestinian, and Samaritan in the west; Jewish-Babylonian (Babylonian-Talmudic), Christian-Mesopotamian (Syriac), and Mandaean in the east. With the Islamic conquest and subsequent Arabization of large parts of the population, the contiguous Aramaic language area dissolved into ever smaller fragments which developed independently of each other. The major varieties of Neo-Aramaic resulting from this process are mutually unintelligible and have to be considered separate languages (here in the sense of dialect clusters; for language in the sense of a written code, see below). Charted out on a map of the Middle East, the Neo-Aramaic languages would appear as an archipelago of islands, large and small, roughly between Lake Van and Lake Urmia in the north and the cities of Damascus and Ahvaz in the south. The situation resembles that of Berber (cf. Lionel Galand, "La langue berbère existe-t-elle?" in *Mélanges linguistiques offerts à Maxime Rodinson*, ed. Christian Robin [Paris: Geuthner 1985], pp. 175-184) and even more closely that of Frisian in Holland and northern Germany. In both cases we have a series of islands of various sizes within a "sea" formed by another language, Arabic in one case, Low German (including Dutch) in the other, and we have a name that seems to refer to one homogeneous language.

The present state of research into Neo-Aramaic allows us to distinguish four major dialect groups:

1. Western Neo-Aramaic.

This is spoken about 60 km to the northeast of Damascus in a group of three villages, Ma'lūla, Bakh'a, and Jubb 'Adīn, each of which has its own dialect (see W. Arnold's contribution to the present volume). Since Ma'lūla is the largest and most important of these places, the language is sometimes called Ma'lūla Aramaic. The speakers number several thousand, all of them bilingual in Aramaic and Arabic. The inhabitants of Bakh'a and Jubb 'Adīn are Muslims (since the eighteenth century), as is a large portion of the people of Ma'lūla, while the rest have remained Christian, mostly of Melkite (Greek Catholic) persuasion. The retention of the "Christian" language after conversion to Islam is noteworthy. Ma'lūla Aramaic is the only remnant, small but vigorous, of the western branch of Aramaic; the remaining dialect groups belong historically to the eastern branch.

For more information cf. Spitaler 1938* and Correll 1978.

2. Central Neo-Aramaic. This has two subgroups: Ṭūrōyo and Mlaḥsô.

a. Ṭūrōyo.

This is spoken in the town of Midyat and a number of villages in the Ṭūr 'Abdīn region of Mardin province, southeast Turkey, whence its name. Due to large-scale emigration triggered by political and economic pressures during the last twenty years, the Ṭūrōyo population of the area has been seriously depleted, and the previous sentence should probably be put in the past tense. Large groups have settled in West Germany and Sweden. The total number of speakers is probably between 15,000 and 20,000; most of them are multilingual, also speaking Kurdish and Anatolian Arabic (and, of course, the official language of the state, Turkish). All speakers are Christians and, although Catholic and Protestant missionaries have made some inroads since the last century, they remain predominantly Jacobite (Syrian-Orthodox). The main dialect split is between the town dialect of Midyat and the village dialects. An attempt to write Ṭūrōyo with Syriac letters was made in the 1880s with the encourgement of the American mission in Mardin (see editor's contribution to the present volume), but seems to have been of little consequence. More recently, the Swedish government has commissioned

---

*References are to G. Krotkoff's bibliography in this volume.

teaching materials in Ṭūrōyo for elementary schools, pursuant to a law that requires every child to be taught in its mother tongue. For this purpose a written form of Ṭūrōyo was developed by Y. Ishaq and his team (see his contribution to this volume), based on an artificial mixed town-village dialect and using a modified Latin alphabet with diacritics. A primer, several workbooks and reading books as well as a Swedish-Ṭūrōyo dictionary have been published so far. There is strong opposition to this undertaking on the part of the Jacobite church hierarchy with its disdain for the "vulgar" language, so the success of this written form of Ṭūrōyo cannot be predicted yet. In cultural journals one sometimes finds Ṭūrōyo texts, often poems, written in Syriac script.

For more information cf. Jastrow 1967 and Ritter 1967.

   b. Mlaḥsô.

This was spoken in a village of the same name not far from the town of Lice in Diyarbakır province more than a hundred km to the northwest of Midyat. The village was destroyed during the Armenian massacres. About twenty years ago O. Jastrow discovered a handful of survivors and made some tape recordings on which he based an article (Jastrow 1985) containing the only information available on this dialect. The people of Mlaḥsô were mainly Jacobites; they were multilingual and spoke Armenian, Kurdish, and Zaza as well. Their own dialect which is clearly related to Ṭūrōyo, but sufficiently different to warrant separate classification, must probably be considered extinct today.

   3. **Eastern Neo-Aramaic** (also called Northeastern Neo-Aramaic to distinguish it from no. 4 below).

This is the largest and most varied dialect group of Neo-Aramaic, probably numbering several hundred thousand speakers altogether. Further research is needed before a definitive dialectal division can be given. The main dichotomy may be between Jewish and Christian dialects. One should note that the phenomenon of communal dialects is very prominent, that is to say that in places where both Christian and Jewish speakers of Aramaic were present, such as Zakho, Urmia, and Sanandaj (to name but a few important ones), their dialects were different from each other, sometimes extremely so.

   a. Jewish dialects.

These were spoken in a number of towns in Turkish Kurdistan (Cizre, Van, Başkale and others), Iraqi Kurdistan (with Zakho as its main center), Persian Azerbaijan (with Salamas and Urmia) and Persian Kurdistan (with Saqqez and Sanandaj for larger places and Karand as its southernmost outpost). Jewish Neo-Aramaic from the area of what is now Iraqi Kurdistan is historically attested since the seventeenth century in manuscripts of Neo-Aramaic Targums. The custom of reciting such Targums alongside the Scripture in services has survived until recently (see Goldenberg and Zaken's contribution to the present volume). Today almost all Jewish speakers of Neo-Aramaic have emigrated to Israel—those from Iran mostly in recent years—and all research is carried out there.

For more information see Garbell 1965(b) and Sabar 1976(b).

b. Christian dialects.

Before the large population shifts as the result of the First World War, Christian Eastern Neo-Aramaic, also called—especially in its written form—Neo-Syriac (see below), was spoken in an almost contiguous area including the plain of Mosul, the plain of Urmia and the intervening mountain areas of Iraqi and Turkish Kurdistan (Hakkâri, Siirt, and Van provinces), as well as in some outposts to the southeast, such as Sanandaj. In these areas the Aramaic speakers were always mixed with and surrounded by Kurds, at the peripheries also Arabs (in the Mosul area) and Azeri Turks (in the Urmia plain). In the plain of Mosul most of the speakers were, and still are, Chaldeans (Rome-united Nestorians), whence their language is sometimes called (Modern) Chaldean. Another—Arabic—name is Fellīḥī. Already in the seventeenth century Neo-Aramaic was reduced to writing in this area ("School of Alqosh") predominantly for composing edifying poetry (see B. Poizat's contribution to this volume). More recently, the Dominican Press in Mosul has produced a number of books in "Chaldean."

The most important and successful written language, however, is the one developed in the 1830s by the American missionaries on the basis of the Urmia dialect. Justin Perkins, who had been sent by the American Board of Commissioners for Foreign Missions to uplift the downtrodden Nestorian community in that area, started by founding schools and a printing press. In consultation with Nestorian priests he decided to use the Nestorian Syriac script and a heavily etymological orthography, although he most probably knew the Chaldean writing tradition which is much less encumbered by etymological considerations. The other missions (Catholic, Anglican, and Russian Orthodox) that later set up shop in Urmia all adopted the same writing system with some orthographical variation. At the beginning of this century, when nationalist ideas became popular among most Middle Eastern nations, some of the intellectual leaders of the Nestorian and ex-Nestorian communities began to adopt a secularist attitude which made them deplore the divisive activities of the various missions and redefine their people as a nation *(umta)* rather than a denomination or a *millet*. It was in this context that they discovered their identity as Assyrians. The details of this highly interesting and complex process cannot be laid out here; suffice it to say that the name and the notions supporting it have had a strong impact on the Nestorian people and are still very much with us today. There has been a strong tendency in recent decades, especially among young people in the diaspora, to extend the idea of Assyrianism to all groups who have Classical Syriac as their church language; there are, however, those among the

Chaldeans and the Jacobites, particularly in the church hierarchies, who are opposed to this "Greater Assyrian" solution. Nevertheless, the name, whatever its compass, has an indisputable reality; as a consequence, the written language of Urmia, earlier on usually named *səryāya* (or *sūrāya*) *swādāya* (colloquial Syriac) or *Neo-Syriac* in western publications, is now called "Assyrian" (in Assyrian: *ātōrāya*—which is the correct Aramaic form—or *asūrāya*—which makes it more closely resemble the western form "Assyrian" and the Persian form *āsūrī*). Since from the point of view of linguistic taxonomy this usage may create confusion, "Assyrian" normally referring to the Akkadian dialect of the ancient Assyrians, some recent authors have dubbed the language "Modern Assyrian." It should be noted in this connection that one of the earliest emigration movements from the Urmia region was directed to Georgia (especially Tiflis) and (what is now Soviet) Armenia. Around the turn of the century several Russian scholars devoted linguistic studies to these people and called them *Aysorui* and their language *Aysorskiy*, a name derived from Armenian *Asori* meaning (Eastern) Syrian Christian. In the thirties, when many minority languages in the Soviet Union were officially provided with Latin alphabets, the Syrians were not left out, and a number of books were published in a specially devised Latin script. But by now Russian scholars who studied this language no longer called it *Aysorskiy* but *Assiriyskiy* (Assyrian)! It was the intervening period and particularly World War I and its aftermath that had put the Assyrian name indelibly upon the record of history.

This brings us to the third group of speakers of Christian Eastern Neo-Aramaic, the so-called Mountain Nestorians in the Hakkâri and adjacent areas. They used to live as semi-independent tribes *(ashīrāte)* much like their Kurdish neighbors, each tribe having its own rather distinctive dialect. In their midst in the village of Qūjānis, not far from the town of Jūlāmarg (Çölemerik), resided the patriarch of the Nestorian church ("the Ancient Apostolic Church of the East," to use the official designation). During the First World War, when the Patriarch and the tribes realized their precarious situation vis-à-vis the Ottoman army and their Kurdish neighbors, they decided to give up their homeland and, in a mass exodus, put themselves under the protection of the Russian army which had then occupied the Urmia region. When after the war the Russians had to recede, the leaders of the Assyrians decided to seek the protection of the British in Iraq—which meant another terrible trek, with heavy loss of life, southward to Ba'qūba, where they were interned by the British. The historical-political events of the ensuing years need not concern us here. A large number of the Assyrians settled in the north, hoping soon to regain their homeland (the "Assyrian question" was before the League of Nations, but all the political aspirations of the Assyrians came to naught). In the early thirties tensions between the Assyrians and the Iraqi state prompted a number of them to cross into Syria, then a French mandate. They were finally settled along the river Khabur in eastern Syria where their villages reflect the old tribal divisions. In Iraq the influx of speakers of so many different dialects has led, in the last forty years or so, to the formation of a supradialectal colloquial language which is not identical with the written Urmia language. E. Odisho was the first to draw attention to this language which he calls the Iraqi Koine (for a specific feature of this language see his contribution to this volume).

Apart from these population movements within the Middle East there has been a steady flow of emigrants to all parts of the world but most strongly to the United States (since before the turn of this century). Today there are large communities in Chicago, Detroit, and Turlock County, California. Among the older generations the dialects are still alive and afford the linguist a host of data that will in all likelihood soon be lost.

Finally, it should be noted that at least two of the peripheral dialects are rather different from the rest: Hertevin in the northwest (see Jastrow 1988) and Sanandaj in the southeast (see E. Panoussi's contribution to this volume).

For more information cf. Nöldeke 1868, Maclean 1895 and 1901, Jacobi 1973, Marogulov 1976, Tsereteli 1978 and Jastrow 1988.

4. Neo-Mandaic.

This is spoken by the Mandaeans in Iran (Khuzistan), but no longer by those in Iraq. It was first discovered and made known to the scholarly public by Macuch 1965(a), who also published one text (1965[b]). In addition, he has announced the publication of the rest of his collection under the title *Neumandäische Chrestomathie mit grammatischer Skizze, kommentierter Übersetzung und Glossar*, which to my knowledge has not yet appeared. New texts have apparently not been collected and, considering the ravages the Gulf War has wrought on the region, it is doubtful that they ever will. There have, however, been as yet unconfirmed reports by Assyrians that speakers of Neo-Mandaic do exist in the United States; these informants called them *Yokhananaye* and reported that they spoke a language somewhat similar to their own. The editor welcomes any information on this matter that readers of this volume may have.

Presentation of the Volume

The present volume surprises by the broad variety of its contents. It starts off, fittingly and auspiciously, with the most complete bibliography to date of everything written on Neo-Aramaic from the linguistic point of view (i.e., historical and most educational works have been excluded). Since publications on Neo-Aramaic are so widely scattered over many countries and languages, everyone with an interst in this topic will be most grateful to Georg Krotkoff for having undertaken this arduous task. The section on phonetics and phonology contains two contributions that have something to do, in one way or another, with the phenomenon of synharmonism characteristic of many Eastern Neo-Aramaic dialects. This refers to the fact that in dialects of this type all words can be assigned to one of two groups, one with an "emphatic," velarized pronunciation, the other with a non-"emphatic" one. Edward Odisho discusses the distribution and phonemic status of the labio-palatal and labio-velar approximants (i.e, the consonantal equivalents of / ü/ and / u/) in this context. Konstantin Tsereteli discusses the fate of the velar spirant / ġ/ in Eastern Neo-Aramaic. It is highly unstable and often vanishes altogether, but not without leaving the telltale sign of an "emphatic" pronunciation ("hard timbre" in Tsereteli). This is convincingly explained by an intermediate stage in which the velar spirant had become /ʻ/. Obviously, this is of some importance for the *'ayn-ghayn* problem in comparative Semitics. Solomon Sara, S.J., has contributed to the domain of morphology and semantics by discussing the function of the feminine gender in Modern Chaldean. Most, if not all, of his findings will be true for the other Eastern Neo-Aramaic dialects, too, but further research is, of course, needed. One might single out here the feminine infinitive which corresponds to the *ism al-marra* in Arabic grammar and the use of the feminine as diminutive. Yona Sabar's lexical study on European loanwords in the Jewish dialect of Zakho gives a fascinating picture of the influx of Western civilization into this rather remote area.

It seems highly significant that there are three contributions to the section on comparative studies. It must have been in the air. The general question posed in these chapters is: how do we bridge the considerable gap between the classical Aramaic languages and Neo-Aramaic and how do we account for the restructuring of the language, particularly its verbal system, during the intervening period? It has long been noticed that the modern dialects are not direct descendants of the classical languages. Reconstruction of some Proto-Neo-Aramaic on the basis of the existing dialects seemed the only correct method in this situation, and that is the approach that Samuel Fox, Robert Hoberman, and Otto Jastrow have taken in their studies of the pronouns. It is particularly satisfying that the volume also offers some new fieldwork. Estiphan Panoussi gives a sketch of his own dialect, the Christian idiom of Sanandaj (Sena) in Persian Kurdistan. When compared to the more central and better known dialects, it certainly exhibits a number of tantalizingly aberrant features which makes a monograph on this gravely endangered dialect a matter of high urgency. Werner Arnold offers a small sample from the apparently huge corpus of texts he collected during several years of fieldwork on Western Neo-Aramaic: one text each from Maʻlūla, Bakhʻa, and Jubb ʻAdīn on marriage customs among Muslims (thus easy to compare) and important grammatical notes. Gideon Goldenberg and his student Mordekhay Zaken publish an oral targum of the Book of Ruth from Zakho which shows some of the features typical of Neo-Aramaic used in translations. This contribution might as well have found its place in the last section somewhat vaguely entitled "philological and literary studies." Bruno Poizat present us with a rather moving specimen of eighteenth-century Neo-Aramaic (Chaldean) poetry, a partial edition and translation of a long poem on the ravages of the plague in the village of Pioz, with extremely valuable notes on the grammar, especially the verb, of this old form of Neo-Aramaic. The text in Syriac script is in the author's own neat handwriting. In my own contribution I draw attention to the only attempt, of which we know, to turn Ṭūrōyo into a written language in the last century. Last, but not least, Yusuf Ishaq describes the process and the method by which Ṭūrōyo became a written language in Latin script in Sweden, a process in which he himself was the main protagonist. I should like to add here a caveat in my capacity as editor. I have not attempted to use a uniform transliteration system, rather I have kept whatever the authors chose to do, except for a few changes due to technical reasons.

Acknowledgments

Finally, it behooves me to thank all those who have contributed to the production of this volume: first and foremost the David Perley Fund for financial support; Eden Naby, who was instrumental in setting up the Perley Fund, for contributing a foreword to our volume; Carolyn Cross for her incredible patience in typesetting and formatting a manuscript that can justly be described as maddening; Frank Moore Cross for accepting this volume for the Harvard Semitic Studies Series; and John Huehnergard, my colleague in the field of Comparative Semitics, for proofreading the galleys with an expert eye. My heartfelt gratitude goes out to all of them.

I. Bibliography

AN ANNOTATED BIBLIOGRAPHY OF NEO-ARAMAIC
Georg Krotkoff

The increased attention which Neo-Aramaic (NA) dialects have received in the past decades makes it desirable to update the existing bibliographies. The only previous attempt at a comprehensive listing was published by Bruno Poizat in 1981 (see entry under this year below), covering materials up to 1979. Being the first pioneering effort of this kind, it contains a number of lacunae and imperfections which the present listing tries to correct. Furthermore, only materials of linguistic interest are listed here, to the exclusion of purely historical and literary works, and of travelogs. For these, as well as for an excellent narrative survey of the field of NA, the reader is referred to Poizat's publication. In contrast to the latter, the arrangement here is purely chronological, and all dialect groups are listed together. Only a small selection of the didactic books published by the Assyrians in the East is included.

Other copious listings of the general literature on the Aramaic-speaking minorities of the Middle East can be found in the following works:

Anschütz, Helga: "Zur Gegenwartslage der syrischen Christen im Tur 'Abdin, im Hakkarigebiet und im Iran," *ZDMG, Supplement* 1,2 (XVII. Deutscher Orientalistentag, Würzburg 1968), 1969, 483-510.

Joseph, John: *The Nestorians and their Muslim Neighbors.* Princeton: Princeton University Press 1961.

A first attempt to gather all information on the periodical literature produced by speakers of NA is:

Yonan, Gabriele: *Journalismus bei den Assyrern.* Ein Überblick von seinen Anfängen bis zur Gegenwart. Reihe Gilgamesch. Materialien zur Kulturgeschichte der Assyrer im 19. und 20. Jahrhundert, Bd. 1. Berlin: Zentralverband der Assyrischen Vereinigungen in Deutschland und Mitteleuropa 1985. [WH]

The necessity for a deadline for a collective work like the present volume dictated an arbitrary end to further search, and the compiler is aware that he must have missed one or the other item which might deserve inclusion, and that he alone bears the responsibility for possible omissions, wrong judgments, and other errors. At the same time he is grateful to Wolfhart Heinrichs, Robert Hoberman, and Yona Sabar for having shared their

3

bibliographical notes with him. In particular, Robert Hoberman very generously contributed information on over thirty additional publications and the transliteration of Hebrew titles. Important remarks and additions due to one particular source are acknowledged with the abbreviations [WH], [RH], [YS], respectively. Most items, even those communicated by others, were checked in their originals, but some remained inaccessible. The transliteration in some titles had to be simplified and adjusted to available fonts. In Russian words "y" stands for both the mid-low vowel and the palatal semivowel.

1838 RÖDIGER, Emil: *Chrestomathia syriaca.* Halle/Saale.
The first edition of this classical Syriac reader contains one text in NA.

1839 RÖDIGER, Emil: "Über die aramäische Vulgärsprache der heutigen syrischen Christen," *Zeitschrift für die Kunde des Morgenlandes* (Göttingen) 2, 77-93, 314-316.
The first report in a German scholarly journal on NA based on American missionary publications. It confirms an earlier report by Niebuhr and compares the text of the Christian credo in NA and classical Syriac.

1856 STODDARD, D. T.: "Grammar of the Modern Syriac Language, as spoken in Oroomiah, Persia, and in Koordistan," *JAOS* 5, 1-180a-h, New York (sic! only beginning with vol. 6 does the place of publication change to New Haven).
This pioneering grammar of NA is remarkably complete and well informed for its time, and it served as point of departure for Nöldeke 1868. The introduction contains a list of the early publications of the missionary press in Urmia.

1861 [Bedjan, Paul, translator] BELLARMINO, (Saint) Robert: *Doctrinae Christianae rudimenta in vernaculam Chaldaeorum linguam Urmiensis Provinciae translata.* Paris/Leipzig [RH].
See also Bellarmino 1886.

1863 FERRETTE, J.: "On a Neo-Syriac Language still spoken in the Anti-Lebanon," *JRAS* 1863, 431-436.

1867 NÖLDEKE, Theodor: "Beiträge zur Kenntnis aramäischer Dialekte I," *ZDMG* 21, 183-200.
Discussion of the Ma'lula material collected by Ferrette (1863). Part II in the following volume deals with Christian Palestinian Aramaic.

1868 NÖLDEKE, Theodor: *Grammatik der neusyrischen Sprache am Urmia-See und in Kurdistan.* Leipzig: T. O. Weigel. Reprint: Hildesheim: Olms 1974.

1871 PRYM, Eugen: "Aus einem Briefe des Herrn Dr. Prym an Prof. Fleischer," *ZDMG* 25, 651-655.
Deals with the recording of Turoyo texts by Prym and Socin.

1873 MERX, Adalbert: *Neusyrisches Lesebuch.* Texte im Dialecte von Urmia, gesammelt, übersetzt und erklärt. Tübingen: Fues.
Texts in Syriac script with parallel German translation. The last few texts with transliteration.

1873 NÖLDEKE, Theodor. Rev. of Merx 1873. *Göttingische gelehrte Anzeigen* 1873, 1961-75.

1874 SOCIN, Albert: Rev. of Merx 1873. *Jenaer Literaturzeitung*, no. 554, cols. 597-8.

1876 LÖWY, Albert: "On a Unique Specimen of the Lishana shel Imrani, the Modern Syriac or Targum Dialect of the Jews in Kurdistan and adjacent Countries; with an Account of the People by whom it is spoken," *Transactions of the Society of Biblical Archaeology*, 4, 98-117. London 1876.
This is a unique occurrence of the label Imrani for this language. Interestingly, it is also found among the names of a number of incomprehensible language samples quoted by the famous Turkish traveller Evliya Chelebi (X,967; communication by Robert Dankoff).

1878 HUART, Clément: "Notes prises pendant un voyage en Syrie," *JA* 7e sér., t. 12, 478-498.

1878 LÖWY, Albert: "On Kurdish Folk Lore in the Kurdo-Jewish Dialect," *Transactions of the Society of Biblical Archaeology*, 6, 600-602.
Condensed report of a paper given at the Society. It contains three short stories in translation and one also in transliteration. This transliteration is more realistic than Löwy's first attempt in 1875. The *lishanet imrani* is also termed *lishanet djabali.*

1879 DUVAL, Rubens: "Notice sur le dialecte de Maalula," *JA* 7e sér., t. 13, 456-459. Annotations to Huart 1878.

1881 DUVAL, Rubens: Rev. of Prym/Socin 1881. *Revue critique* n.s., t. 12, no. 33, 125-129.

1881 PRYM, Eugen and Albert SOCIN: *Der neu-aramaeische Dialekt des Ṭûr Abdîn.* 2 vols. Göttingen: Vandenhoeck & Ruprecht.
A large collection of Turoyo texts (stories and fairy tales) in a very detailed phonetic transcription in vol. 1 and their translations in vol. 2.

1881 NÖLDEKE, Theodor: Rev. of Prym/Socin 1881. *ZDMG* 35, 218-235.

1882 SOCIN, Albert: *Die neu-aramaeischen Dialekte von Urmia bis Mosul.* Texte und Übersetzung. Tübingen: Laupp.
Texts in various dialects in precise handwritten transcription; some also in Syriac script. German translation at the end of volume.

1882 NÖLDEKE, Theodor: Rev. of Socin 1882. *ZDMG* 36, 669-682.
The same volume contains on pp. 708-711 folkloristic remarks on Socin's texts by Felix Liebrecht.

1883 DUVAL, R.: *Les dialectes néo-araméens de Salamas.* Textes sur l'état actuel de la Perse et contes populaires, publiés avec une traduction française. Paris.
Texts in the dialects of the Christians and Jews of Salamas. Phonetic transliteration in cursive handwriting, translation in letter press.

1883 GUIDI, Ignazio: "Beiträge zur Kenntnis des neuaramäischen Fellihi-Dialektes," *ZDMG* 37, 293-318.

1883 NÖLDEKE, Theodor: Rev. of Duval 1883. *ZDMG* 37, 598-609.

1884 DUVAL, Rubens: "Lettre à M. Barbier de Meynard," *JA* 8e sér., t. 3, 106-108.
Report on manuscripts of the Nestorian breviary obtained by P. Bedjan.

1884 SOCIN, Albert: Rev. of Duval 1883. *Literaturblatt für orientalische Philologie* 1, 407-410; and 2 (1885), 32.

1885 BEDJAN, Paul, translator: *Imitatio Christi, nunc primum ex latino in Chaldaicum idiomatis Urmiae Persidis translata.* Paris: Maisonneuve.

1885 DUVAL, Rubens: "Inscriptions syriaques de Salamas, en Perse," *JA* 83 sér., t. 5, 39-62.
Publication of several inscriptions found on tombstones in the cemeteries in and around Chosrava and collected with the aid of P. Bedjan.

1886 BEDJAN, Paul: *Manuel de piété ou livre de prières, de méditations et des offices, en lange chaldéenne.* Paris: Maisonneuve (2nd ed. 1893).

1886 BELLARMINO, (Saint) Robert: *Doctrina Christiana lingua Chaldaica idiomatis Urmiae Persidis.* Revised by Paul Bedjan. Rome. [RH]
See also Bedjan 1861.

1886 DUVAL, Rubens: Rev. of Bedjan 1885, 1886. *JA* 8e sér., t. 7, 371-375.

1888 BEDJAN, Paul: *Histoire Sainte.* [RH] [Paris?]
Most references to Bedjan are due to Polotsky 1961. On Bedjan's remarkable life (1838-1920) see A. Rücker, *Oriens Christianus,* n.s. X/XI (1923), 146-151.

1890 BLISS, F. J.: "Ma'lula and its Dialects," *Palestine Exploration Fund, Quart. Stat.* 1890, 74-98.

1892 [MACLEAN]: *Grammāṭiqī d-lišāna ḥadtā d-Suryāyē madinḥāyē.* Urmi: Press of the Archbishop of Canterbury's Mission. [WH]

1893 MACLEAN, Arthur John: "Vernacular Syriac as spoken by the Eastern Syrians." *Transactions of the Ninth International Congress of Orientalists* (London, Sept. 5-12, 1892), Vol. 2, 33-45. London.

1893 GOTTHEIL, Richard J. H.: "The Judaeo-Aramaean Dialect of Salamas," *JAOS* 15, 297-310. Compares Gen. 1 in different dialects.

1894 KALASHEV, A.: "Aysorskiye teksty [Assyrian texts]," *SMOMPK,* vol. 20, sect. 3, 33-96.

1894 KALASHEV, A.: "Russko-aysorskiy i aysorsko-russkiy slovar' [Russian-Assyrian and Assyrian-Russian Dictionary]," *SMOMPK*, vol. 20, sect. 2, 1-408.

1894 LIDZBARSKI, Mark: "Beiträge zur Grammatik der neuaramäischen Dialecte," *ZA* 9, 224-263.

1894 LOPATINSKIY, L.: "Yevreysko-arameyskiye teksty [Jewish-Aramaic texts]," *SMOMPK*, vol. 20, sect. 9, 1-32.

1894 LOPATINSKIY, L.: "Zametka k aysorskim tekstam [a remark on the Assyrian texts]," *SMOMPK*, vol. 20.

1894 LOPATINSKIY, L.: "Zametka k yevreysko-arameyskim tekstam [a remark on the Jewish-Aramaic texts]," *SMOMPK*, vol. 20.

1895 MACLEAN, Arthur John: *Grammar of the Dialects of Vernacular Syriac.* Cambridge: University Press (reprint Amsterdam: Philo Press, 1971).
The subtitle says: "As spoken by the eastern Syrians of Kurdistan, North-West Persia and the plain of Mosul with notices of the vernacular of the Jews of Azerbaijan and of Zakhu near Mosul with an introduction and a collection of proverbs." This is the only grammar which attempts to be comparative. The phonetic side is obscured by the use of the Nestorian script throughout.

1895 SACHAU, Eduard: *Skizze des Fellichi-Dialekts von Mosul.* Abhandlungen der Königlich-Preussischen Akademie der Wissenschaften zu Berlin. Berlin.
A highly dependable and perceptive grammatical sketch with examples and valuable observations. The transliteration is somewhat normalized, but Rosenthal's reservations (1939, p. 261) regarding its faithfulness to the pronunciation are not justified.

1896 DUVAL, Rubens: "Notice sur les dialectes néo-araméens," *Mémoires de la sociéte de linguistique de Paris*, 9, 125-135.
Phonetic comparisons between dialects of NA.

1896 LIDZBARSKI, Mark: *Die neu-aramäischen Handschriften der Königlichen Bibliothek zu Berlin in Auswahl herausgegeben, übersetzt und erläutert.* 2 vols. Semitistische Studien 4/9. Weimar: Emil Felber (reprint Hildesheim: Olms 1973).

1896 NÖLDEKE, Theodor: Rev. of Lidzbarski 1896, Sachau 1895, Maclean 1895. *ZDMG* 50, 302-316.

1896 SACHAU, Eduard: "Über die Poesie in der Volkssprache der Nestorianer," *Sitzungsberichte der Königlich-Preussischen Akademie der Wissenschaften zu Berlin*, 1896, 179-215.

1897 MARGOLIOUTH, D. S.: Rev. of Maclean 1895. *JRAS* 1897, 168-171.

1897 ODDO [ODO, AUDO], Mar Touma: *Assyrian Dictionary.* Mosul: Dominican Press (reprint Ann Arbor: Edwards Brothers, 1978).
This Assyrian-Assyrian dictionary was originally printed in two volumes which are now combined into one.

1898 PARISOT, Jean: "Contribution à l'étude du dialecte néo-syriaque du Tour Abdin," *Actes du 11e Congrès Intern. des Orient.*, 4e sect., 178-198. Paris: Leroux.

1898 PARISOT, Jean: "Le dialecte de Maalula," *JA* 9e sér., t. 11, 239-312, 440-519; t. 12, 124-176.

1899 LABAREE, Benjamin: "Maclean's Grammar of the Dialects of Vernacular Syriac," *AJSLL* 15, 87-99.

1900 YOHANNAN, Abraham: *A Modern Syriac-English Dictionary*, Part 1. [Letter Aleph only.] New York: Columbia U. P.

1901 MACLEAN, Arthur John: *Dictionary of the Dialects of Vernacular Syriac*. Oxford: Clarendon Press (reprint Amsterdam: Philo Press 1972).
The subtitle says: "As spoken by eastern Syrians of Kurdistan, North-West Persia and the plain of Mosul with illustrations from the dialects of the Jews of Zakhu and Azerbaijan, and of the western Syrians of Tur'abdin and Ma'lula, and an introduction."

1901 S. A. C.: Rev. of Maclean 1901. *JRAS* 1901, 609-611.

1902 PARISOT, Jean: "Le dialecte néo-syriaque de Bakha et Djub'adin," *JA* 9e sér., t. 19, 51-61.

1903 ROSENBERG, I.: *Lehrbuch der neusyrischen Schrift- und Umgangssprache*. Grammatik, Konversation, Korrespondenz und Chrestomathie. Bibliothek der Sprachenkunde, Teil 77. Wien, Pest, Leipzig: Hartleben.
A practical introduction into the literary language of the Urmia mission with samples of correspondence.

1904 BEDJAN, Paul: *Mois de Marie*. Paris.

1904 DE MORGAN, J.-J.: "Le dialecte Israélite de Sihneh." In: *Mission scientifique en Perse*, t. 5: *Etudes linguistiques*, 312-322. Paris. Compare Perles 1904.

1904 PERLES, Felix: "Über das Semitische im jüdischen Dialekt von Sihneh," *OLZ* 12, 483-6.

1905 KAMPFFMEYER, G.: "Neusyrische Sprichwörter im Dialekt von Urmia," *MSOS*, II. Abt., 1-24.

1905 ODDO [ODO, AUDO], Mar Touma: *Grammatiqi dlishana swadaya* [Grammar of the colloquial language]. Urmia.

1906 ZETTERSTEEN, Karl Vilhelm. "Ein geistliches Wechsellied in Fellihi." In: *Orientalistische Studien, Theodor Nöldeke gewidmet*. Ed. C. Bezold. Vol. 1, 497-503. Giessen: Töpelmann.
A strophic poem in Nestorian script only.

1909 SARGIS, Arkhimandrit: *Russko-sirskiy leksikon* [Russian-Syriac dictionary]. Urmia.

1912 BEDJAN, Paul: *Vies des Saints*. Paris.

1912 MUSHE, Yokhanan: *Pshiqate dlishana suryaya swadaya* [Grammar of colloquial Syriac). Urmia (Reprint: Tabriz 1928). [Poizat SL 38].

1912 RHÉTORÉ, J.: *Grammaire de la langue soureth ou chaldéen vulgaire selon le dialecte de la plaine de Mossoul et des pays adjacents.* Mossoul: Imprimerie des Pères Dominicains.
A detailed and systematic morphology of the Fellihi dialect. Uses the Nestorian script.

1913 IDELSSOHN, Avraham-Tsevi: "Sippurim ba-lashon ha-aramit ha-ḥadasha," *Hashiloah* (Odessa) 29, 121-130, 240-250, 319-327, 466-476, 522-561. [Cf. Poizat SL 40 and 41.]

1913 OSIPOFF, S.: "Syriaque." In: *Le Maître Phonétique* 28, 79-80.

1914 RHÉTORÉ, P. Jacques: *Cantiques et poesies diverses sur des sujets religieux.* Mossoul: Imprimerie des Pères Dominicains.
On unpublished manuscripts by R. see Poizat SL 35-37, T 6.

1915 BERGSTRÄSSER, Gotthelf: "Neuaramäische Märchen und andere Texte aus Maʻlūla hauptsächlich aus der Sammlung E. Pryms und A. Socins," *AKM* 13,2 (Reprint 1966).
The German translation of these texts is in *AKM* 13,3.

1918 NÖLDEKE, Theodor: "Texte im aramäischen Dialekt von Maalula," *ZA* 31 (1917-18), 203-230. Remarks on Bergsträsser 1915.

1919 BERGSTRÄSSER, Gotthelf: "Neue Texte im aramäischen Dialekt von Maʻlūla," *ZA* 32, 103-163. Additions in *ZA* 33 (1920), 68-69.

1919 SCHAHBAZ, D.: "Erzählungen, Sprichwörter der heutigen Syrer in Nordpersien. Texte im Dialekt von Urmia," *MSOS*, III. Abt., 112-126.

1920 ELLOW, Agha Petros [Gen. A. Petros Eliya d-Baz]: *Assyrian, Kurdish and Yazidis* (sic?). Baghdad: Govt. Press.
A possibly garbled reference in G. Yonan: *Assyrer heute.* [WH]

1921 BERGSTRÄSSER, Gotthelf: "Glossar des neuaramäischen Dialekts von Maʻlūla," *AKM* 15, 4.
A copy dedicated by the author to Nöldeke is preserved in the library of the Hebrew University. [RH]

1923 SIEGEL, Adolf: *Laut- und Formenlehre des neuaramäischen Dialekts des Tur ʻAbdin.* Beiträge zur semitischen Philologie und Linguistik, Heft 2. Hannover: Lafaire.
Based on Prym/Socin 1881 and superseded by Jastrow 1967.

1926 HART, R.: *Colloquial Syriac as Spoken in the Assyrian Levies.* Mosul: Assyrian Press.
This book was privately reprinted and distributed under the title *Syriac made easy for Assyrian-Americans* (ca 1974) by John Yonan, 2243 W. Berwyn Ave., Chicago 60625. [RH]

1926 LITTMANN, Enno: Revs. of Bergsträsser 1915 and 1921, and of Siegel 1923. *OLZ* 29, 803-9 and 1003-8.

1928 BERGSTRÄSSER, Gotthelf: *Einführung in die semitischen Sprachen. Sprachproben und grammatische Skizzen.* München: Max Hueber.

Two more printings till 1977. Pages 80-96 are devoted to the NA of Ma'lula and Urmia. English translation see Bergsträsser 1983.

1929 BEIT QELAYTA, Yosep d-: *Grammaire de l'araméen oriental en lange vulgaire.* Mossoul. See Poizat SL 44.

1930 COHEN, Marcel: "Documents araméens du 16e siècle," *JA* 216, 147-156.

1930 RIVLIN, L. L.: "Sippur David ve-Golyah bi-Leshon Targum," *Siyyon* 5690, 109-121.

1930 BAR-ADON, Pesakh: "Mehaaramit hameduberet etsel hayehudim hakurdiyim," *Tsion (Yediot)* 1, 1(1930/1931), 12-13. [YS]

1933 BERGSTRÄSSER, Gotthelf: "Phonogramme im neuaramäischen Dialekt von Ma'lula. Satzdruck und Satzmelodie," *Sb. der Bayerischen Akademie der Wissenschaften, phil.-hist. Abt.,* Jg. 1931/32, 7.
An attempt to capture intonation and stress in longer speech periods disregarding word boundaries.

1933 COHEN, Marcel: "Observations sur le néo-syriaque d'Ourmiah," *GLECS* 1, 25 and 27-8.

1933 YUSHMANOV, N. V.: "Assiriyskiy yazyk i evo pis'mo," *Pis'mennost'i revol'utsiya* 1, 112-128. Moscow-Leningrad.

1935 MAROGULOV, Q. I.: *Grammatiqij qa madrasi d guri* [A NA grammar for adults]. Moscow. [French translation, see Marogulov 1976.]

1935 YUSHMANOV, N. V.: "Zagadochnoye 'm' novosiriyskovo dialekta" [The enigmatic *m* of the Neo-Syriac dialect], *Yazyk i myshleniye* 5, 93-96. Moscow-Leningrad.

1937 REICH, S.: *Etudes sur les villages araméens de l'Anti-Liban.* Documents d'Etudes Orientales, t. 7. Damas: Institut Français.

1938 SPITALER, Anton: "Grammatik des neuaramäischen Dialekts von Ma'lula (Antilibanon)," *AKM* 23, 1 (Reprint 1966).
The standard description of the Ma'lula dialect, except its syntax (for which now see Correll 1978). In the introduction a survey and evaluation of earlier works on Ma'lula.

1938 YUSHMANOV, N. V.: "Singarmonizm urmiyskovo dialekta." In: *Pam'ati akademika N. Ya. Marra,* 295-314. Moscow-Leningrad.
Synharmonism is Yushmanov's term for the suprasegmental feature of vowel and consonant harmony peculiar to some NA dialects.

1939 ROSENTHAL, Franz: *Die aramaistische Forschung seit Th. Nöldekes Veröffentlichungen.* Leiden: Brill.
NA studies are surveyed in ch. B/4 *Das Neu-Jungaramäische* (Ma'lula), 160-172, and ch. C/4 *Das Neu-Ostaramäische,* 255-269.

1939 ROSENTHAL, Franz: "Spitalers Grammatik des neuaramäischen Dialekts von Ma'lūla," *Orientalia* 8, 346-360.

1942 RIVLIN, Y. Y.: "Siphrutam shel Yehude Zakho." In: *Gulak-Klein Memorial Volume* (5702), 171-186.

1943 ORAHAM, Alexander Joseph: *Dictionary of the Stabilized and Enriched Assyrian Language and English.* Chicago: Consolidated Press.
A labor of love but dubious scholarship with sometimes hilarious English definitions of English words.

1945 RIVLIN, Y. Y.: "Pitgamim Bi-Leshon Targum," *Reshumot,* n.s. 1, 207-215. Continued n.s. 2, 209-214.
Jewish Neo-Aramaic proverbs.

1946 TSERETELI, Konstantin: "Urmiyskiy singarmonizm" [The synharmonism of Urmia; in Georgian], *SANGruzSSR,* vol. 7, no. 7, 467-468.
Between 1946 and 1957, K. T. published ten articles on NA in Georgian in serials of the Academy of Sciences of the Georgian SSR. They are listed on p. 33 of Tsereteli 1958 (Essay). Not all titles could be found in Russian.

1946 TSERETELI, Konstantin: "Osnovy urmiyskovo singarmonizma" [The principles of synharmonism in Urmia; in Georgian], *SANGruzSSR,* vol. 7, no. 9.

1948 TSERETELI, Konstantin: "Sluchai palatalizatsii soglasnykh v urmiyskom dialekte arameyskovo yazyka" [Cases of palatalization of consonants in the Urmia dialect of Aramaic; in Georgian], *SANGruzSSR,* vol. 9, no. 8, 507-511.

1952 TSERETELI, Konstantin: "O geminatsii v urmiyskom dialekte arameyskovo yazyka" [On gemination in the Urmia dialect; in Georgian], *SANGruzSSR,* vol. 13, no. 9, 569-574.

1952 TSERETELI, Konstantin: "Prit'azhatel'nyye mestoimeniya v urmiyskom dialekte arameyskovo yazyka" [Possessive pronouns in the Urmia dialect of Aramaic; in Georgian], *SANGruzSSR,* vol. 13, no. 8, 491-494.

1953 TSERETELI, Konstantin: [An article in Georgian], *SANGruzSSR,* vol. 14, no. 1.

1954 BROCKELMANN, Carl: "Das Aramäische, einschließlich des Syrischen." In: *Handbuch der Orientalistik,* 3. Band, 2 u. 3. Abschnitt. Leiden: Brill. On pp. 157-162 a brief sketch of the characteristics of NA based on Spitaler, Siegel, Nöldeke, Maclean and Sachau.

1954 TSERETELI, Konstantin: [An article in Georgian], *TIYaANGruzSSR,* vol. 1.

1955 SEGAL, J. B.: "Neo-Aramaic Proverbs of the Jews of Zakho," *JNES* 14,4, 251-270.

1957 SPITALER, Anton: "Neue Materialien zum aramäischen Dialekt von Ma'lūla," *ZDMG* 107, 299-339.

1957 TSERETELI, Konstantin: "Sistema spr'azheniya glagolov v sovremennykh assiriyskikh (vostochno-arameyskikh) dialektakh" [The system of verbal inflection in modern Assyrian (East-Aramaic) dialects; in Georgian with Russian summary], *TIYaANGruzSSR*, vol. 2, 125-156.

1957 TSERETELI, Konstantin: "Sledy kauzativa na sha/sa v urmiyskom dialekte" [Traces of a causative with sha/sa in the Urmia dialect; in Georgian], *SANGruzSSR* 18, no. 1.

1957 YAURE, Lazarus: "A Poem in the Neo-Aramaic Dialect of Urmia," *JNES* 16, 73-87.

1958 GARBELL, Irene: "Lishanit targum." In: *Le Maître Phonétique* 109, 8-10.

1958 RIVLIN, Joseph Joel: *Targume Yehude Kurdista'n: Kurdish Targum Language Texts*. Semitic Texts Series, 1. Chicago: The College of Jewish Studies. [RH]

1958 TSERETELI, Konstantin: *Essay of Comparative Phonetics of the Modern Assyrian Dialects* [in Georgian with Russian summary]. Institute of Linguistics Publications. Tbilisi: Academy of Sciences of the Georgian SSR.
Tsereteli's major contribution. The Russian summary of forty pages has been translated into German (see Tsereteli 1961).

1958 TSERETELI, Konstantin: *Khrestomatiya sovremennovo assiriyskovo yazyka so slovar'om* [A reader of the modern Assyrian language with a dictionary]. Tbilisi: State University Publishing House.
This collection of NA texts contains grammatical exercises, proverbs, fables, translations from Georgian literature, and parts of the Bible in the Nestorian script, as well as a substantial dictionary. In the preface, Assyrian books published in Tiflis and Moscow after 1926 are listed.

1959 AVIDANI, Alwan: *Seder Hagada shel Pesakh/ Ivri Kurdi*. Jerusalem. [YS]

1959 FRIEDRICH, Johannes: "Neusyrisches in Lateinschrift aus der Sowjetunion," *ZDMG* 109, 50-81.

1959 RIVLIN, Yosef Yoël: *Shirat Yehude ha-Targum* [NA Biblical epics of Kurdish Jews with a Hebrew translation]. Jerusalem: Bialik Institute.

1960 FRIEDRICH, Johannes: "Zwei russische Novellen in neusyrischer Übersetzung und Lateinschrift," *AKM*, XXXIII,4.
Tolstoy's "After the Ball" and Pushkin's "Stationmaster" in NA with facing German translation. Vocabulary.

1960 GARBELL, Irene: "'Al mehkaro shel Y. Y. Rivlin be-shirat Yehude ha-Targum" [On the research of Y. Y. Rivlin on the poetry of the Targum Jews], *Leshonenu* 24, 111-112. On Rivlin 1959.

1960 POLOTSKY, H. J.: "Yehude ha-Targum u-Leshonam" [The Targum Jews and their language], *Gesher* 6.

1960 TSERETELI, K. G.: "K sravnitel'no-istoricheskomu izucheniyu foneticheskikh osobennostey sovremennykh vostochno-arameyskikh dialektov" [On a comparative historical study of the phonetic peculiarities of modern East-Aramaic dialects], *Trudy 25vo mezhdunarodnovo kongressa vostokovedov* [Proceedings of the 25th Int. Congr. of Orientalists] t. 1, 337-343. Moskva: Izd. Vost. Lit. 1963 (Kraus reprint 1972).

1961 CANTARINO, Vicente: "Der neuaramäische Dialekt von Gubb 'Adin (Texte und Übersetzung)." Chapel Hill, N.C.
A doctoral dissertation defended in Munich in 1957.

1961 KROTKOFF, Georg: "Beobachtungen zum Neu-Ostaramäischen," *ZDMG* 111:339-95.
A paper read at the Deutsche Orientalistentag in Göttingen announcing newly found evidence of velarized affricates in NA.

1961 MOLITOR, J.: *Chaldäisches Brevier*. Ordinarium des ostsyrischen Studiengebiets. ? [information incomplete]

1961 POLOTSKY, H. J.: "Studies in Modern Syriac," *JSS* 6, 1-32 (= Collected Papers. Jerusalem 1971, 585-616).
Important survey of literature, including a list of Assyrian publications in the USSR, as well as a discussion of various grammatical matters.

1961 SEGERT, Stanislav: "Neue Darstellung der vergleichenden Phonetik der modernene aramäischen Dialekt von K. Cereteli," *AO* 29, 96-105.

1961 CERETELI [TSERETELI], Konstantin G.: "Abriß der vergleichenden Phonetik der modernen assyrischen Dialekte." In: Altheim, Franz: *Geschichte der Hunnen*, Bd 3, 218-266. Berlin: De Gruyter.
German translation by Dr. Norbert Reiter of the Russian summary of Tsereteli 1958 (Essay).

1962 BANNERTH, Ernst: Rev. of Friedrich 1960. *WZKM* 58, 250.

1962 FRIEDRICH, Johannes: "Das Neusyrische als Typus einer entarteten semitischen Sprache," *AION-L* 4, 95-106.
Concentrates on the features of NA which deviate from typical Semitic structure.

1962 FRIEDRICH, Johannes & L. YAURE: "Onkel Sälu und Qämbär. Eine neusyrische Verserzählung von D. Iljan. Text, Übersetzung und Erläuterungen," *ZDMG* 112,6-49.

1962 MACUCH, Rudolf: "Zu J. Friedrichs Arbeiten über das Neusyrische in Lateinschrift," *OLZ* 57, 117-125.

1962 POLOTSKY, H. J.: Rev. of Friedrich 1960. *Orientalia* 31, 273-283.

1963 FRIEDRICH, Johannes: "Neun und zehn im Neusyrischen," *Zeitschrift für vergleichende Sprachforschung auf dem Gebiete der indogermanischen Sprachen*, 78, p. 55. Göttingen: Vandenhoeck & Ruprecht.

1963 FRIEDRICH, Johannes: "Aus einer neusyrischen Fibel," *RSO* 38, 9-21.

A few short texts from a NA primer (publ. in Moscow in 1936) in Latin script and German translation with lexical annotations.

1963 RUNDGREN, Frithiof: "Erneuerung des Verbalaspekts im Semitischen. Funktionell-diachronische Studien zur semitischen Verblehre," *Acta Universitatis Upsalensis. Acta Societatis Linguisticae Upsalensis*, N.S. 1:3. Uppsala: Almqvist & Wiksells.

In this treatise which is one of several devoted by the author to the study of Semitic verbal systems, pp. 72-87 and 97 deal with NA on the basis of Friedrich 1960. [RH]

1963 STARININ, V. P.: Rev. of Tsereteli 1958 (Khrestomatiya). In: *Semitskiye yazyki* [1], 234-5 (for details see next entry).

1963 TSERETELI, Konstantin: "Obraztsy sovremennoy assiriyskoy rechi (vanskiye teksty)" [Samples of modern Assyrian speech. Texts from Van]. *Semitskiye yazyki* [Semitic Languages]. Ed. G. Sharbatov. [Issue 1], 202-218. Moscow: Acad. of Sc. of the USSR.

Two stories in transliteration with Russian translation and notes.

1963 TSERETELI, Konstantin: Rev. of Friedrich 1959. *Semitskiye Yazyki*, 242-246 (details in prev. entry).

1963 TSERETELI, Konstantin: "The comparative-historical study of the category of tense in modern Aramaic dialects." XXVI International Congress of Orientalists [New Delhi 1964]. Papers Presented by the USSR Delegation. Moscow.

Paper for private distribution, identical to Tsereteli 1968 (On the...).

1964 GARBELL, Irene: "Flat Words and Syllables in Jewish East New Aramaic of Persian Azerbaijan and the Contiguous Districts (A Problem of Multilingualism)." In: *Studies in Egyptology and Linguistics in Honor of H. J. Polotsky*, ed. H. B. Rosen. Jerusalem: The Israel Exploration Society.

1964 TSERETELI, K. G.: *Sovremennyy assiriyskiy yazyk* [The Modern Assyrian Language]. Yazyki narodov Azii i Afriki. Moskva: Nauka.

A concise grammatical survey based on the dialect of Urmia.

1964 TSERETELI, Konstantin: "Über die Reflexivstämme in den modernen aramäischen Dialekten,"*RSO* 39, 125-132.

1965 ARSANIS, G. V.: "Rol' assiriyskikh prosvetiteley i pisateley v stanovlenii sovremennovo assiriyskovo yazyka" [The role of the Assyrian educators and writers in the formation of modern Assyrian]. In: *Semitskiye yazyki*, vol. 2, 600-706. Moskva: Nauka.

Two other articles by Arsanis are listed by Poizat without dates (SL 55 and 56, the latter obviously misquoted).

1965 GARBELL, Irene: "The Impact of Kurdish and Turkish on the Jewish Neo-Aramaic Dialect of Persian Azerbaijan and the Adjoining Regions," *JAOS* 85, 159-177.

1965 GARBELL, Irene: *The Jewish Neo-Aramaic Dialect of Persian Azerbaijan. Linguistic Analysis and Folkloristic Texts*, Janua Linguarum, Series Practica 3. The Hague: Mouton.
Very rich corpus of folk tales and legends. The linguistic analysis of this phonologically very peculiar dialect is thorough, but due to its one-sidedly structuralist approach difficult to use. Divides the entire vocabulary into "plain" and "flat" words.

1965 MACUCH, Rudolf: *Handbook of Classical and Modern Mandaic.* Berlin: Walter de Gruyter.
Information on modern spoken Mandaic is mixed with the description of classical Mandaic. The appendix contains an English-modern Mandaic word list.

1965 MACUCH, Rudolf: "The Bridge of Shushtar. A Legend in Vernacular Mandaic with Introduction, Translation and Notes." In: *Studia Semitica Philologica necnon Philosophica Ioanni Bakoš dicata*, ed. S. Segert, 153-172. Bratislava.

1965 MATVEYEV, K. P.: "Kategoriya grammaticheskovo roda zaimstvovannykh im'on sushchestvitel'nykh v sovremennom assiriyskom yazyke" [The category of grammatical gender of borrowed substantives in the modern Assyrian language], *Semitskiye yazyki*, 2, 162-167 [for details see following entry].

1965 TSERETELI, Konstantin:: "Sintaksicheskaya funktsiya chastitsy 'de' ve sovremennykh arameyskikh dialektakh" [The syntactic function of the particle *d* in modern Aramaic dialects], *Semitskiye yazyki*, ed. G. Sharbatov, issue 2, 152-162. Moscow: Nauka.

1965 TSERETELI, Konstantin: "A Type of Nominal Syntagm in Modern Aramaic Dialects," *BSOAS* 28,2, 227-232.

1965 TSERETELI, Konstantin: *Materialy po arameyskoy dialektologii. Tom I. Urmiyskiy dialekt* [Materials on Aramaic Dialectology. Vol. 1. The Urmia Dialect]. Oriental Institute of the Academy of Sciences, Georgian SSR. Tbilisi: Metsniereba.

1966 KADARI, Menakhem-Tsevi: Rev. of Garbell 1965. *Kiryat Sefer* 41, 499-504. [YS]

1966 ROSENTHAL, Franz: Rev. of Macuch 1965 (Handbook). JAOS 86, 54-57.

1966 SABAR, Yona: "Tafsirim la-miqra' u-fiyutim bi-leshonam ha-Aramit shel Yehude Kurdista'n" [Commentaries and Hymns in the Neo-Aramaic of the Kurdish Jews]. *Sefunot* 10, 337-412. Jerusalem: Ben-Zvi Institute.

1967 FOURCADE, J. F.: "Mission à Maalula," *GLECS* 11 (1966-67), 93-102.

1967 GORDON, Cyrus H.: Rev. of Macuch 1965 (Handbook). *JNES* 26, 133-135.

1967 JASTROW, Otto: *Laut- und Formenlehre des neuaramäischen Dialekts von Mīdin im Ṭūr 'Abdīn*. Bamberg: Rodenbusch. 2nd printing 1970. Reprint with new introduction and bibliography: Wiesbaden: Harrassowitz 1985.
A doctoral dissertation of the University of the Saarland. Sets the standard for Turoyo.

1967 RITTER, Hellmut: *Ṭūrōyo. Die Volkssprache der syrischen Christen des Ṭūr 'Abdīn*. A: Texte. Band I. (Band II: 1969; Band III: 1971). Beirut: Orient-Institut der DMG.
The largest collection of NA texts in phonetic transcription and German translation covering some 2000 pages.

1967 ROSENTHAL, Franz, editor: *An Aramaic Handbook*. Porta Linguarum Orientalium, N.S. 10. Wiesbaden: Harrassowitz.
The contributions on NA are by A. Spitaler (Maʿlula), H. J. Polotsky (Urmi and Zakho), H. Ritter (Turoyo), 62-111.

1967 SEGERT, Stanislav: Rev. of Tsereteli, Materialy (1965). *AO* 35, 492-3.

1967 SPITALER, Anton: "Wiederherstellung von scheinbaren alten vortonigen Längen unter dem Akzent im Neuaramäischen und Arabischen." In: *Festschrift für Wilhelm Eilers*, ed. G. Wiessner, 400-412. Wiesbaden: Harrassowitz.

1967 TSERETELI, Konstantin: "The Static Verb in Modern Aramaic Dialects." In: *Studi sull'Oriente e la Bibbia* (P. Giovanni Rinaldi Festschrift), 83-89. Genova.

1968 ARSANIS, G. V.: "Sovremennyy assiriyskiy yazyk" [The modern Assyrian language], *Yazyki Narodov SSSR* [The Languages of the Peoples of the USSR], ed. P. Ya. Skorik, vol. 2, 489-507. Leningrad: Nauka.

1968 BLAU, Joshua: Revs. of Ritter 1967 (vol. 1) and Jastrow 1967. *BSOAS* 31, 605-610

1968 JASTROW, Otto: "Ein Märchen im neuaramäischen Dialekt von Mīdin (Ṭūr 'Abdīn)," *ZDMG* 118, 29-61.

1968 RITTER, Hellmut: "Die beste Frau. Eine Ṭūrōyo-Erzählung aus dem Ṭūr'abdīn." In: *Studia orientalia in memoriam Caroli Brockelmann*, ed. M. Fleischhammer, 155-159. Halle (Saale): Martin-Luther-Universität.

1968 RITTER, Hellmut: "'Aneze und Šammar in zwei Ṭōrānī (Ṭūrōyō) Erzählungen aus dem Ṭūr'abdīn." In: *Festschrift Werner Caskel*, ed. E. Gräf, 245-252. Leiden: Brill.
German summaries of stories nos. 29 and 30 in Ritter 1967.

1968 TSERETELI, Konstantin: "Compound Tense Forms in Modern Aramaic Dialects," *AION* n.s. 18, 247-252.

1968 TSERETELI, Konstantin: "On the comparative-historical study of the category of tense in modern Aramaic dialects." *Proceedings of the Twenty-Sixth International Congress of Orientalists, New Delhi 4-10 January, 1964.* Vol. 2, 38-41. New Delhi: Rabindra Bhavan. Same as Tsereteli 1963 (The Comparative...).

1968 TSERETELI, Konstantin: "Zur Determination und Indetermination der Nomina in den modernen aramäischen Dialekten." In: *Studia orientalia in Memoriam Caroli Brockelmann,* ed. M. Fleischhammer, 201-206. Halle (Saale): Martin-Luther-Universität.

1968 TSERETELI, Konstantin: *Grammatika sovremennovo assiriyskovo yazyka* [in Georgian]. Tbilisi. Same as Tsereteli 1964.

1969 CORRELL, Christoph: "Materialien zur Kenntnis des neuaramäischen Dialekts von Baḫ'a." München [Dissertation]. Texts, translation, vocabulary, and grammatical notes.

1969 GABRIYELOVA, A.: "Obrazets arameyskoy rechi salamasskikh yevreyev" [A sample of the Aramaic speech of the Jews of Salamas], *Vostochnaya filologiya* 1, 47-58. Tbilisi.

1969 HETZRON, Robert: "The Morphology of the Verb in Modern Syriac (Christian Colloquial of Urmi)," *JAOS* 89, 112-127.

1969 KROTKOFF, Georg: Rev. of Garbell 1965 (The Jewish, etc.). *WZKM* 62, 346-48.

1969 KROTKOFF, Georg: Rev. of Macuch 1965 (Handb.). *WZKM* 62, 348-50.

1969 KUTSCHER, E. Y.: "Two Passive Constructions in Aramaic in the Light of Persian." In: *Proceedings of the International Conference on Semitic Studies held in Jerusalem, 19-23 July 1965.* Pp. 132-151. Jerusalem: The Israel Academy of Sciences and Humanities. NA is discussed on pp. 144-146.

1969 MALONE, Joseph L.: Rev. of Macuch 1965 (Handb.). *Language* 45, 191-203.

1969 NAKANO, Aki'o: "Preliminary Reports on the Zaxo Dialect of Neo-Aramaic," *JAAS* (Tokyo) 2, 126-142.

1969 RUDOLPH, Kurt: Rev. of Macuch 1965 (Handb.). *OLZ* 64, 39-44.

1969 SARMAS, William: *Persian-Assyrian Dictionary.* Teheran: Assyrian Youth Cultural Society.

1969 SEGAL, J. B.: Rev. of Garbell 1965 and Macuch 1965 (Handb.). *BSOAS* 32, 383-385.

1969 SIMONO, Nemrod and Kurosh BENYAMIN: *Turas mamlla yan grammatiqi blishana suraya swadaya* [Grammar of the colloquial Syriac language]. Teheran.

1969 TSERETELI, Konstantin: Rev. of Rosenthal 1967. *JAOS* 89, 774-777.

1970 GREENFIELD, Jonas: Rev. of Garbell 1965. *JAOS* 90, 293-295.

1970 NAKANO, Aki'o: "Texts of Gzira Dialect of Neo-Aramaic," *JAAS* (Tokyo) 3, 166-203.

1970 TSERETELI, Konstantin G.: *Grammatica di assiro moderno*. Napoli: Istituto Orientale di Napoli.
The Italian translation of Tsereteli 1964.

1971 BLAU, Joshua: Rev. of Ritter 1967, vol. 2. *BSOAS* 34, 396-397.

1971 CERULLI, Enrico & F. A. PENNACCHIETTI: *Testi neo-aramaici dell'Iran settentrionale*. Napoli: Istituto Orientale di Napoli.
Texts in the Urmia dialect with translation and glossary.

1971 JASTROW, Otto: "Ein neuaramäischer Dialekt aus dem Vilayet Siirt (Ostanatolien)," *ZDMG* 121, 215-222.
The first report on a NA dialect in eastern Turkey (village Härteven) which is different from Turoyo. Cf. Jastrow 1988.

1971 TSERETELI, Konstantin: Rev. of Ritter 1967. *Oriens* 21-22 (1968-69), 503-508.

1972 COHEN, David: "Neo-Aramaic." In: *Encyclopedia Judaica*. New York: Macmillan.

1972 TSERETELI, Konstantin: "Analytical Verbal Forms in Modern Aramaic Dialects," *AION* n.s. 22, 17-23.

1972 TSERETELI, Konstantin: "Neuaramäisch." *Berliner Byzantinische Arbeiten*, vol. 43 *(Von Nag Hammadi bis Zypern)*, 47-64.

1972 TSERETELI, Konstantin: "The Aramaic Dialects of Iraq," *AION* n.s. 22, 245-250.

1973 BARUKH, Shemuel and Yosef BINYAMIN: *Sefer Taame Hamitsvot*. Jerusalem [YS].

1973 BLAU, Joshua: Rev. of Ritter 1967, vol. 3. *BSOAS* 36, 131-133.

1973 DEGEN, Rainer: Rev. of Tsereteli 1970. *WO* 7, 182-185.

1973 JACOBI, Heidi: "Grammatik des thumischen Neuaramäisch (Nordostsyrien)," *AKM* 40,3.
Due to the mixed population of refugees from different regions along the Khabur, it is questionable that this language can be treated as a genuine dialect. The grammatical analysis does not reveal anything which has not been known before. Verbal forms with the prefix *qam-* are not discussed although the texts furnish three examples. Rev. Degen 1977 and Rundgren 1977.

1973 NAKANO, Aki'o: *Conversational Texts in Eastern Neo-Aramaic (Gzira Dialect)*. Study of Languages and Cultures of Asia and Africa, A Series, No. 4. Tokyo: Institute for the Study of Languages and Cultures of Asia and Africa.
Very interesting texts on everyday life recorded from a Jewish informant born in Israel from parents who immigrated from Cizre, Turkey. The dialect is very close to those of the Zakho-Amadia corridor. Glossary and notes. Manuscript completed in 1971.

1973 SOLOMON, Zomaya S. and Robert K. HEADLEY, Jr.: "The Phonology of Modern Spoken Syriac," *Anthropological Linguistics*, vol. 15, 136-147.

A discussion of the articulation of NA sounds based on the dialect of Tkhuma.

1974 AVINERY, Iddo: "Sippur ba-niv ha-Arami shel Yehudey Zakho" [A tale in the Neo-Aramaic dialect of the Jews of Zakho]. In: *Henoch Yalon Memorial Volume*, 8-16. Jerusalem.

1974 CORRELL, Christoph: "Ein Vorschlag zur Erklärung der Negation *ču (čū)* in den neuwestaramäischen Dialekten des Antilibanon," *ZDMG* 124, 271-285.

1974 MACUCH, Rudolf und Estiphan PANOUSSI: *Neusyrische Chrestomathie*. Porta Linguarum Orientalium, N.S.XIII. Wiesbaden: Harrassowitz.
A wide range of texts in Syriac script. The introduction contains a sample in transliteration and phonetic transcription showing the considerable difference between the two. Substantial glossary.

1974 SABAR, Yona: "First Names, Nicknames and Family Names among the Jews of Kurdistan," *Jewish Quarterly Review* 65, 43-51.

1974 SABAR, Yona: "Ha-yesodot ha-'Ivriyim ba-niv ha-Arami she-be-fi Yehude Za'kho be-Kurdista'n" [The Hebrew Elements in the Neo-Aramaic Dialect of the Jews of Zakho]. *Leshonenu* 38, 206-219.

1974 SABAR, Yona: "Nursery Rhymes and Baby Words in the Jewish Neo-Aramaic Dialect of Zakho (Iraq)," *JAOS* 94, 329-336.

1974 SABAR, Yona: "The Socio-Linguistic Aspects of the Bilingual Hebrew Neo-Aramaic Contact in Israel." *Hebrew Abstracts* 15, 44-47.

1974 SARA, Solomon I.: *A Description of Modern Chaldean*, Janua linguarum, Series practica, 213. The Hague: Mouton.
The book claims to be the description of the dialect of Mangesh in Iraqi Kurdistan. Its material, however, is not distinguishable from normalized Fellihi. The fact that the author acts as his own informant is not an advantage, since he left the village at age eight. Too much space is allotted to phonology at the expense of morphology and syntax. The structuralist formalism of the description obscures rather than elucidates the otherwise well-known facts. Rev. Poizat 1981.

1974 SIMONO, Nemrod: *Meltā dlišānā atorāyā swadāyā wper'oh* [The verb in the Assyrian vernacular and its derivatives]. Teheran.
French translation: Poizat 1981.

1975 ODISHO, Edward Y.: "The Phonology and Phonetics of Neo-Aramaic as spoken by the Assyrians in Iraq." Unpublished Ph.D. dissertation, University of Leeds.

1975 SABAR, Yona: "Ha-yesodot ha-'Ivriyim ba-nivim ha-Aramiyim shel Yehude Azerbaija'n" [The Hebrew Elements in the Neo-Aramaic Dialects of the Jews of Azerbaijan], *Leshonenu* 39, 272-294.

1975 SABAR, Yona: "The Impact of Israeli Hebrew on the Neo-Aramaic Dialect of the Kurdish Jews of Zakho: A Case of Language Shift," *Hebrew Union College Annual* 46, 489-508.

1975 SARMAS, William: *Assyrian Self Teacher.* Cannes: Private printing. On the author and his privately printed word lists, see Poizat 1981 ("Bibliographie"), *SL* 119-122.

1976 AVINERY, Iddo: "The Israeli Contribution to the Study of Neo-Syriac," *Afroasiatic Linguistics* 2:10, 39-47.

1976 LIPINSKI, E.: Rev. of Jacobi 1973. *Bibliotheca Orientalis* 33, 234-236.

1976 MACUCH, Rudolf: *Geschichte der spät- und neusyrischen Literatur.* Berlin: Walter de Gruyter.
Important additions and corrections in Brock 1978.

1976 MAROGULOV, Q. I.: "Grammaire néo-syriaque pour écoles d'adultes (dialecte d'Urmia)," traduit par Olga Kapeliuk. *GLECS* Suppl. 5. Translation of Marogulov 1935.

1976 MATVEYEV, K. P.: "Obraztsy sovremennykh assiriyskikh poslovits i pogovorok (dialekty Al'bak, Gavar)," *Semitskiye yazyki,* issue 3, 203-205. Moscow: Nauka.
On modern proverbs and sayings.

1976 PENNACCHIETTI, Fabrizio A.: "Un manoscritto Curdo in Karšuni da Arādin (Iraq)," *AION,* n.s. 24, 548-552.
On a manuscript of a Kurdish grammar in Syriac and in Nestorian script.

1976 PENNACCHIETTI, Fabrizio A.: "Zmiryata-d rawe: 'Stornelli' degli Aramei Kurdistanei." In: *Scritti in onore di Giuliano Bonfante,* 639-663. Brescia: Paideia Editrice.

1976 SABAR, Yona: "Lel-Huza: Story and History in a Cycle of Lamentations for the Ninth of Ab in the Jewish Neo-Aramaic Dialect of Zakho, Iraqi Kurdistan," *JSS* 21, 138-162.

1976 SABAR, Yona: *Pəšaṭ wayəhi bəšallaḥ.* A Neo-Aramaic Midrash on Beshallaḥ (Exodus). Introduction, Phonetic transcription, Translation, Notes and Glossary. Wiesbaden: Harrassowitz.

1976 SABAR, Yona: Rev. of Macuch/Panoussi 1974. *JAOS* 96, 438-9.

1976 SEGAL, J. B.: Rev. of Jacobi 1973. *JRAS,* 156.

1976 TSERETELI, K. G. : "Arameyskiye dialekty Iraka." In: *Semitskiye yazyki,* issue 3, 169-171. Moscow: Nauka.

1976 TSERETELI, K. G.: "Obraztsy sovremennoy assiriyskoy rechi (salamasskiye teksty)" [Samples of modern speech (texts from Salamas)]. In: *Semitskiye yazyki,* issue 3, 208-219. Moscow: Nauka.

1976 VAN DEN BRANDEN, A.: Rev. of Sara 1974. *Bibliotheca Orientalis* 33, 236-237.

1977 DEGEN, Rainer: Rev. of Jacobi 1973. *WZKM* 69, 124-5.

1977 ODISHO, Edward Y.: "The opposition / tʃ/ vs. / tʃh/ in Neo-Aramaic," *Journal of the International Phonetic Association,* vol. 7,2, 79-83.

1977 RUNDGREN, Frithiof: Rev. of Jacobi 1973. *Acta Orientalia* 38, 350-361.

1977 TSERETELI, Konstantin: "Zur Frage der Klassifikation der neuaramäischen Dialekte," *ZDMG* 127, 244-253.

1978 AVINERY, Iddo: "A Folktale in the Neo-Aramaic Dialect of the Jews of Zakho," *JAOS* 98, 92-96.

1978 BROCK, Sebastian: Rev. of Macuch 1976. *JSS* 23, 129-138.

1978 CORRELL, Christoph: *Untersuchungen zur Syntax der neuwestaramäischen Dialekte des Antilibanon*, AKM 44,4. Rev. Caquot 1985.

1978 ODISHO, Edward Y. and C. SCULLY: "Contrasting Patterns of Laryngeal Activity for Stops in Neo-Aramaic," *Proceedings of the Institute of Acoustics, 5-7 April, 1978*. Cambridge, England. A spectrographic investigation.

1978 OELSNER, J.: Rev. of Macuch/Panoussi 1974. *OLZ* 73, 259-261.

1978 SABAR, Yona: "Multilingual Proverbs in the Neo-Aramaic Speech of the Jews of Zakho, Iraqi Kurdistan," *IJMES* 9, 215-235.

1978 SARA, S. I.: Rev. of Sabar 1976 (Pəšaṭ). *Journal of Biblical Literature* 97, 124-125.

1978 TSERETELI, K. G.: *The Modern Assyrian Language*. Languages of Asia and Africa. Moscow: Nauka.
English translation of Tsereteli 1964 *(Sovremennyy)*. Expanded bibliography.

1978 TSERETELI, Konstantin: *Grammatik der modernen assyrischen Sprache (Neuostramäisch)*. Leipzig: Enzyklopädie.
German translation of Tsereteli 1964 *(Sovremennyy)* by Dr. Peter Nagel. Conjugational tables in Nestorian script, an index, and expanded bibliography added.

1979 COHEN, David: "Sur le système verbal du néo-araméen de Maʻlula," *JSS* 24, 219-239.

1979 DEGEN, Rainer: Rev. of Sabar 1976 (Pəšaṭ). *WO* 10, 143.

1979 MEEHAN, Charles and Jacqueline ALON: "The Boy whose Tunic Stuck to Him: A Folktale in the Jewish Neo-Aramaic Dialect of Zakho (Iraqi Kurdistan)," *Israel Oriental Studies* 9, 174-203. Tel-Aviv.

1979 ODISHO, Edward Y.: "An emphatic alveolar affricate," *Journal of the International Phonetic Association*, vol. 9,2, 67-71.
A technical discussion of the same phenomenon as announced in Krotkoff 1961.

1979 POLOTSKY, H. J.: "Verbs with Two Objects in Modern Syriac (Urmi)," *Israel Oriental Studies* 9, 204-227.

1979 RITTER, Hellmut: *Ṭūrōyo. Die Volkssprache der syrischen Christen des Ṭūr ʻAbdīn. B: Wörterbuch*. Das Autorenmanuskript zum

Druck in Faksimile gebracht von Rudolf Sellheim. Beirut: Orient-Institut der DMG.

This posthumously published work does not contain the verbs of Turoyo, which Ritter had planned to present separately, and the publication of the existing manuscript remains one of the most urgent tasks in NA studies.

1981 GROSSFELD, Bernard: Rev. of Sabar 1976 (Pəšaṭ). *JAOS* 100, 64-65.

1981 GAI, Amikam: "A Note on the Negation of the Aorist and the Future in Modern Syriac." In: *Studies Presented to Hans Jakob Polotsky*, ed. D. W. Young, p. 50. East Gloucester, MA: Pirtle & Polson.

1981 POIZAT, Bruno: Rev. of Sara 1974. *GLECS* Tomes XVIII-XXIII (1973-1979), 193-4.

1981 POIZAT, Bruno: "Un traité sur le verbe néo-araméen: présentation et traduction (partielle) d'un ouvrage en soureth (suret) de Nimrod Simono," *GLECS*, Tomes XVIII-XXIII (1973-1979), 169-192.
A partial French translation of Simono 1974.

1981 POIZAT, Bruno: "Une bibliographie commenté pour le néo-araméen," *GLECS*, Tomes XVIII-XXIII (1973-1979), 347-414.

1981 SABAR, Yona: "A Midrashic Commentary on the Book of Jonah in the Neo-Aramaic of the Jews of Kurdistan." In: *Jewish Thought in Islamic Lands*, ed. M. Zohory, 131-143. Jerusalem. [YS]

1981 SABAR, Yona: "Bibliography of Secondary Literature on New Aramaic," *Jewish Language Review* 1, 123-125. Addendum: 2 (1982), 98. [YS]

1981 SABAR, Yona: "Qistit Hanna: Sippur Hannah ve-shiv'at baneha ba-Aramit she-be-fi Yehude Kurdista'n" [The story of Hannah and her seven sons in the Aramaic spoken by the Jews of Kurdistan], *Pe'amim* 7, 83-99. Ben-Zvi Institute. [YS]

1982 BOYARIN, Daniel: Rev. of Sabar 1976 (Pəšaṭ). *Maarav* 3, 99-114.

1982 JASTROW, Otto: Rev. of Ritter 1979. *WZKM* 74, 305-308.

1982 KROTKOFF, Georg: *A Neo-Aramaic Dialect of Kurdistan*. Texts, Grammar and Vocabulary. American Oriental Series, vol. 64. New Haven: American Oriental Society.
A description of NA based on a corpus of texts recorded from an informant from the village of Aradhin near Amadia. The texts cover the life of the village. Some grammatical features of NA are discussed for the first time.

1982 KROTKOFF, Georg: Rev. of Tsereteli 1978. *BASOR* 248, 76-77.

1982 SABAR, Yona: " 'Al Tivam shel ha-targumim la-Miqra' (Sefer Bere'shit) ba-nivim shel Aramit ḥadashah Yehudit" [On the character of the Bible translations (Book of Genesis) in the dialects of modern Jewish Aramaic], *Leshonenu* 46, 124-140. [YS]

1982 SABAR, Yona: "Perush darshani le-sefer Yonah ba-Aramit Ḥadashah shel Yehude Kurdista'n [A homiletical commentary to the book of

Jonah in the modern Aramaic of the Jews of Kurdistan]. In: *Hagut 'Ivrit be-Artsot ha-Islam* [Jewish thought in Islamic lands], ed. Menahem Zohori *et al.*, 130-143. Jerusalem: Berit Ivrit Olamit. [YS]

1982 SABAR, Yona: *The Folk Literature of the Kurdistani Jews: An Anthology.* Translated from Hebrew and Neo-Aramaic Sources with Introduction and Notes. Yale Judaica Series, vol. 23. New Haven: Yale U. P.

1982 SABAR, Yona: "The Quadriradical Verb in Eastern Neo-Aramaic Dialects," *JSS* 27, 149-176.

1982 TSERETELI, Konstantin: "On One Suprasegmental Phoneme in Modern Semitic," *JAOS* 102, 343-346.

1983 BERGSTRÄSSER, Gotthelf: *Introduction to the Semitic Languages.* Specimens and Grammatical Sketches. Translated with Notes and Bibliography and an Appendix on the Scripts by Peter T. Daniels. Winona Lake, IN: Eisenbrauns. [See 1928]

1983 HARVIAINEN, Tapani: "Diglossia in Jewish Eastern Aramaic," *Studia Orientalia* (Helsinki) 55,2, 97-113.

1983 HOBERMAN, Robert D.: "Verb Inflection in Modern Aramaic: Morphosyntax and Semantics." Unpublished Ph.D. dissertation, University of Chicago.
This deeply penetrating study uses the best insights of modern linguistics. It is soon to be published in the American Oriental Series.

1983 ISHAQ, Yusuf *(et al.)*: *Toxu qorena* [Come, let us read]. Stockholm: Skolöverstyrelsen.
A reader in Turoyo which documents the creation of a new literary language. [WH]

1983 SABAR, Yona: *Sefer Bere'shit ba-Aramit Hadashah be-Nivam shel Yehude Zakho* [The Book of Genesis in Neo-Aramaic in the Dialect of the Jewish Community of Zakho]. Including selected texts in other Neo-Aramaic dialects and a glossary. Publications of the Hebrew University Language Traditions project. Jerusalem: Magnes Press.

1983 SABAR, Yona: "Tafsir la-haftarah shel shemini de-Fesah ba-Aramit hadashah shel Yehude Kurdistan." In: *Studies in Aggadah and Jewish Folklore.* Folklore Research Center Studies, 7, 317-336. Jerusalem: Magnes Press. [YS]

1983 SABAR, Yona: "Shne perushim darshiyim le-haftarat Asof Asifem (Yirmiyah 8:13-9:23) le-Tish'ah be-Av ba-nivim ha-aramiyim she-be-fi Yehude Kurdista'n (Za'kho ve-'Amidyah)" [Two commentaries on the Haftara Asof Asifem for the ninth of Ab in the NA dialects of the Jews of Kurdistan]. In: *Arameans, Aramaic, and the Aramaic Literary Tradition*, ed. Michael Sokoloff, 11-41 (Hebrew section). Ramat-Gan: Bar-Ilan University Press.

1984 SABAR, Yona: *Midrashim ba-Aramit Yehude Kurdista'n la-Parashiyot Va-Yeḥi, Be-Shallaḥ, ve-Yitro* [Homilies in the Neo-Aramaic of the Kurdistani Jews on the Parashot Wayḥi, Beshallaḥ and Yitro]. Edition, Hebrew translation and glossary. Publications of the Israel Academy of Sciences and Humanities. Section of Humanities. Jerusalem.

1984 SABAR, Yona: "The Arabic Elements in the Jewish Neo-Aramaic Texts of Nerwa and 'Amadiya, Iraqi Kurdistan," *JAOS* 104, 201-211.

1985 BROCK, Sebastian: Rev. of Krotkoff 1982. *BSOAS* 48, 149-150.

1985 CAQUOT, André: Rev. of Correll 1978. *JA* 273, 455-6.

1985 HOBERMAN, Robert D.: Rev. of Sabar 1983 *(Sefer Bere'shit)*. *JAOS* 104, 734-735.

1985 HOBERMAN, Robert D.: "The Phonology of Pharyngeals and Pharyngealization in Pre-Modern Aramaic," *JAOS* 104, 221-231.

1985 ISHAQ, Yusuf *(et al.)*: *Toxu qorena, kṭowo d cwodo. A.* Stockholm: Statens Institut för Läromedelsinformation. [WH, cf. 1983]

1985 JASTROW, Otto: see 1967.

1985 KROTKOFF, Georg: "Studies in Neo-Aramaic Lexicology." In: *Biblical and Related Studies presented to Samuel Iwry*, eds. Ann Kort and Scott Morschauser, pp. 123-134. Winona Lake: Eisenbrauns.
Etymologies and discussion of problem words in NA.

1986 GREENFIELD, Jonas: Rev. of Krotkoff 1982. *JAOS* 106, 842-843.

1986 JASTROW, Otto: "Mlaḥsŏ: An Unknown Neo-Aramaic Language of Turkey," *JSS* 30 (1985), 265-270.

1986 JASTROW, Otto: Revs. of Krotkoff 1982 and Sabar 1983 *(Sefer Bere'shit)*. *ZDMG* 135, 642-3.

1986 JASTROW, Otto: "The Turoyo Language Today," *JAAS* (Chicago) 1, 7-16.

1986 ODISHO, Edward: "Comments on the Epic of Kateeny," *JAAS* (Chicago) 1, 47-8, 17§-34§.
Short introduction to and samples of an epic of some 2000 verses. Extracts in Nestorian script and transcription.

1986 POLOTSKY, H. J.: "Neusyrische Konjugation." In: *On the Dignity of Man.* Oriental and Classical Studies in Honour of Frithiof Rundgren, edd. Tryggve Kronholm and Eva Riad (= *Orientalia Suecana*, vol. 33-35). Stockholm: Almqvist & Wiksell, 323-332. [WH]

1986 TOSCO, Mauro: Rev. of Krotkoff 1982. *AION* 46, 520-523.

1986 RUNDGREN, Frithiof: Rev. of Krotkoff 1982. *Acta Orientalia* 47, 172-173.

1987 HOBERMAN, Robert D.: Rev. of Sabar 1984 *(Midrashim)*. *JAOS* 107, 551-552.

1988 HOBERMAN, Robert D.: Rev. of Krotkoff 1982. *JSS* 33, 340-346.

1988 HOBERMAN, Robert D.: "The History of the Modern Aramaic Pronouns and Pronominal Suffixes," *JAOS* 108, 557-575.

1988 JASTROW, Otto: *Der neuaramäische Dialekt von Hertevin (Provinz Siirt)*. Wiesbaden: Harrassowitz.
Grammar, texts with German translation, glossaries (separate glossary of verbs). Cf. Jastrow 1971.

1988 ODISHO, Edward: *The Sound System of Modern Assyrian (Neo-Aramaic)*. Wiesbaden: Harrassowitz.
Study of the phonetics and phonemics of the Iraqi Koine, with introductory chapters on the ethnolinguistic history of the Assyrians and the character of the Koine vis-à-vis the Standard Written Language and the dialects.

The following titles are either forthcoming or in preparation and are listed as communicated by their authors or editors. The articles in the present volume are not included.

198? HOBERMAN, Robert D.: "Agglutination and Composition in Neo-Aramaic Verb Inflection." In: *Studia Linguistica et Orientalia Memoriae Haim Blanc Dedicata*, ed. A. Borg, S. Somekh, and P. Wexler. Wiesbaden: Harrassowitz (in press).

198? HOBERMAN, Robert D.: Rev. of Krotkoff 1982. *JSS*.

198? HOBERMAN, Robert D.: *The Syntax and Semantics of Verb Morphology in Modern Aramaic: A Jewish Dialect of Kurdistan*. American Oriental Series. [See Hoberman 1983.]

198? MACUCH, Rudolf: "Neumandäisch," *Porta Linguarum Orientalium*.

198? PENNACCHIETTI/TOSCO: "Testi neo-aramaici sovietici," *IO* Napoli.

198? SABAR, Yona: *A Dictionary of Jewish Neo-Aramaic*.

198? SABAR, Yona: "A Midrashic Commentary on Isaiah 10:32-12:6 in the Neo-Aramaic of the Kurdish Jews." In: *Dov Noy Festschrift*.

198? SABAR, Yona: "Substrata and Adstrata Elements in Jewish Neo-Aramaic." In: *Studia Linguistica et Orientalia Memoriae Haim Blanc Dedicata*. Wiesbaden: Harrassowitz.

198? SABAR, Yona: *The Book of Exodus in Neo-Aramaic*. Companion volume to Sabar 1983 *(Sefer Bere'shit)*.

198? SABAR, Yona: "The Nature of Oral Translation of the Book of Exodus in the Neo-Aramaic Dialect of the Jews of Zakho." In: *Festschrift S. Segert*.

198? SABAR, Yona: *The Neo-Aramaic Dialects and the Other Languages Spoken by the Jews of Kurdistan*. Studies on the History of the Iraqi Jewry and their Culture, IV.

198? SABAR, Yona: *Yona Gabbay's Popular Folktales of Kurdistan*.

Regrettably, two important works remain in manuscript, and, although their publication is among the most urgent tasks in NA studies, it is at this point uncertain if and when they will become available to scholars in the field. One is the part on the verb of H. Ritter's Turoyo dictionary (see Ritter 1979 and Jastrow 1982), the other H. J. Polotsky's description of the dialect of Zakho which is reportedly in the custody of the Department of Linguistics of the Hebrew University, Jerusalem.

Abbreviations

AION(-L) — Annali dell'Istituto Orientale di Napoli (Sezione linguistica).

AJSLL — American Journal of Semitic Languages and Literatures.

AKM — Abhandlungen für die Kunde des Morgenlandes (Wiesbaden).

AO — Archiv Orientálni (Prague).

BASOR — Bulletin of the American Schools of Oriental Research.

Bd. — Band.

BSOAS — Bulletin of the School of Oriental and African Studies (London).

GLECS — Comptes rendus du Groupe Linguistique d'Etudes Chamito-Sémitiques (Paris).

IJMES — International Journal of Middle Eastern Studies.

JA — Journal Asiatique (Paris).

JAAS (Chicago) — Journal of the Assyrian Academic Society (recently founded in Chicago; president Dr. Edward Odisho; 1st vol. 1986).

JAAS (Tokyo) — Journal of Asian and African Studies (of the Institute for the Study of Languages and Cultures of Asia and Africa, Tokyo).

JAOS — Journal of the American Oriental Society.

Jg. — Jahrgang.

JNES — Journal of Near Eastern Studies (Chicago).

JRAS — Journal of the Royal Asiatic Society (London).

JSS — Journal of Semitic Studies (Manchester).

MSOS — Mitteilungen des Seminars für Orientalische Sprachen (Berlin).

OLZ — Orientalistische Literaturzeitung.

Rev. — Review.

RSO — Rivista degli Studi Orientali (Rome).

SANGruzSSR — Soobshcheniya Akademii Nauk Gruzinskoy SSR (Tbilisi).

Sb. — Sitzungsberichte.

SMOMPK — Sbornik materialov po opisanii mestnostey i plem'on Kavkaza (Tbilisi).

TIYaANGruzSSR — Trudy Instituta Yazykoznaniya Akademii Nauk Gruzinskoy SSR (Tbilisi).

WO — Die Welt des Orients.

WZKM — Wiener Zeitschrift für die Kunde des Morgenlandes.

ZA — Zeitschrift für Assyriologie.

ZDMG — Zeitschrift der Deutschen Morgenländischen Gesellschaft.

II. Phonetics and Phonology

PHONETIC AND PHONOLOGICAL DESCRIPTION
OF THE LABIO-PALATAL AND LABIO-VELAR
APPROXIMANTS IN NEO-ARAMAIC

Edward Y. Odisho

Introduction

The phonology of the Neo-Aramaic (NA) dialects, in general, or of the Iraqi *Koine* (IK), in particular,[1] does not display strikingly unfamiliar features. However, certain phonological aspects of IK, as well as other varieties of NA, are interesting to note as being more characteristic than others. Those aspects are:

First, the phonological relevance of aspiration not only to *plosives*, but also to *affricates*. To illustrate, the system has

---

[1]Iraqi *Koine* designates the common dialect of daily communication among the Assyrians of Iraq which emerged after their resettlement in the urban areas of Iraq. Originally, the early settlers were speakers of scores of regional and tribal dialects, but, due to the creation of the Standard Written Form of NA introduced by the missionaries in the 19th century and the intermingling and intermarriages among the speakers of various regional and tribal dialects, a spoken norm of NA developed gradually and consolidated itself as the speech of the first, second and later generations born in the major urban areas of Iraq. This does not mean that the regional and tribal dialects have disappeared. On the contrary, they are still used by the grandparents and the rural population of Assyrians.

Unfortunately, the political turmoil in the Middle East has led to the immigration of thousands of Assyrians to the United States and European countries. For instance, Chicago today accommodates no fewer than 60,000 speakers of NA, most of whom are from Iraq and Iran. Of great interest is the fact that linguistically these two groups are easily distinguished because each one has developed a spoken *koine* that is characteristic to it. However, there is still greater dialectal diversification among the Assyrians from Iraq than among the Assyrians from Iran. Among the former group one can still hear typical representations of Tiari (both upper and lower), Tkhuma, Jilu, Baz, Mar Bishu, Shamsdin, Barwar, etc. dialects, whereas the latter group speaks what could broadly be labeled as 'general Urmian.'

29

/pʰ/ vs. /p/
/tʰ/ vs. /t/
/cʰ/ vs. /c/
together with
/tšʰ/ vs. /tš/

It is the last pair that is of phonetic and phonological interest since it is not commonly encountered in other languages[2] (Odisho 1975; 1977). The above opposition represents palato-alveolar sounds. IK has also an *emphatic unaspirated alveolar affricate*, /tṣ/ (Odisho, 1979).

Second, instead of the velar plosive pair /k/, /g/, IK has the palatal plosive pair of /cʰ/ or /c/ vs. /ɟ/ which is of a more restricted occurrence in languages.[3]

Third, IK is heavily laden with a wide range of double-plosive clusters in initial position, e.g. /pʰtʰ/, /tʰpʰ/, /bd/, /ɟd/, /dq/, /qd/, /qb/, /cʰtʰ/, /cʰpʰ/, etc. (Odisho, 1975).

Fourth, unlike most languages, IK is reminiscent of French in that it has a *labio-velar approximant* [w] as well as a *labio-palatal approximant* [ɥ]. It is the occurrence of the latter and its phonetic and phonological relationship to the former that this paper intends to investigate.

A Phonetic Statement

In the orthography, [w] and [ɥ] appear in the form of the alphabet characters 'waw' ● or 'beth' ⇉ with the dot indicating *Rukaxa* for which some traditional Semitists use the misnomer 'aspiration.' In modern linguistic terminology, *Rukaxa* designates spirantization because the conversion of ↲

---

[2]In 1913 *Le Maitre Phonétique* published the first ever phonetic text of Neo-Aramaic in IPA. It was the contribution of Osipov (Osipoff) who, according to D. Jones (1950), was a remarkable linguist and phonetician. The text had, however, been the cause of a dispute between Jones and P. Passy. The latter, a leading French phonetician, had reacted so strongly to Osipov's phonetic representation of the feature of aspiration that he described the language (i.e., NA) as 'langue excentrique' (Passy, 1913). According to Polotsky (1961), 'this epithet refers to the bewildering abundance of aspiration marks in Osipov's text and to their occurrence in unexpected surroundings.' By the 'unexpected surroundings' Polotsky undoubtedly means the affricate sounds.

[3]Some investigators tend to transcribe this pair as /k/, /g/. They do this either because they are not aware of the palatal nature of this pair or because they prefer the more familiar symbols of /k/, /g/ to the less familiar ones of /cʰ/, /ɟ/. This sort of graphic substitution has two drawbacks: (a) it fails to give a precise description of the sounds involved and (b) it may mislead the unfamiliar learner into thinking that those sounds are actually velar, not palatal. Of almost all the dialects of NA spoken by the Assyrians, /k/, /g/ are predominantly retained only in the Jilu dialect. On the other hand, in most of the Urmian dialects /cʰ/, /ɟ/ are further advanced and palatalized; thus they sound like the affricates /tšʰ/, /dž/.

ʝ, ܐ d, ܐ ch, ܓ ph, ܠ tʰ into ܝ ɣ, ܕ ð, ܟ x, ܦ f, ܬ θ involves the change of *plosives* into *spirants* (fricatives). It is only in the case of ܕ that the process does not represent spirantization because the diacritical sign converts the plosive into an *approximant*, more commonly known as 'semi-vowel' or 'frictionless continuant.'[4] Thus, the change with / b/ involves *approximation* rather than *spirantization*.

In IK there are three central approximants: [j], [w] and [ɥ].[5] In general phonetic terms, they are described as palatal, labio-velar and labio-palatal, respectively.[6] They represent the non-syllabic versions of the long vowels [i, u, y] (Ladefoged, 1982). [j] is excluded from this discussion because it involves no phonetic or phonological controversy. [ɥ] is different from [w] in two major features: in the place of articulation and in the lip position. [ɥ] has an advanced tongue position which is primarily palatal, while [w] has a retracted tongue position which is primarily velar. The lips with [ɥ] are more rounded and tensioned, thus displaying a very small labial aperture. With [w], the lips are relatively less rounded and tensioned, and the labial aperture is somewhat larger. Both features contribute to the overall distinctness of the two sounds. For those who are familiar with phonetic material in other languages, one has to mention the common presence of those two sounds in French as in 'huit' (eight) [ɥit] and 'oui' (yes) [wi]. However, unlike French, their occurrence in IK tends to be synchronically motivated, hence raising the issue of their phonological relatedness as one unit.

The phonetic material in IK indicates that [ɥ] is basically associated with the front vowels, namely [i] as in [ɥi] (be); [ɪ] as in [ɥɪdlɪ] (he did); [ɛ] as in [ɥetha] (being); and [a] as in [ɥarda] (flower). In contrast, [w] is associated with central and back vowels: [u] as in [wudun] (you do, pl.) and [ɔ] as in

---

[4]In the traditional terminology, sounds like / w, j, ɥ/, etc., are given the label 'semi-vowel' or 'frictionless continuant' *(Principles of the International Phonetic Association*, 1949). In the 1979 volume of the *Journal of the International Phonetic Association*, which is issued by the IPA, the international chart of sounds was revised with many radical changes, one of which was the replacement of the terms 'semi-vowel' and 'frictionless continuant' with the term 'approximant.' This particular change was, most likely, brought about under the influence of Professor P. Ladefoged, who has been a member of the IPA Council for a long time and had originally coined the term which D. Abercrombie (1967) then popularized.

[5]In an attempt to elicit the phonetic realization of the IK [ɥ] in the speech of the Assyrians of Iran, six speakers were asked to pronounce words containing the relevant sound. The results were highly consistent in that all [ɥ] realizations in IK were replaced with the labio-dental approximant [ʋ]. In fact, this substitution is a salient difference between the Iraqi *Koine* and the Iranian *Koine* of NA.

[6]Ladefoged uses the terms 'labial-velar' and 'labial-palatal' instead of 'labio-velar' and 'labio-palatal' to make them look more consistent with his own description of sound categories (Ladefoged, 1971).

[ɟawɔ] (in it, 3rd P.f.). By central vowels I mean the vowels that occur in emphatic *(mufaxxama)* contexts. Experimental evidence for both NA (Odisho, 1975) and Arabic (Al-Ani, 1970) shows that the front spread and unrounded vowels [i, ɪ, ə, a] are highly susceptible to emphasis; they are retracted and lowered, thus becoming more compatible with the articulation of [w]. In fact, in IK there are no occurrences of [ɥ] in emphatic contexts. In the following pairs of words, which are solely distinguished by the presence or absence of the features of emphasis, [ɥ] of the plain words uniformly converts to [w]:

Plain	Emphatic
[raɥɪ] 'a kind of Tiari folk song'	[rɑwɪ] 'becomes drunk'
[ɥada] 'doing'	[wɑdɑ] 'promise; appointment'
[haɥi] "they be"	[hɑwi] 'my air'
[naɥɪ] 'nits'	[nɑwɪ] 'oozes'
[saɥa] 'old'	[sɑwɑ] 'thirst'

This replacement of [ɥ] with [w] in the emphatic contexts is not unexpected if we understand the nature of the tongue configuration required for emphasis. A major articulatory maneuver that executes emphasis is the backward gesture of the tongue. In other words, the tongue tends to push itself backwards to bring about the necessary pharyngeal constriction (al-Ani, 1970; Ali and Daniloff, 1972; Odisho, 1975). It is this backward gesture of the tongue that causes a retraction in the location of [ɥ] from palatal to velar, hence emerging as [w]. With many sounds, especially the alveolars /t/, /d/, the shift in the place of articulation is only nominal as the tongue has its tip anchored at the alveolar ridge. [ɥ] being a labio-palatal approximant, there is no anchorage involved, thus the tongue easily gives in to the backing gesture.

A Phonological Statement

In an earlier work (Odisho, 1975), the nature of [ɥ] was not satisfactorily identified. It was thought then that IK had /w/ as the primary phonological unit with some secondary contextual variants. More lip rounding was reported for one of its variants, but the failure to realize the change in the place of articulation of that variant made the investigation fall short of identifying it as [ɥ]. Further investigation since then has firmly established [ɥ] as a characteristic sound in IK. From the phonological point of view, it is obvious that [ɥ] and [w] are in complementary distribution, since the occurrence of [w] is confined to emphatic contexts. Another phonological revision relevant in this respect is my tendency to treat [ɥ] as the underlying (abstract) form from which [w] is derived according to a simple and neat rule:

$$\text{ɥ} \longrightarrow \text{w} / \underline{\quad} \begin{bmatrix} \text{v} \\ +\text{back} \end{bmatrix}$$

The rationale for this treatment stems from the fact that, when the native speakers of IK embark on learning foreign languages, the dominant trend is to replace the /w/ and /v/ in those languages with [ɥ]. They usually experience great difficulty in mastering /w/ and /v/. The frequent recurrence of [ɥ] in the English and Arabic speech of an Assyrian constitutes a major clue for his/her ethnic and linguistic identification.

Most interesting of all is the fact that the very existence of /ɥ/ in the system is apparently tied up with the presence of the palatal triplet /cʰ, c, ɟ/ rather than the velar triplet /kʰ, k, g/. In other words, /ɥ/ as a palatal is more compatible with the palatal category; in fact, from the articulatory point of view, it is very difficult to combine [ɥ] in the form of clusters with any member of the velar category. This may indicate that languages with a palatal category of plosives are more likely to have a [ɥ] while those with a velar category of plosives will lean towards a /w/. However, to seek more definitive statements in this regard, further investigation is indispensable.

References

Al-Ani, S. H. (1970). *Arabic Phonology.* The Hague: Mouton.

Abercrombie, D. (1967). *Elements of General Phonetics.* Edinburgh: Edinburgh University Press.

Ali, H. H. and Daniloff, R. (1972). 'A Contrastive Cinefluorographic Investigation of the Articulation of Emphatic-Nonemphatic Cognate Consonants,' *Studia Linguistica,* Vol. 26, No. 2.

International Phonetic Association, The Principles (revised 1949, 1971, 1979). London: University College.

Jones, D. (1950). *The Phoneme: its Nature and Use.* Cambridge: Heffer.

Ladefoged, P. (1971). *Preliminaries to Linguistic Phonetics.* Chicago: Chicago University Press.

——— (1982). *A Course in Phonetics.* New York: Harcourt Brace Jovanovich.

Odisho, E. Y. (1975). 'The Phonology and Phonetics of Neo-Aramaic as Spoken by the Assyrians in Iraq.' Unpublished Ph.D. thesis, Leeds University.

——— (1977). 'The Opposition /tš/ vs. /tšh/ in Neo-Aramaic,' *Journal of the International Phonetic Association,* 7, 79-83.

——— (1979). 'An Emphatic Alveolar Affricate,' *Journal of the International Phonetic Association,* 9, 67-71.

Osipov, S. (1913). 'Siriæk,' *Le Maitre Phonétique,* 28, 79-80.

Passy, P. (1913). 'Langue excentrique,' *Le Maître Phonétique,* 28, 120.

Polotsky, H. (1961). 'Studies in Modern Syriac,' *Journal of Semitic Studies,* 6, 1-32.

THE VELAR SPIRANT ġ IN MODERN EAST ARAMAIC DIALECTS

Konstantin Tsereteli

1. As is known, in the classical northwest Semitic languages the phonetic law of spirantization of plosives was operational, according to which in the postvocalic position the plosives b p d t g k changed to the corresponding spirants ḇ p̄ ḏ ṯ ḡ ḵ. Subsequently, the latter were pronounced as labiodental v and f, interdental ḏ and ṯ, and velar ġ and ḫ. Thus, in the northwest Semitic languages, in particular Aramaic, there appeared a series of spirants (originally not characteristic of these languages) which, in the classical languages, represented allophones of the above plosives. However, in Modern Aramaic dialects the law of spirantization has ceased to function, and in many dialects the former allophones have acquired an independent phonological status by turning into phonemes (Tsereteli 1980). Thus, a velar voiced spirant ġ has appeared among the new phonemes. The fate of this sound in the history of Semitic languages in general is highly interesting and has long since been the object of study by Semitists.

According to the evidence of classical Semitic languages, the consonant ġ is attested in Ugaritic (⊁), Arabic (غ), and in the South Arabian inscriptions (Sab. ℸ). In all the other Old Semitic languages the sound ġ is not expressed graphically; instead of it, wherever it is expected, we find the grapheme which normally expresses pharyngeal voice spirant ' with the exception of Akkadian, in which ' corresponds to it, the latter occurring in place of ' as well. (An almost analogous phenomenon is also observable with the Semitic voiceless velar spirant ḫ: it is absent in all languages which lack its voiced correlate; the Ethiopic language is an exception, in which, although it has no ġ, ḫ exists along with the pharyngeal ḥ, as in Ugaritic, Arabic, and Sabaean.) This state of affairs complicates the reconstruction of the series of velar spirants in the Proto-Semitic phonological system.

Among Modern Aramaic dialects, the velar voiced spirant ġ occurs systematically in the West Aramaic dialects of Maʻlūla. There, not only has the spirantized ḡ been preserved as ġ, but the initial plosive g has changed to the spirant ġ as well (as is the case with all the other plosives, except the labials: k > ḫ, d > ḏ, t > ṯ; Tsereteli 1980: 212-213): ġabrōna "man," ġofna "vine," ġamla "camel" (cf. MEA gōra from gaḇrā; gipna, gamla, and so on), roġma "stone," reġra "leg," etc.

In the Central Aramaic Ṭūrōyo dialect the spirantized ḡ is also preserved as ġ: raġlo "leg" (< raḡlā), raġyo "raw" (< raḡyā), mfalaġ "divide!", but fälgo, filgo "half," and so on. In Modern East Aramaic dialects the velar voiced spirant ġ is pronounced rather rarely (cf. also Sara 1974:36) and is largely the consequence of a conditioned phonetic change of the voiceless spirant ḥ before voiced consonants (excepting the sonorants): U ġda "one" (< ḥda), ġdēta "joy" (< ḥdēta), maġdir "turn it over!" (< maḥdir), maġbir "tell me!" (< maḥbir), ġzīle "they saw" (< ḥzīle), and others, but the voiceless spirant ḥ before vowels and sonorants remains voiceless: pḥīli "cried" (< bḥīli), dḥiri "remembered" (often: tḥiri), ḥmärä "ass," ḥniqlɨ "got drowned; strangled," etc.

More often than not ġ occurs in loanwords: āġa (< Tur.) "lord, master," baydaġ (< P) "flag," damġa (< Tur.) "brand," dāmiġ "to brand," zāġa (< Az) "cave," ġalibūta (< Ar with Aram. ending -ūtā) "victory" and v. ġālib "to vanquish," ġulāma "servant" (< Ar) (Sara 1974:39) and others.

In Aramaic words proper the spirant ġ occurs very rarely. If it does, the voiced spirant ġ is rendered in writing through the corresponding grapheme ܓ [ġ].

We shall now discuss these words.

1) šāġiš [šāġiš] "to disturb, stir up; to make a tumult; to be agitated." žġušya (< šġūšyā) "agitation; disturbance, tumult," root: šġš. In classical Syriac the root šgš is used in this meaning: šġūšyā and šəgaš. Mention should here be made of the Modern Aramaic verb šaš, šáʾiš "to shake (intr.), to stagger," n.act. šāša šyāša (cf. Krotkoff 1982:169 - šʾaša, šya:ša), in the intensive: "to shake; to rock" (tr.), usually written with ʾ: [šāʾiš], but along with it: [šāʾiš] and [šā(g)š] (Maclean 1901:299). In interpreting the word šāġiš, Maclean points to OS [šgš], referring the reader to [šāʾiš] (Maclean 1901:310). Cf. in Arabic the verb sġs in stem II: "to agitate."

2) rāġiš ~ rāʾiš (Maclean 1901:295), rʾa:ša from rgš (Krotkoff 1982:168) "to feel; to wake up." Cf. OS rgš: rəḡaš "to be restless; to rage; to feel," reḡšā "a sense"; BA rgš, caus. "to come running agitated," H rgš: "to be restless, to be in restless motion," riḡšā "agitation, confusion."

Thus, in the present case the OS rgš has two connotations: "to feel" and "to be restless." The BA and H rgš has the latter meaning, whereas in Modern East Aramaic dialects rḡš is used only in the former meaning of "to feel," hence riḡša "feeling," raḡūša "sensitive" (Sargis 1909:647 - [riḡšā], [rāḡōšā]). The meaning "to wake up" evidently developed from this (cf. Cerulli 1971:117). It should be noted that in East Aramaic the verb in question is pronounced with a hard timbre: rišłɨ "woke up," rāyɨš "to wake up," and so on (cf. Kalashev 1894:360, with a hard timbre). This is the case when velarization is a reflex of the pharyngeal ʾ. Hence, in Modern Assyrian dialects this root is written with ʾ: [rʾš], although the spelling of these words with g also occurs: [rā(g)š] (Maclean 1901:289; Cerulli 1971:117); [rāʾyūšā] along with [rāḡūšā].

Along with the root rgš in Semitic languages we have the root r'š with an analogous meaning: H ra'aš "earthquake," v. r'š "to shake, to be shaken; to suffer," Ar ra'asa and ra'aša "to shiver, to shake," ra'š, ra'aš "shiver." Although the root r'š occurs in Old Syriac as well, its meaning ("to rend, to trample, to demolish") is hardly related to the above root.

It follows from the foregoing that to the OS rgš "to be restless; to feel" there correspond two roots in Hebrew: rgš and r'š, with almost identical meanings: r'š "to shake" and rgš "to be in restless motion." It is analogous in Arabic: rǧs (stem VIII) "to be in a state of agitation, confusion" and r's (r'š) "to shake, shiver."

3) U šrāya and šrāǧa "lamp; candle" (Kalashev 1894:405: šraya, šraǧa, šra; Maclean 1901:311: U šrāǧā, šrā, šrāyā). Cf. OS šrāǧā "lamp; candle," hence the verb šəraǧ "to light" (cf. Ar srǧ, IV: "to light, kindle," sirāǧ "lamp"), Mand šrg in the same meaning.

From the root šgr come: OS šəgar "to kindle, to stoke," Ar sǧr "to kindle a fire, to stoke an oven," but Mand šrg "to kindle." In Modern East Aramaic dialects the verbs "to light" and "to kindle" are formed from the same root š'r (< šgr): šāyir, šar, šā'ir (Maclean 1901:299 [šā(g)r] and [šā'ir], ibid., p. 310 [šā'ir]; in Kalashev this verb is formed from the root šyr, but with a hard timbre [1894:402]).

Thus, in West Semitic the root šrg alternates with šgr. In some of these languages, these two roots are used with a certain differentiation of meaning: (1) "to light" and (2) "to kindle." As is seen from the foregoing, there are two roots in Old Syriac: šrg "to light, to illuminate" and šgr "to kindle, to stoke." The same tendency is observable in Neo-Aramaic: šrāǧa "lamp" (along with šra, šrāya) and šā'ir "to stoke, kindle." The same in Mandaean: šraga "lamp," but šgr "to burn, to enflame." However, in Arabic the roots srǧ and sǧr occur in the same meaning: "to light, to kindle."

4) U dāgil "to deceive," but Al Ash zāǧil (Maclean 1901:83), U dägälä, but in Kalashev dagala (Kalashev 1894:272) and Al Ash zaǧāla "deceiver, liar." Cf. Mand dagala, OS dgl, II: "to deceive," daggālā "deceiver, liar," daggālūtā "deception; lie, falsehood"; Ar dagala "to lie."

It is interesting to note that in the Urmia dialect the 2nd radical g is preserved (from gg); however, in some other Modern East Aramaic dialects (Alqosh, Ashitha) ǧ is attested in this case in place of g, which is quite unexpected, for a geminated plosive in postvocalic position preserves its occlusive nature.

5) raǧūla ~ ravūla "gorge; valley" [rāǧūlā], [rāwūlā]; Al râ-ûlâ (Maclean 1901:289, OS rāgōlā). In Kalashev, without g: ravula, ravulta (Kalashev 1894:356). In Pera Sarmas' Dictionary this word occurs in two forms: with ǧ and with w instead of ǧ: [rāǧūlā] and [rāwūlā] (Sarmas 1965:325).

6) In Neo-Aramaic, the word aǧīra "hired servant" is attested in Pera Sarmas' Dictionary (p. 17). In the same dictionary we find another word formed from

the same root: aǧra "pay, payment." The latter word occurs in Ṭūrōyo as well: aǧro (Ritter 1979:29) and in Maʻlūla: aǧra (Bergsträsser 1963:30). In the Alqosh dialect g(ǧ) is missing in this word: yāyir "to hire," īra "hired servant, hireling," although Maclean writes these words with a "mute" g: [yā(g)ir] and [ʼī(g)īrā] (Maclean 1901:115 and 3). Cf. OS ʼeḡar in the same meaning: ʼaḡrā, Mand agra "payment." This root occurs in other Semitic languages as well: H OA Akk ʼgr; Ar ʼǧr (II) "to pay the price; to hire."

7) In the Ṭūrōyo, Alqosh, and Ashitha dialects the radical g in the form of ǧ is preserved in the word "bit, bridle": T lǧōmo (Ritter 1979:295); Al Ash liǧāma, liǧēma (Maclean 1901:145). In other East Aramaic dialects the second radical consonant is missing: łāma (Kalashev 1894:314, in Russian transcription - лама), but the word has a hard timbre, and hence is sometimes written with the pharyngeal spirant ʻ : [laʻmā], along with [la(g)mā], [lagmā] and [lāmā] (Maclean 1901:150; Sarmas 1965:189; Sargis 1909:583). However, in the denominative verb łāǧim "to bridle" ǧ is preserved in the eastern dialects as well (Kalashev 1894:314).

In Classical Syriac, two words are attested in the meaning of "bridle": ləḡāmā "bridle, bit" and luḡmā "bridle; jaw"; cf. also Mand lugma "cheek," Ar liǧām (possibly from Aramaic) and P lägām "bridle."

8) MEA paǧra "body" < paḡrā. (Kalashev 1894:34: paǧra), T faǧro (Ritter 1979:147); cf. OS and Targ paḡrā; paḡranāya "bodily" < paḡrānāyā.

9) MEA sāǧid "to bow down, to worship; to make obeisance" (Kalashev 1894:366: siǧädtä, säǧid); sǧīda "worthy" < sḡīḏā. Cf. OS səḡeḏ, the same in Targ səḡaḏ, and Ar saḡada.

10) MEA māziǧ "to mix, stir" (something in a liquid) < māziḡ; mzīǧa "diluted" < mzīḡā (Kalashev 1894:355: mäziḫ). OS məzaḡ, the same.

11) syāǧa "fence; ledge; wall" but Al [syā(gʼ), syaʼa] (Maclean 1901:225, Krotkoff 1982:148, 156) < syāḡā, cf. OS and Targ syāḡā—id., Targ səyūḡā "fenced," H sūḡ (SWG) "fenced, enclosed" as well as the denominative verb sāḡ (OS) and sīḡ (Targ) "to fence, enclose," Ar. siyāǧ.

12) U salǧa [salǧā] "accuracy," salǧāna [sálǧānā] "accurate"; cf. Kalashev 1894:364: sälgä and sälgänä.

2. In Modern East Aramaic dialects we observe some cases where neither the plosive g (as is the case in these dialects) nor the spirant ḡ (as found in Maʻlūla and Ṭūrōyo) stands for the spirantized consonant ḡ, i.e. ḡ > φ. Two cases should be distinguished here: (a) when ḡ vanishes without a trace, and (b) when hard timbre remains after the omission of ḡ (ǧ). (Cf. Krotkoff 1982:13). The following words may serve as examples of the former case:

1) MEA māna "shield" < maḡanā. Cf. OS məḡannā, Targ məḡan, as well as H māḡēn, Ar miḡann (< GNN).

2) Tkh Ash nāya, Ti nāha (Maclean 1901:209) "dawn" < naḡhā, cf. OS nəḡah, Mand NG' "to dawn," BA naḡhā "daylight," H nāḡah "to illuminate, shine."
3) Al yāyir "to hire" and īra "hired servant" < yāḡir, 'īḡīrā (cf. above).
4) MEA šāda "almond" < šaḡdā (Krotkoff 1982:169: Mos še:ðe). Cf. OS šeḡdā, Targ šiḡdā.

As noted above, sometimes g > ∅, but the hard timbre remains in the word (as a reflex of the dropped g/ǧ):

1) U pāli "to divide," inf. plāyə (Krotkoff 1982:166: pla'a, pli:ya) < plg; cf. Maclean 1901:252: [pālig], [pālī], Cerulli 1971:108: [mplg] and [mpl'], but pälgä "half." Cf. T fəlgo, M flǧ II "to divide in two," felka "half." In Kalashev the word "to divide" is also with a hard timbre: pałi (p. 348), but "half" is with a soft timbre: pälgä (p. 350). The participle of the same verb "to divide," without ǧ but with a hard timbre, occurs in the Chrestomathie of Macuch and Panoussi: pułłitə "divided" (p. 108).

2) zāyə [za'yā] < za'yā (U) "animal's or bird's young," but T zōǧa, cf. Targ zə'ī "to be small." Th. Nöldeke seems to be right in pointing to the origin of za'yā from z'r (Nöldeke 1974:53), which is corroborated by the parallel use of zə'ī and zə'īr in the Targums in the meaning of "being small" (Levy 1959:266). However, we are here interested in z'y ∼ zgy in Modern Aramaic dialects.

3) nrg, hence Targ narḡā (Levy 1959:129), OS nārḡā "axe." Among Modern Aramaic dialects the 3rd radical g has been preserved only in Ṭūrōyo: närgo (Ritter 1979:358). In East Aramaic dialects g is dropped, but the word is pronounced with a hard timbre: narə (cf. also Kalashev 1894:341, in Russian transcriptions: нappa; Krotkoff 1982:165: narə), being spelt in two variants: [nar'ā] and [narḡā] (see, e.g. Maclean 1901:218; Sargis 1909:549).

Semantically close to the root nrg is ngr, which occurs both in Middle Aramaic (Classical Syriac, Judeo-Aramaic) and in Neo-Aramaic: Targ nəḡar "to saw; to work in wood" (Levy 1959:91), OS nəḡar "to chop," in the intensive: naggar "to carpenter," MEA nāgir "to carpenter" (Maclean 1901:209). The word "carpenter" is formed from the same root: Targ naggārā, OS naggārā, Mos nagāra (Maclean 1901:209); in Pera Sarmas: [nagārā], but naǧar (U) from Ar naǧǧār. It should be noted that in the word narə the short vowel is pronounced in a stressed open syllable; in addition, sometimes a long r is heard here, hence in Kalashev нappa is given with a double r.

3. The following can be concluded from the foregoing:

1) In Modern East Aramaic dialects—in words originally Aramaic (or in old borrowings)—the velar voiced spirant ǧ, occurring rather rarely, derives from the plosive phoneme g, originally spirantized in postvocalic position. In such cases the phoneme ǧ is rendered in writing through a corresponding grapheme ܓ [ǧ].
2) In some words the consonant g(ḡ) is omitted, which is usually reflected in writing: the word is spelled without g(ǧ) or with the given letter, but with a

special sign showing that the g(ġ) is not pronounced: ⅃ [(g)].

3) In the latter case (when g/ġ is dropped) the vowels of this word are often velarized, as is also the case in words etymologically containing the pharyngeal voiced spirant ' (cf. ɑynɑ "eye" < 'aynā, šmīḷi "he heard" < šmī'li, etc.). In such cases the letter 'ayn frequently occurs in writing in place of the expected g/ġ; sometimes, however, letters rendering the pharyngeal consonant ' and the velar consonant g/ġ alternate in one and the same word (cf. [nargā] ~ [nar'ā], [laġmā] ~ [la'mā]). Thus, judging by the reflex of the omitted consonants (in the present case, velarization), here one may speak of the alternation of ' ~ ġ in East Aramaic dialects. Evidently this accounts for the use of ' instead of the omitted g/ġ in the words under discussion.

4) Cases are also observable in the above examples in which g ~ ' alternation is attested in related roots (evidently of the same origin), as šgš "to be agitated," "to revolt," and š'š "to shake, to be unsteady"; rgš "to feel," "to be restless" and r'š "to wake up, to start," which occasionally finds parallels in other Semitic languages as well: H rgš "to be in a restless state, to be in restless motion," and r'š "to shake," Ar rġs and r'š (the same).

4. Proceeding from the presence of velarization in words of the indicated type, a root with ' could be reconstructed for them: pl' "to divide," from plġ (< plg).

The alternation of the velar voiced spirant ġ with the pharyngeal voiced spirant ' is known in classical Semitic languages: Ar SA Ug ġ ~ H A Eth ' (cf. Ar ṣaġīr and BA zə'īr "small"; Ar ġarb and H 'ereḇ "evening," etc.); hence, such alternation in Modern East Aramaic dialects does not appear impossible from the standpoint of Semitic phonology. Here I would like to recall the Greek and Latin rendering of the Hebrew pharyngeal voiced spirant ' by the Greek γ and Latin g, along with φ.

5. As noted above, the MES ġ is characterized by a low frequency, in contradistinction to its voiceless correlate ḫ, which exhibits high frequency. Thus, the MEA ġ is a marked phoneme (which cannot be said in the same way with regard to the central Aramaic dialect of Ṭūrōyo, and hardly at all regarding the West Aramaic dialect of Ma'lūla). It should be noted that the omission of g/ġ—leading to the velarization of a word, i.e., manifesting the characteristic feature of the pharyngeal spirant ' in these dialects—perhaps points to the fact that ġ turned into ' prior to its disappearance (and then disappeared with the rest of the 'ayns, leaving only a trace in the form of velarization). Only thus can one account for the velarization of a word that once had a velar spirant ġ. If this is actually the case, then we are dealing with a certain repetition of the history of velar consonants in Aramaic: P.-S. ġ > ', which later > φ. Thus, e.g., plg > plġ > pl' > plφ (cf. P.-S. tġr A tar'ā, MEA tɑrɑ "door, gate").

Thus, the velar voiced spirant ġ which in Modern Aramaic dialects results from g, becomes φ, possibly through ', i.e., g > ḡ > ġ > ' > φ.

6. The phonological characteristics of the entire series of velar consonants in Modern East Aramaic dialects calls for a special study—both in its synchronic and diachronic aspects. The purpose of this paper has been to present the phonological status of the velar voiced spirant $\dot{g}$ and its historical development in Modern East Aramaic dialects.

References

BERGSTRÄSSER, G. 1963. *Einführung in die semitischen Sprachen.* Darmstadt.

CERULLI, E. 1971. *Testi Neo-Aramaici dell'Iran settentrionale.* Raccolti da Enrico Cerulli con glossario di Fabrizio Pennacchietti, I. Napoli.

KALASHEV, A. 1894. "Russko-aysorskiy i aysorsko-russkiy slovar," *SMOMPK* XX. Tiflis.

KROTKOFF, G. 1982. *A Neo-Aramaic Dialect of Kurdistan.* New Haven.

LEVY, J. 1959. *Chaldäisches Wörterbuch.* Köln.

MACLEAN, A. J. 1901. *A Dictionary of the Dialects of Vernacular Syriac.* Oxford.

MACUCH, R. and E. PANOUSSI. 1974. *Neusyrische Chrestomathie.* Wiesbaden.

NÖLDEKE, Th. 1974. *Grammatik der neusyrischen Sprache.* Hildesheim.

RITTER, H. 1979. *Ṭūrōyo, die Volkssprache der syrischen Christen des Ṭūr 'Abdîn.* B. *Wörterbuch.* Beirut.

SARA, S. I. 1974. *A Description of Modern Chaldean.* The Hague-Paris.

Sargis, the archimandrite. 1909. *Russko-sirskiy leksikon.* Urmia.

SARMAS, Pera. 1965. *Assyrian Vocabulary.* Teheran.

TSERETELI, K. 1980. "Zur Frage der Spirantization der Verschlußlaute in den semitischen Sprachen," *ZDMG* 130.

Abbreviations and Symbols

A — Aramaic
Akk — Akkadian
Al — Alqosh Neo-Aramaic dialect
Ar — Arabic
Ash — Ashitha Neo-Aramaic dialect
Az — Azeri
BA - Biblical Aramaic
caus. — causative
Eth — Ethiopic
H — Hebrew
inf. — infinitive
intr. — intransitive
M — Ma'lūla Neo-Aramaic dialect
Mand — Mandaic
MEA — Modern East Aramaic
Mos — Neo-Aramaic dialect of Mosul
n.act. — nomen actionis
OA — Old Aramaic
OS — Old Syriac, Classical Syriac
P — Persian
P.-S. — Proto-Semitic
SA — South Arabian
Sab. — Sabaean
T - Ṭūrōyo, Neo-Aramaic dialect of Ṭūr 'Abdīn
Targ — Targumic
Ti — Tiari Neo-Aramaic dialect
Tkh — Tkhumi Neo-Aramaic dialect
tr. - transitive·
Tur — Turkish
U — Urmia Neo-Aramaic dialect
Ug — Ugaritic
v. — verb
< — results from, derives from
> — results in, becomes
* — reconstructed form
[ ] — for graphemic transliterations

III. Morphology and Lexicology

FEMININE GENDER IN MODERN CHALDEAN FORM AND FUNCTION

Solomon I. Sara, S.J.

The lexicon of any one language is constituted of a list of unique items that combine to form the messages of that language. No language, however, uses a unique form for every semantic nuance in its representational inventory of reality, nor for every nuance that may occur in all its possible messages. To effect a certain economy of form and function, a language utilizes many of the same forms in varying combinations and contexts to attain its goal. This study will show how language attains economy by employing the same form multifunctionally. The illustrations in this study are taken from Modern Chaldean, and they will provide a summary presentation of the uses of the feminine gender in that language.

Modern Chaldean is a Semitic language related to classical Syriac and Aramaic directly, and to Hebrew, Arabic and the other Semitic languages more remotely. Gender is an obligatory category of the noun system of these languages. It is marked by means of suffixes to the base forms at the level of morphology. Gender is also manifested at the level of syntax, i.e., the phrase and the clause levels. The manifestation at the level of the phrase is indicated by the agreement in gender among the head noun and its modifiers. The manifestation at the level of the clause is indicated by the agreement in gender between the pronominal suffixes of the verb and the nominal subject of the clause. Every noun in Modern Chaldean is either masculine of feminine.

The Gender Marker

The noun system of Modern Chaldean is divided into two subclasses, the masculine and the feminine. The feminine is the marked member and the masculine is the unmarked member of the opposition. The feminine noun is marked by the addition of one of the feminine suffixes to the nominal stem, i.e., /-ta, -θa, - i/. Some nominals come in pairs; e.g.,

1. *Feminine*   *Masculine*

    suus-ta   suus-a   'mare/horse'
    xmaar-ta   xmaar-a   'donkey/ass'
    beetiik-ta   beetiik-a   'sparrow,' f,m

koodin-ta	kaawidn-a	'mule,' f,m
zoor-ta	zoor-a	'small,' f,m
smooq-ta	smooq-a	'red,' f,m
naatoor-ta	naatoor-a	'guard,' f,m
xoor-ta	xoor-a	'friend,' f,m

In the above cases the feminine is marked with the /-t(a)/ suffix added to the stem form of the nominal. The feminine base form will change according to the morphophonemic rules, e.g., in the above cases the vowel in the closed syllable caused by the addition of /-ta/ will be shortened; e.g., /susta, xmarta, etc./.

Other nouns occur only in the feminine form with no corresponding masculine form; e.g.,

2. *Feminine*

maa-θa	'village'
naa-θa	'ear'
gin-θa	'garden'
duk-θa	'place'
xam-θa	'maiden'
šab-θa	'saturday'
sik-θa	'stick'
magree-θa	'razor'
ṣabee-θa	'finger'
miz-ta	'hair'
qiš-ta	'bow'
ʔaruu-ta	'friday'
bee-ta	'egg'

In the above forms the feminine is marked with the /-θa/-ta/ suffixes and they do not have corresponding masculine forms. They do not come in pairs like the previous forms.

There are other nouns that are marked for gender by the suffix /- i/. e.g.,

3. *Feminine*

hann-i	'Joan'
ʔaad-i	'habit'
kaaw-i	'window'
maʔn-i	'meaning'

There are also nouns that do not exhibit an overt feminine gender marker even though they are feminine nouns; rather they have the unmarked or the masculine ending. e.g.,

4. *Feminine*

baaq-a	'bouquet'
dipn-a	'side'
ʔar-a	'earth'

Ɂeen-a   'eye'
Ɂiiḍ-a   'hand'
Ɂaql-a   'foot'
Ɂaqirw-a   'scorpion'
šimš-a   'sun'

There is gender agreement in syntactic constructions for the type of nouns listed above similar to the morphologically marked ones as illustrated below:

5. *feminine*   *masculine*
   /suusta smooqta/   /suusa smooqa/
   'red mare'   'red horse'

   /xmaarta koorɨ/   /xmaara koora/
   'blind donkey'   'blind ass'

   /maaθa ḥaruqta/
   'distant town'

   /xamθa xliiθa/
   'pretty maiden'

   /baaqa kriiθa/
   'short bundle'

   /Ɂara wišta/
   'dry ground'

   /twira Ɂaqli/   /twirɨ xaasi/
   'My leg broke.   'My back broke.'

The Diminutive

A class of nouns that is invariably marked for gender is the diminutive class of nouns. The morphological marker for the diminutive form itself is the affix /-ik-/ added to the base form. Since gender is an obligatory category of nouns, a gender marker is suffixed to the diminutivized form, and this form is the invariable feminine marker /-θa/. e.g.,

6. *Base*   *diminutive*
   danw-a m.   danw-ik-θa f.   'tail/tailette'
   dast-a f.   dast-ik-θa f.   'bundle/handle'
   čamč-a m.   čamč-ik-θa f.   'spoon/tiny spoon'
   dɨqn-a m.   dɨqn-ik-θa f.   'beard/goatee'
   Ɂeen-a f.   Ɂeen-ik-θa f.   'eye/beady eye'
   Ɂeew-a m.   Ɂeew-ik-θa f.   'cloud/cloud patch'
   kund-a m.   kund-ik-θa f.   'short-tailed/shorter'
   neer-a m.   neer-ik-θa f.   'stream/rivulet'
   karm-a m.   karm-ik-θa f.   'vineyard/small...'
   kaas-a f.   kaas-ik-θa f.   'belly/tiny belly"
   kɨxw-a m.   kɨxw-ik-θa f.   'star/starlet'

qȧnn-a f.	qȧnn-ik-θa f.	'nest/tiny nest'
qaṣr-a m.	qaṣr-ik-θa f.	'castle/miniature...'
parr-a m.	parr-ik-θa f.	'feather/small...'
baabuj-a m.	baabuj-ik-θa f.	'slipper/tiny...'
zand-a m.	zand-ik-θa f.	'forearm/glove'

The list is not exhaustive, only illustrative of the process. The form is productive, but many forms do not seem to be in use, or meaningful. One can create contexts that will make diminutives meaningful and understood. There is a tendency to use a periphrastic structure to attain the same effect. It is much more common to use the adjective /zoorta - zoora/ 'small, f,m' with the noun than to create the morphologically complex formation of the diminutive. It is obvious that there is more articulatory effort in the formation of the diminutive form, due to its length, than in the use of the adjective.

The point of significance here is that the base form may be masculine or feminine, but the derived diminutive form is invariably feminine, marked with the suffix /-θa/. More on the use of these two forms of the apparently similar concepts, i.e. the diminutive and the periphrastic structures, will be discussed below.

Events

There is a class of derived nouns that are marked with the feminine gender marker exclusively. These nouns are derived from the verb form. The gender marker is added to the infinitive form of the verb, and the resulting form is a noun that has the general notion of a "single event, single session, single occurrence of the action specified." e.g.,

7.
infinitive	*derived nominal*	
ʔiixaala	ʔiixaal-ta	'eat/eating event'
zmaara	zmaar-ta	'sing/singing event'
nšaaqa	nšaaq-ta	'kiss/kissing event'
rwaaya	rwee-θa	'drink/drinking event'
gnaawa	gnoo-θa	'steal/stealing event'
bnaaya	bnee-θa	'build/building event'
qyaama	qyaam-ta	'rise/rising event'
bxaaya	bxee-θa	'cry/crying event'
draaya	dree-θa	'put/putting event'

This process is very productive. It has, however, certain limits where the semantics of the resulting form may not be acceptable. e.g.,

7a.
makpooni	*makpanta	'cause hunger/*'
maloopi	*malapta	'teach/*'
mamooθi	*mamaθta	'cause to die/*'
magwoori	*magwarta	'cause to marry/*'

These are causative forms. The causative, however, is not the reason for the non-acceptability of the above derivations. There are acceptable causative derivations in this category, as in the following:

7b. mbarboozi   mbarbaz-ta   'scatter/single time'
     meeqoori   meeqar-ta   'oppress/single time'
     manxoopi   manxap-ta   'embarrass/single time'

Alternate Plural

A fourth place where the feminine gender suffix occurs is in the plural of a class of masculine nouns. It is an alternate plural formation to the regular masculine plural formation. It regularly adds an additional connotation to the plurals of these masculine nouns which the regular plural does not support. e.g.,

8. *Two Plurals*

singular	*1st plural*	*2nd plural*
baab-a m.	baab-i m.	baab-awaaθa m.
'father'	'fathers'	'forefathers'
maam-a m.	maam-i m.	maam-awaaθa m.
'uncle, p'	'uncles'	'uncles in the clan'
xaal-a m.	xaal-i m.	xaal-awaaθa m.
'uncle, m.'	'uncles'	'uncles in the clan'
naaš-a m.	naaš-i m.	naaš-waaθa m.
'person'	'people'	'our people'
ʔaxoon-a m.	ʔaxoon-i m.	ʔaxoon-waaθa m.
'brother'	'brothers'	'brethren'
maar-a m.	maar-i m.	maar-waaθa m.
'owner'	'owners'	'known owners'
ʔeeḍa m.	ʔeeḍi	ʔeeḍ-awaaθa m.
'feast'	'feasts'	'religious feasts'

The second plural formation may be used in the plural sense to indicate multiplicity, but over and above that it also has the added semantic sense of some other particularity; e.g., 'forefather,' 'uncle' in the more extensive sense than the biological. So also does 'people,' meaning our people, in the sense of relatives, acquaintances, ethnic groups, etc., and 'owners,' in the sense of a known group of people and not the generic concepts of multiplicity of that concept. The label 'second plural' has no special significance besides that of distinguishing it from the 'first plural.' Many nouns in Modern Chaldean have two or more plurals.

The point of significance is that the plural ending is homophonous with that of the feminine plural ending, and it has the same semantic import of plurality with additional connotations. It does not, however, behave as a

feminine noun in terms of syntactic structure agreement. It agrees with
masculine forms of adjectives and verbal pronominal affixes. The plural
forms of these nouns have the same gender as their corresponding singular
nouns. Even though the plural suffix is feminine in form, the noun is still
masculine. The feminine plural ending is illustrated below: e.g.,

8a.   *singular*   *plural*
      maaθa f.   maaθ-waaθa f.   'town/s'
      xaaθa f.   xaaθ-waaθa f.   'sister/s'
      dunyɨ f.   duny-aaθa f.   'world/s'

Uses of the Diminutive

The use of the diminutive gives an added social and personal implication to
the notion of smallness. Reference to reduction in size is much more
commonly achieved by the use of the periphrastic structure. The diminutive
use goes beyond the notion of smallness to the notions of endearment,
delicacy, approval, or to their opposites like disapproval, meagerness,
shabbiness, derogation and similar concepts. All these obviously occur in
their proper linguistic and social contexts. The choice of the diminutive form
in place of the periphrastic structure implies social attitude towards the object
communicated about which would otherwise not be the case, as the examples
in the following sections illustrate.

Diminutive and Endearment

9a.   /ʔiixul b-čamčux/   /ʔiixul b-čamčikθux/
      'Eat with your spoon.'   'Eat with your little spoon.'

      /xɨlli danwux/   xɨlli danwikθux/
      'I love your tail.'   'I love your tailette.'

The above examples show that a mother feeding her baby and a pet owner
admiring a pet are being more than informative about the baby and the pet by
the use of the diminutive. They are indicating their attitudes toward the
addressees. The emotions of affection, tenderness and endearment are
conveyed by the use of the diminutive, an effect that would not have been
possible by the simple use of the noun.

Diminutive and Derogation

9b.   /dɨqneḥ d-gabbaarelɨ/
      'His beard is that of giants.'

      /dɨqnikθeḥ d-gabbaarela/
      'His meager beard is that of giants.'

      /danwa d-suuseḥ mxa ʔaθra xɨnneelɨ/
      'His horse's tail is out of this world.'

      /danwikθa d-suuseḥ mxa ʔaθra xɨnneela/
      'The tiny tail of his horse is out of this world.'

The uses of the diminutive in these contexts do not express admiration, delicacy or refinement, rather the meaning is that the object referred to, i.e. the beard or the tail, is to be ridiculed and dismissed as not worthy of the name.

Obviously the context plays a key role in the meaning and the interpretation of these structures and their full semantic and pragmatic imports. The point at issue is that the diminutive is a means of indicating one's attitude toward the subject under discussion and is not a mere size indicator.

Diminutive and Taboo

There is another aspect to the use of the diminutive that is relevant to certain taboo words. References to sex or sex organs in certain contexts is not socially acceptable. There are, of course, contexts in which these terms will, in all their starkness, be employed. One common use of these terms is in cussing. Cussing is a mode of speech that occurs in special contexts, i.e. in insults, during heated arguments, fights, brawls and similar incidents. In what are referred to as polite contexts, however, references to genitalia are not made by their names, but often are either not mentioned at all or are referred to obliquely; i.e., the meaning is indicated without using the words themselves. These are taboo words.

There is, however, a linguistic process around the taboo, a less objectionable way of using these words than would otherwise be possible, a process that will be inoffensive to the hearers. The process is the use of the diminutive form. Somehow the diminutization neutralizes and "de-taboos" these words sufficiently to make them pronounceable in certain polite contexts without offending one's hearers; e.g.,

9c.	šorma f.	šormikθa f.	'arse, anus'
	buuṭa ˙ m.	buuṭikθa f.	'penis'
	quuṭa m.	quuṭikθa f.	'pudendum, f'

Obviously there are many other taboo words that refer to sex organs or other topics. The point of significance is that there is a linguistic mechanism that sanitizes the terms and makes them usable. The regular taboo form may be masculine or feminine, but the diminutive form is invariably feminine in its linguistic form and linguistic function. The use of taboo words discussed here pertains to adult speech only. The use of diminutives with reference to babies or children is common and is outside the purview of this discussion and does not affect its argument.

Feminine and Smallness

There is one more use of the feminine form that we need to mention in this discussion. There are many forms in Modern Chaldean in which the feminine is not solely a gender marker but rather has a definite reference to size in addition to the gender. Such nouns refer to the same object except that the marked member is invariably the smaller one of the two, e.g.,

10. *regular*   *small size*

ʔaloola	'street'	ʔaloolta	'alley'
duuka	'space'	duukθa	'place'
diqna	'beard'	diqinθa	'chin'
masirqa	'comb'	masriqθa	'small comb'
magla	'scythe'	magilta	'sickle'
talma	'jar'	talimθa	'pitcher'
kiisa	'bag'	kiista	'shoulder bag'

This brief sketch indicates some of the mechanisms of language in effecting economy of form and function. This survey does not claim to be complete. When working within the confines of a single dialect, one finds that our lexical sources are very meager. Consequently it has not been possible to account exhaustively for all the lexical items that may have bearing on this topic.

Sources:

MACLEAN, Arthur John. 1901. *A Dictionary of the Dialects of Vernacular Syriac*. Oxford: Clarendon Press (Reprint: Amsterdam: Philo Press 1972).

RHÉTORÉ, J. 1912. *Grammaire de la langue soureth ou chaldéen vulgaire selon le dialecte de Mossoul et des pays adjacents*. Mossoul: Imprimerie des Pères Dominicains.

SARA, Solomon I. 1974. *A Description of Modern Chaldean*. Janua Linguarum, Series Practica, 213. The Hague: Mouton.

GENERAL EUROPEAN LOANWORDS
IN THE JEWISH NEO-ARAMAIC DIALECT
OF ZAKHO, IRAQI KURDISTAN
Yona Sabar

1. Introduction[1]

Neo-Aramaic, like other old and new Semitic languages, has incorporated a certain number of loanwords from European languages.[2] These loanwords are mostly from the semantic areas of modern technology, general western culture and medicine. Most of these words were probably incorporated in the spoken Neo-Aramaic dialect of the Jews of Zakho during the 1940's, just prior to their emigration en masse to Israel during 1950-51. They have been gleaned from my *Dictionary of Jewish Neo-Aramaic* (in progress) and from my personal knowledge of the dialect.

Zakho was a central Kurdish town of about 30,000 people, of whom about 5,000 were Jews (the largest Jewish community in Kurdistan at that time). The rest were mostly Muslim Kurds, and a substantial number of Christian Assyrians, Armenians, and some Arabs, mostly Iraqi officials.

Direct contact between the Jews of Zakho and speakers of European languages was practically non-existent. Only rarely would European travelers reach the distant border town of Zakho. Therefore, we have to assume that most of the European loanwords were incorporated via the intermediary urban languages, i.e., Arabic (mainly the spoken dialects of Mosul and

---

[1]A paper based on this article was presented at the annual meeting of the Middle East Studies Association at New Orleans, on November 23, 1985. I am grateful to my colleague Dr. Ralph Jaeckel for his kind help regarding the possible origin of some Turkish loanwords, and my brother Dr. Shalom Sabar for his help regarding the origin of several Italian loanwords. Special thanks to Professor Wolfhart Heinrichs for his most useful and keen editing remarks and suggestions.

[2]For specific studies on such loanwords in modern Arabic, see Smeaton, Sa'id; on modern Hebrew, see Weiman; on modern Persian, see Jazayery; on Turkish, see Kahane, Kahane and Tietze; for general studies on language expansion see the bibliography in Smeaton, pp. 183-190; Blau, Joshua (on Hebrew and Arabic); Stetkevych.

Baghdad), Turkish (especially during the first quarter of the century, when the Turkish cultural influence was still strong, to be gradually replaced by Arabic), and probably Persian and Kurdish.

Zakho is located not too far from the common borders of Iraq with Turkey, Syria, and Iran; hence, a strong cultural influence and linguistic borrowing from these countries. In the 1940's the contact of the Jews of Zakho with the much larger Jewish communities of the major cities of Mosul and Baghdad was greatly intensified thanks to the intoduction of motorized vehicles (bus till Mosul, and train to Baghdad). Many traveled back and forth to these urban centers, and some stayed there as immigrants, thus establishing a bilingual (Neo-Aramaic and Arabic) community.

After the collapse of the Ottoman rule, British-English cultural and linguistic influence became quite common in the major urban cities of Iraq.[3] This is indicated not only by borrowing many words from English, but also by the common use of English proper names, especially by Jews and Christians of Iraq, e.g., Albert, Edward, George, Maurice; Daisy, Doris, Juliet, Nancy. It seems that the French and Italian loanwords belong to the earlier stage of borrowing, probably via Turkish or Syrian Arabic. While borrowing from Russian is rare in Zakho, it is common in the Christian and Jewish Neo-Aramaic dialects of Urmi (Persian Azerbaijan), due to the common borders with the Soviet Union and Neo-Aramaic-speaking immigrants in Russia.[4]

2. General Notes

An effort was made to track each word in the various available dictionaries of the contact languages, i.e., Iraqi Arabic, Anatolian Arabic, modern written Arabic, Syrian Arabic, Turkish, Kurdish, and Persian.

Not every word could be found in the various dictionaries. Especially those for the spoken dialects are by nature incomplete. For various reasons (some practical, some nationalistic-puristic) they lack many words, especially European loanwords, even when those are common in the everyday speech of the masses. For example, the *Dictionary of Iraqi Arabic* is actually only of the colloquial Arabic spoken in Baghdad, excluding the distinct spoken dialects in other major cities of Iraq (e.g., Mosul, Kirkuk in the north, Basra in the south). Moreover, the entries belong to the spoken Arabic used by an *educated Muslim Baghdadi* in everyday speech,[5] thus excluding again the other distinct Jewish and Christian Arabic dialects of Baghdad.[6]

Furthermore, foreign European loanwords often have a short life, usually accompanying the newly imported cultural or technical item only in its initial

---

[3]On the intensive contacts between British officials and the Jews of Mosul see Laniado, pp. 97-101.

[4]Cf. Tsereteli, p. 95; Garbell, Glossary, *passim* (see below, end of section 5).

[5]See Woodhead and Beene, p. IX.

[6]See Blanc; Mansour's dictionary on the Arabic of the Jews of Baghdad includes so far only the first seven letters of the (Arabic) alphabet ('-ة).

introduction, but later on, due to nationalistic or other reasons, is replaced with a normative native word, e.g., in Iraqi Arabic *warwar* "revolver" was later on replaced by *musaddes, šemendefer* "train, railroad"—by *qiṭār.*[7]

The original European donor language of certain words, such as *rādyo* "radio," may not always be clearly determined, due to the fact that the word is general in several European languages.

3. Phonological Observations

In addition to the original Semitic stock of consonants, Neo-Aramaic also includes some common in European languages, i.e., the palatals *j, c, z,* and the labiodental *v,* due to extensive borrowing from the non-Semitic contact-languages (Turkish, Persian and Kurdish), which include some or all of the above consonants. Similarly, Iraqi Arabic retains, especially in foreign words, non-native consonants, such as *p* (classial Arabic has only *f*) and *c,* common already in loanwords from Persian and Turkish, e.g., carak "one-fourth" (P.), *paskir* "hand towel" (T.), *pančar* "puncture, flat tire" (En.). The latter sound, *c,* is, however, native in the *gilit* dialects of IA as a conditioned reflex of classical Arabic *k.*

Some of the following phonetic changes usually occurred already in the intermediary lending language, with some additional modifications in Neo-Aramaic as well:

Velarized (*tafxim,* "emphatic") pronunciation is a typical feature of many loanwords,[8] e.g., *BITIL* "bottle," *PANZĪF* "benzine," *BATĀTA* "potato," *PAYSIGIL* "bicycle," *JIGĀRA* "cigarette," *QĀSA* "case, safety-box"; but also (non-velarized): *jandirma* "gendarme," *yārda* "measuring yard," *lōrd* "lord, a wealthy person."

Original *b* may shift to *p*:[9] *potine* "boots" (< Fr. *bottine*), *PANZĪF* "benzine," *PAYSIGIL* "bicycle," *PĀPŪR* "steamboat" < A. *bābūr* (< It. *vapore*). There is one case of the opposite shift *(p < b)*: *BATĀTA* "potato"; but in the NA dialects of Aradhin: *patāta,* and IA: *putēta.*

v > b (via Arabic and/or Turkish): *'ABUQAT* "advocate, eloquent speaker"[10] (< It. *avvocato* ?), *'AMBARSĪTA* "university."[11]

p > f (via Arabic): *'AFLĀTON* "Plato, genius."

---

[7]See Smeaton, p. 98; Mansour, p. 96; Yushmanov, pp. 24-25; Jazayery, p. 96. In modern Hebrew many European loanwords, introduced in earlier years, are gradually being replaced by newly coined native words, e.g., *yukra* "prestige" instead of *prestija*; *blamim* "brakes" instead of *breks*; *neker* "puncture in a tire" instead of *pančer.* Cf. Blau, Joshua, pp. 50-141.

[8]Sabar, 1975, p. 278; cf. Tsereteli, "On One Suprasegmental Phoneme in Modern Semitic," *JAOS* 102/2 (1982), pp. 343-346.

[9]Cf. Blanc, p. 18 (b).

[10]T. *avukat.*

[11]In Israeli NA only, and probably via Hebrew *'universita.*

s/z > *c/j* (via Turkish): ciminto "cement," *cinko* "zinc," *JIGARA* "cigarette" (but cf. Aradhin: *sigāla*).[12]

g > *ḡ* (via Arabic): *ḠRAM* "gram," *MAGNATIS* "magnet," *telḠIRAF* "telegraph."

k > *q* (via Turkish): *FABRĪQA* "factory" (< Sp. *fabrica*), *qāpūt* "overcoat" (< Fr. *capot*), *mozīqa* "music, harmonica," *QĀSA* "case, safety-box," *QAMARA* "sedan, taxi" (< It. *camera*).[13]

k > *g* (via IA): *PAYSIGIL* "bicycle," *MĀTIRSIGIL* "motorcycle," *gāzino* "casino, modern cafe."[14]

k > *j* (Arabic): *JINFĀS* "canvas, sack cloth."

l > *r*. *fanēra* "flannel (undershirt)," *PANTARŪN* "European pants" (< It. *pantalone*), *spītar* "hospital" (but in the Jewish NA of Urmi: *spital*).

' > ': *'almōda* "à-la-mode, western fashion (in women dressing)"; *'alatrik* "electric light," *'inglēzi* "English," *'AMBARSĪTA* "university," *'injil* "Gospels" (< A. *'injīl*).[15]

Varia: *PANZĪF* "benzine," *PANZĪFXĀNA*[16] "gas station"; *TUXTOR*[17] "doctor"; *BĀMYA* "okra" (< Gr. *mbamia*); *WARWAR*[18] "revolver, hand gun"; *TRAMBĒL* "automobile" *FARGŌN*[19] "(train) wagon"; *grēfon* "grapefruit"; *kestāye* "Christian (neighborhood in Zakho)"; *šamindarfēr*[20] "train" (< Fr. *chemin de fer*).

[12]See Blanc, p. 149.

[13]Note that *q* is the normal reflex in Ottoman orthography of European *k* when followed by a back vowel. Cf. also the spelling, and probably the pronunciation, of Greek-Latin loanwords in post-Biblical Hebrew, e.g., *qysr* "Caesar," *qprysyn* "Cyprus"; cf. Arabic *qubruṣ*; also *qaṣr* < Latin *castra* "camp, castle."

[14]Cf. Mansour, p. 72: *bang* "bank"; on the various reflexes of *k/q* in Arabic dialects see Blanc, pp. 25-30.

[15]See Sabar, 1984, p. 203, n. 14. The case of *'almōda* could be explained as a popular etymology: IA *'al* plus *mōda*.

[16]The change of the second *n* to *f* appears only in the NA reflex. The ending -*xāna* (T/P) "a place for, house of" is common in IA, e.g. (Woodhead-Beene, pp. 127f.): *xastaxāna* "hospital," *musāfirxāna* "inn."

[17]A case of assimilation *(d–t* > *t–t)*. The spirantization *k* > *x* probably reflects Eastern Turkish pronunciation.

[18]Cf. Smeaton, p. 76: "Of particular interest here is how the arabicization, which quite fortuitously results in a reduplicating form, benefits in expressivity from the onomatopoeic function of that form."

[19]The insertion of *r* in both *trambēl* and *fargōn* (in IA as well) is obscure; cf. below, n. 20, and end of section 6. The case of *trambēl* could be explained as a contamination of En. *tram* (cf. T. *tramvay*) and En. *automobile*. See, however, G. Krotkoff, "Studies in Neo-Aramaic Lexicology," *Samuel Iwry Festschrift* (1985), p. 127.

[20]The insertion of *r* in this word (only in the NA reflex) is perhaps due to a folk etymology connecting the first element with *samindar* "beet"; see, however, above, n. 19.

While the accent on NA words is usually on the penult syllable, in loanwords it may be retained on the original final syllable, as in the intermediary language (mostly IA): *FARGŌN* "wagon," *'utēl* "hotel," *ciklēt* "candy," etc.

4. Morphological Observations

Many loanwords are not Aramaicized, i.e., not suffixed by the -*a* ending (typical to Aramaic nouns), e.g.: *BANK* "bank," *čiklēt*[21] "candy," *kupōn* "coupon." There are, however, many exceptions, probably belonging to an older stratum,[22] e.g.: *qandēla* "candle."

The common plural ending is -*at* (< Arabic -*āt*), or -*e* (Aramaic), e.g.: *ciklētat* "chiklets," *PĀKĒTAT* "packets (of cigarettes)," *sākōyat* (sg. *sāko*) "jackets"; *PŌLĪSAT/PŌLĪSE* "policemen," *JIGĀRE* "cigarettes,"[23] *QAPTĀNE* "captains," *KĀRTE* "(playing) cards" (sg. and pl.).

The gender of a loanword may be m. or f. without an apparent reason; however, those ending with -*a* usually are f., e.g.: *makīna* "machine," *JIGĀRA* "cigarette," *qandēla* "candle"; exceptions: *yārda* "yard" (m.), *jandirma* "gendarme." Cf. *TRAMBĒL* "automobile," m., but in the NA dialect of Aradhin *trumbēla*, f.

5. Lexical Observations

Not all the European loanwords are from recent times. Some obviously are older, having been in general use in other Near Eastern languages, and some go back as far as old Syriac and Greek, e.g., *'abanōs* "ebony," originally from Old Egyptian *hebni* (cf. Hebrew *hovne*), *'ALMAS* "diamond" (Gr. *alamas*), *TIRYAQ* "opium" (Gr. *theriake*), *mistakke* "mastic," *qandēla* "candle," *LAMPA* "lamp," *nergīza* "narcissus." It is interesting to note that some of these old loanwords are quite obsolete, being used only in certain expressions, e.g.: *XAMŪSA X-TIRYAQ* "as sour as *theriake*," *wīsa mux kēpid 'abanōs* "as dry as the stone of *abanos*" (nobody knowing what exactly these words mean, except that they have this typical quality; hence "stone" instead of "wood" in the expression with "ebony").

The semantic areas of the more recent European loanwords may be divided into the following major categories: (a) Modern technology, e.g.: *makina* "machine," *FABRĪQA* "factory," *TRAMBĒL* "automobile," *latrīk* "electric (light)," *rādyo* "radio," etc. (b) Modern culture in general: *sīnama* "cinema," *mozīqa* "music, harmonica," *gāzīno* "casino, modern cafe," *kupōne* "(rationing) coupons," *'utēl* "hotel," *PANDĀN* "fountain pen," *WARWAR* "revolver," etc. (c) Modern clothing: *fānēra* "flannel (undershirt)," *blūz*

---

[21]Cf. T. *çiklet* "chewing gum" (< brand name "Chicklet") and IA *čukleet* (1) "chocolate," (2) "various types of wrapped candies," apparently a contamination of "chocolate" and "Chicklet."

[22]Cf. Sabar, in progress.

[23]Cf. the broken plural *jigāyir* in IA, suggesting a higher degree of integration.

"blouse," *qāpūt* "overcoat," *PĀLTO* "overcoat," *PANTARŪN* "(European) pants"; *potīne* "boots," *silik* "silk, rayon," *poplīn* "poplin."[24] (d) Modern vegetables and food: *TAMĀTA* "tomatoes," *BATĀTA* "potatoes," *FĀSŌLYA* "beans," *BĀMYA* "okra," *grēfon* "grapefruit";[25] *kēk* "(European) cake," *ZĀLATA* "salad," *LOQANTA* "(modern) restaurant." (e) Modern medicine: *TUXTOR* "doctor" (in contrast to *ḥakim* "traditional healer"), *swisra* "nurse, sister,"[26] *spītar* "hospital," *tintiryok* "tincture of iodine," *sulfīdyazōk* "sulfa pills," *spīrto* "(medical) spirit," *'asfanīk* "phenic acid," *trāxōma* "trachoma"; *vāzarin* "vaseline."

Loan translations from European languages are common in the written national languages of the Near East, at least in the written standard register, usually coined by language academies, e.g., Hebrew *gan yeladim* and Arabic *rawḍat 'aṭfāl* "kindergarten."[27] In Neo-Aramaic, however, having no national academy, such loan translations are rare. The only term which seems to be such is *sanduq zamāra* "phonograph," literally "singing box."

I know of only one loanword which serves as a component with a native element, and that is *makīn-XYATA* "sewing machine," *makīn-pisra* "meat mincer." Only one word, *telefun* has a verbal derivative, *mtalfōne* "to phone."

Due to the lack of comprehensive dictionaries of modern Neo-Aramaic dialects, it is difficult to compare the European loanwords in the various dialects. One may assume that some are common to all of them, as they appear in other Near Eastern languages in general, e.g., *makīna* "machine," *LAMPA* "lamp," *qandēla* "candle," *PŌLIS* "police," *'utēl* "hotel," etc. However, in some cases which we came across the etymons in the various Neo-Aramaic dialects have a different pronunciation or are replaced by a different word altogether, e.g.: "cigarettes" are *JIGĀRE* in Jewish Zakho, *jgāre* in Turoyo,[28] *sigāle* in Aradhin,[29] *paprōs* (< Russian) in Christian Urmi;[30] "potatoes" are *BATĀTA* in Jewish Zakho, *patāta* in Aradhin,[31] *kirtōpa* (< German via Russian) in Christian Urmi;[32] "automobile" is *TRAMBĒL* and

---

[24]An interesting case is *mōzlīn* "muslin," a fine thin cotton fabric originally made in Mosul but later imported from Europe; cf. Fr. *mousseline*, It. *mussolino*. See Kutscher, p. 96.

[25]Only in Israeli NA; cf. n. 11, above.

[26]See below, List of Words, ad *swisra*.

[27]See Blau, Joshua, chaps. 4, 6. My colleague Professor Edward Odisho, an Assyrian living now in Chicago, informs me that he and other nationality-conscious speakers of NA often use in their daily speech a few such loan translations, e.g., *pres-qāla* "radio broadcasting," *pres-xezwa* "television."

[28]Jastrow, p. 204.

[29]Krotkoff, pp. 74, 147.

[30]Maclean, p. 255.

[31]Krotkoff, p. 141.

[32]Maclean, p. 141.

m. in Jewish Zakho, but *trumbēla* and f. in Aradhin,[33] *otobos* in Turoyo,[34] *OTMABEL* in Jewish Urmi;[35] "trucks" are *trakkāt* in Telkef,[36] *lōrīyat* in Jewish Zakho; "table" is *mēza* in Jewish Zakho, but *USTOL* in Christian Urmi (< Russian).[37]

List of the Loanwords

(† indicates medieval loans from Western languages into Syriac and/or Arabic, etc.)

†*'abanōs* ebony; IA < A < Gr. < Egyptian.

'ABUQĀT eloquent, tricky speaker, lawyer; < AA *abūqāt* < T. *avukat* < It. *avvocato*; cf. Palestinian Arabic *'abukātu*, pl. *'abukātiyye.*

†*'AFLĀTŌN* genius, very tricky person; A < Gr. Plato. Cf. AA *Asfatūn* "a proper name"?

†*'ALMAS* diamond; IA < A < Gr.

'asfanìk phenic acid; IA/T < En. < Fr. Cf. Krotkoff: *asfenik.*

'utèl hotel; IA < Fr. Cf. Ishaq: *utel*, AA *ūtēl.*

'alatrìk, latrìk electric light; IA/T < E; cf. Mansour, p. 4: *'atrik*; AA *'atrik, 'alatrìk.*

'almōda à la mode, western style dressing (for women); < T. < It. *alla moda.*

'AMBARSĪTA university (only in Israeli NA); H < E.

'ingilēzi, 'ingiliz, 'ingiliznāya English; cf. Blanc, p. 147: *englēzi* (Jewish), *inglīzi* (Muslim/Christian); AA *əngliz/ənglēzi.*

'injīl New Testament; IA/A *'injīl* < Geez *wangel* < Gr. *evaggelion*; cf. Ishaq: *ewangalyun*; AA *ənjīl.*

BĀMYA okra, gumbo; A/T < Gr. *mbamia*; cf. Mansour, p. 69.

bank bank; A/T < E; cf. Mansour, p. 72: *bang.*

BATĀTA potato; A < It.; cf. IA *putēta*; Mansour, p. 4: *patēta*; Krotkoff: *patāta*; T: *patates.*

BITIL bottle; IA: *BUTIL* < E; cf. Mansour, p. 50: *BITIL*; Krotkoff: *BUTTUL.*

blūz blouse; IA < Fr.; cf. Mansour, p. 64 ("woman's shirt," vs. *QMIS* "man's shirt"); see Kutscher, p. 95.

buks, buksa box, a blow with a closed hand; IA ? < En.

čakèt jacket; IA/T < E; cf. Mansour, p. 137; Garbell; AA *cākēt(a).*

čiklèt wrapped candy (vs. *sakrōkat* bare candy); IA < En.

---

[33]Krotkoff, pp. 41, 152.
[34]Ishaq, p. 79.
[35]Garbell, p. 323.
[36]Sabar, 1978, p. 413.
[37]Tsereteli, p. 95.

čiminṭo cement; T < It.; cf. Krotkoff; Ishaq; K (Blau); AA *cəmənṭo.*
činko zinc, enamel ware; T < It. *'zinco.*
čiryo cheerio, said before drinking a toast; IA ? < En.
†*DĪNAR* dinar (an Iraqi monetary bill); A < Gr. L *denarius.*
†*dirhim* dirham (an Iraqi coin); A < Pahlavi < Gr. *drachma.*
FABRĪQA factory; T/A < Sp.; cf. Maclean, p. 246: *fabrīq*; AA *fabrīqa.*
fanēra flannel (undershirt); T/IA *fanīla* < It. *flanella*; AA *fanēla.*
FARGŌN train car, wagon; IA(EA); see end of section 3.
FĀSŌLYA beans; A < L *phaseolus*; cf. K (Blau): *fasuli*; Mansour, p. 87:
    pasuliyyi.
fircha brush; T/A < E; cf. Mansour, p. 85: *parča.*
FIRNA baker's oven; IA/A/T < It. *forno.*
†*FIRRANG* the Franks, Europeans (archaic); P < E; see *PAPA.*
GARRĀJ inter-city bus station; IA(EA); cf. Ishaq: *garaž.*
gāzīno modern cafe, casino; A (Wehr): *kāzīno* < E.
grēfon grapefruit (only in Israeli NA); PA *grēfūt* < En.
ḠRAM gram; A < E; AA *ḡrām,*
jandirma gendarme; IA < Fr.; cf. Jastrow, p. 204; AA *gandərma.*
JIGĀRA cigarette; T/IA < E; see Blanc, p. 149; end of section 5.
JINFĀS sackcloth, canvas; IA/A < R < L *canabis* hemp.
JĀPĀN yellowish plain cloth used for native underwear or sheets; perhaps
    imported from Japan ?; cf. Kutscher, pp. 95-97; AA *čāpūn* "grobes Leinen,
    leinenes Tuch" (no etymology given).
kāda folded bread with cheese inside; K < Fr *gateau.*
KĀRTE playing cards; ? < En. ?
kēk European style cake; IA < EN.
†*kestāye* Christians, only as a name of the Christian neighborhood in Zakho.
kupōne coupons (for food rations during the 1940's); IA < EN.
LAMPA kerosene lamp; IA < E (It.); cf. Krotkoff; Ishaq; Maclean, p. 149:
    "paraffin or European lamp, opp. *šrā'a* a native lamp."
lasṭik rubber (string or band to hold socks, etc.); IA(EA)/T < E elastic; cf.
    Krotkoff; Mansour, p. 11; K (Blau); AA *asṭīk/lasṭīk.*
latrīk see *'alatrīk.*
LOQANṬA restaurant; IA(EA)/T < It. *locanda* "inn"; AA *lōqanṭa.*
lōrd lord, wealthy person; T < En.
lōri, pl. *-yat*, lorry, truck; A (Wehr) < En.; cf. Krotkoff: *lōrīya*; Smeaton, pp.
    72f., 87; see end of section 5.
luks gas mantle lantern, "Lux"; IA < En.; cf. Krotkoff; AA *lüks.*
†*MAḠNAṬĪS magnet; IA/A* < Gr.
MAḠĀZA modern department store; IA (Blanc, p. 157) < P *maqāze* < Fr.
    magasin, itself originally A; see Kutscher, p. 46.
makīna machine; *makīn-XYAṬA* sewing machine; *makīn (dyāqit)pisra* meat
    mincer; IA/A < It.; cf. Jastrow, p. 207.
†*MARMAR* marble; A/T < Gr./L *marmaros.*

MĀTIRSIGIL motorcycle; IA(EA) < En.

mētar meter; IA/A/T < En.; cf. Jastrow, p. 208: *mitro*.

†*MATRAN* archbishop; A < Gr. *metropolites*; cf. K (Blau): *mitran*.

mēza table (in general, vs. *medo* Sabbath or holiday set table); IA/P *mez* < Sp./Portuguese *mesa*. See Blanc, p. 157.

milyon million; T/A < E.

mirjāne Margaret, Pearl (common woman's name); IA/A < Gr. *margarites*; cf. Maclean, p. 197: *merjan*; AA *mərgān*. Cf. *RAJINA*.

mīstakke mastic, resin of mastic tree; IA/A < Gr. *mastiche*.

mōzīqa ceremonial music; harmonica; T *mizik* "band, harmonica" < E; cf. K. (Wahby): *moziqe* "music, band." AA *mīzəqa* "Musik" < T *mizika*.

mōzlīn muslin; T *muslin* < E; see n. 24.

nērgizạ narcissus, marigold; P/T/K < Gr. *narkissos*; cf. Maclean, p. 218.

PĀKĒT packet of cigarettes; T/IA < E; cf. Garbell; AA *pākēṭ(a)*.

PĀLTO woman's overcoat; T/IA < Fr. *paletot*; cf. Ishaq; Garbell: *PALTON*; Mansour, p. 89; A (Wehr): *BALTO*; K (Wahby).

PAMPẠ pump; IA(EA) < En.

PANDĀN fountain pen; IA < En.; cf. K (Wahby, p. 102).

PANTARŪN European style pants (vs. native *sarwal* baggy pants); IA/T < It. *pantalone*; cf. K (Wahby): *PANTOL*; Garbell, p. 324: *PARTRON*; Mansour, p. 90; *PANTRUN*; AA *panṭūṛ* < T *potur* (!).

PANZĪF, PANZĪN benzine; *PANZIFXĀNA* gas station; IA(EA): *BANZĪN* < En.; cf. Smeaton, pp. 126, 141; T *benzin*.

†*PĀPA* or *PAPID FIRRANG* Pope, Frankish king; IA/T/P < E.

PĀPŪR ship, steamship; K (Wahby): *PAPOR* It. *vapore*; cf. A: *BĀBŪR*, *WĀBŪR*; T *vapur*; AA *pāpūre*.

PASSAPORT, PASTAPUR passport; T < It. *passaporto*; cf. A (Hava): *BĀSABŪRṬ*; SA: *BĀSBŌR*; Mansour, p. 86: *pasport*.

†*PĀTRIK* patriarch; T < Gr.; AA *bəṭrək/baṭrak*.

PAYSIGIL bicycle; IA(EA) < En.; cf. Blanc, p. 18; Mansour, p. 44.

pirtiqala orange; IA/T < E Portugal? (see *Türkçe Sözlük* ad *portakal*); cf. Mansour, p. 86; *PIRTQAL, pirtqal*; A: *burtuqāl, burtuqān*; Garbell: *PORTQAL, PIRTAQAL*.

PŌDRA talc powder; IA *POTRA* < It.; cf. K (Wahby): *PODRE*.

PŌLIS police; IA/T/K < En.; cf. Ishaq: *polis*; Jastrow, p. 202: *bōlīs*.

poplīn poplin; IA (Mansour, p. 83) < En.; cf. A (Wehr): *boblīn*.

PŌSTA post, mail; IA/T < It.; cf. K (Wahby) *poste*; Ishaq; AA *pōsta*.

potīne boots; IA < Fr. *bottines*; cf. K (Wahby); Jastrow, p. 209; Mansour, p. 83: *patin*.

QAMĀRA sedan car, taxi; IA < It. *camera* chamber; cf. A (Wehr) "cabin."

qanapa padded bench; IA/T < It./Sp. *canapé*; cf. En. canopy; Fr. *canapé* < L/Gr. *kanoperion* a bed with mosquito curtains; K (Wahby): *qenepe*.

†*qandēla* small oil lamp; OS/A < E < L *candela*; cf. Maclean: "chandelier, lamp, esp. in a church"; K (Wahby): *qendil*.

†*qānūn* canon, rule; A/OS < Gr. *kanon*; cf. K (Wahby).

QAPTAN captain (of ship); IA/T < E.

qāpūt felt overcoat; T *kaput* "military cloak" < Fr. *capot* "hooded overcoat"; cf. K (Wahby); AA *qāpūṭ.*

QĀSA case, coffer; T *kasa* < It. *cassa.*

†*QĀTA* (m.), *QATŪSA* (f.), cat; OS < L *catus*; cf. Jastrow, p. 210: *qātin.*

QOMANDAR commander, officer; cf. Jastrow, p. 210: *qumandar*; A (Wehr): *qomandan*; T: *kumandan, komutan* < E.

quruš Piaster (a Turkish coin); IA/T < It. *grosso*/Ger. *Groschen.*

RĀDYO radio; IA(EA)/T < E.

RAJĪNA Regina (common woman's name); A ? < En. < L "Queen"; cf. *mirjāne.*

sāko jacket (European style); IA: *sāqu*; A (Wehr): *sāku* sack coat, lounge jacket < It. *sacco* "sack"?

samāwar samovar; P/T < R; cf. Garbell: *SAMAWAR* ; Tsereteli, p. 95: *simavar*; Maclean: *samawar*; K (Wahby): *semawer.*

silik silk, rayon; IA < En.

sīnama cinema, movie theater; IA(EA)/A/T < E; AA *sīnama.*

spīrto medicinal spirit, alcohol; IA(EA) < It.; cf. Krotkoff: *spirtu*; A (Wehr): *isbirito.*

spītar hospital (mostly in Israeli NA); PA < E; cf. Smeaton: *sbaital, sbaitar*; Garbell: *spital* < R < Ger.

sulfītyāzŏk sulfa pills; IA/T ? < E; cf. A (Wehr): *sulfīd* sulfide.

swisra nurse, medical sister; corruption of En. *sister* and Ger. *schwester*? or A *swisra* Switzerland ??

†*SABUN* soap; A < E < L/Gr. *sapon* < Gaulish (originally a liquid for hair coloring); see Kutscher, pp. 61f.

ŠŌFĒR chauffeur, driver of a bus; T/SA < Fr.

ŠAMINDARFĒR train; IA < Fr. *chemin de fer*; see Mansour, p. 96: *šamandafar* > *trēn/rēl* > *QITAR*; cf. K (Blau) *šimendifer*; Garbell: *šamandafer.*

telefun telephone; *mtalfŏne* to phone; T: *telefon*/IA(EA): *talafon* < E; AA *talafŏn.*

telḠIRĀM/telḠIRĀF telegram, telegraph; T: *telgraf*; IA: *talaḡrāf*; Mansour: *telegraf* < E; AA *talgərāf.*

tikkēt ticket; IA: *tikit* < En. Cf. Sabar (1978), p. 413: *tikit.*

tintiryŏk tincture of iodine; IA < En.

tiyyātro theater, musical show; A (Wehr) <It. *teatro.*

TAMĀTA tomatoes (also: *banjāne smŏqe* "red eggplants"; cf. *banjāne kŏme* "(black) eggplants"; IA < It.; cf. SA: *BANDORA* < It. *pomo d'oro.*

TAMPATŪR cork; IA(EA): *tabbadūr* < It. *tappo* "cork" + *duro* "firm, tight"?

TARAMPA trumpet (?), a musical instrument in ceremonial band; cf. T: *trampete* "side drum," *tulumba* pump < It. *tromba* trumpet, pump ?; cf.

Smeaton: *TRUNBAH* pump; Mansour: *TRIMBA*.

†*TIRYAQ* opium, antidote; IA/ A < Gr. *theriake*. Cf. Garbell: *taryaq* hashish.

TĀWLA backgammon; IA(EA): *TAWLE*/T: *tavla* < It. *tavola*; cf. Blanc, p. 153.

†*TILLĒSIM* talisman (translates Biblical H *ḥosen*); IA/ A < Gr.

TRAMBEL automobile; IA < E; see end of section 5; cf. AA *ōtōbōz/ṭrəbēl*.

TRAXŌMA trachoma; IA(EA)/ A (Wehr); cf. Sabar (1978), p. 413.

TUXTOR doctor, physician (vs. *ḥakim* traditional healer); IA: *daktor, duktor*; Krotkoff: *duktūra*; Ishaq: *doktor*; AA *ṭaxṭōr*. See n. 17.

VĀZARIN vaseline, petroleum jelly; T/IA ? < E.

WARWAR revolver, hand gun; IA < En. Cf. K (Wahby): *werwer*; n. 18.

yārda yard (measure); IA/ A/T < En. via It. *iarda* or Sp. *yarda* which would account for the -*a* ending in A/T/ NA.

ZĀLATA salad; IA < It./ L.

List of Abbreviations and References

A = Arabic; AA = Anatolian Arabic (see Vocke-Waldner); E = (general) European; En. = English; Fr. = French; Ger. = German; Gr. = Greek; H = (modern) Hebrew; IA = Iraqi Arabic (see Woodhead-Beene); IA(EA) = see Clarity-Stowasser-Wolfe; It. = Italian; K = Kurdish (see Blau, Joice; Jaba; Wahby-Edmonds); L = Latin; NA = Neo-Aramaic; P = Persian; PA = Palestinian Arabic (personal knowledge); R = Russian; SA = Syrian Arabic (see Stowasser-Ani); Sp = Spanish; T = Turkish.

BLAU, Joice, *Kurdish-French-English Dictionary*, Bruxelles, 1965.

BLAU, Joshua, *The Renaissance of Modern Hebrew and Modern Standard Arabic*, Berkeley, 1981.

BLANC, Haim, *Communal Dialects in Baghdad*, Cambridge, Mass., 1964.

CLARITY, B. E.—STOWASSER, K.—WOLFE, R. G., *A Dictionary of Iraqi Arabic, English-Arabic*, Washington, D.C., 1964.

GARBELL, I., *The Jewish Neo-Aramaic Dialect of Persian Azerbaijan*, The Hague, 1965; glossary, p. 284-342.

HAVA, J. G., *Al-Farā'id, Arabic-English Dictionary*, Beirut, 1964.

HONY, H. C., *A Turkish-English Dictionary*, Oxford, 1967.

ISHAQ, Yusuf, *Toxu Qorena (Turoyo)*, Stockholm, 1983; glossary, pp. 71-83.

JABA, M. A.—JUSTI, M. F., *Dictionnaire Kurde-Français*, St. Pétersbourg, 1879.

JASTROW, Otto, *Laut- und Formenlehre des neuaramäischen Dialekts von Miḏin im Ṭūr 'Abdīn*, Wiesbaden, 1985 (3rd ed.); glossary of loanwords, pp. 200-213.

JAZAYERI, M. A., "Western Influence in Contemporary Persian: A General View," *Bulletin of the School of Oriental and African Studies* 39/ 1 (1966), pp. 79-96.

64 Yona Sabar

KAHANE, H. R.—KAHANE, R.—TIETZE, A., *The Lingua Franca in the Levant: Turkish Nautical Terms of Italian and Greek Origin*, Urbana, 1958.

KUTSCHER, E. Y., *Words and Their History* (Hebrew), Jerusalem, 1961.

KROTKOFF, G., *A Neo-Aramaic Dialect of Kurdistan*, New Haven, 1982; glossary, pp. 117-170.

LANIADO, E., *The Jews of Mosul* (Hebrew), Haifa, 1981.

MANSOUR, J., *The Judaeo-Arabic Dialect of Baghdad: Dictionary (part 1)*, Haifa, 1981.

MACLEAN, A. J., *A Dictionary of the Dialects of Vernacular Syria*, Oxford, 1901. Reprint, Amsterdam, 1972.

SABAR, Y., "The Hebrew Elements in the Jewish Neo-Aramaic Dialects of Azerbaijan," *Leshonenu* 39 (1975), pp. 272-294.

SABAR, Y., "From Tel-Kēpe in Iraqi Kurdistan to Providence, R.I.: The Story of a Chaldean Immigrant to the USA in 1927," *JAOS* 98 (1978), pp. 410-415.

SABAR, Y., "The Arabic Elements in the Jewish Neo-Aramaic Texts of Nerwa and 'Amādīya, Iraqi Kurdistan," *JAOS* 104 (1984), pp. 201-211.

SABAR, Y., "Substrata and Adstrata Elements in Jewish Neo-Aramaic," in progress.

SA'ID, M. F., *Lexical Innovation through Borrowing in Modern Standard Arabic*, Princeton, 1967.

SMEATON, B. H., *Lexical Expansion due to Technical Change as Illustrated by the Arabic of al-Hasā, Saudi Arabia*, Bloomington, 1973.

STEINGASS, F., *A Comprehensive Persian-English Dictionary*, London, 1963.

STETKEVYCH, J., *The Modern Arabic Literary Language, Lexical and Stylistic Developments*, Chicago, 1970.

STOWASSER, K.—MOUKHTAR, A., *A Dictionary of Syrian Arabic: English-Arabic*, Washington, D.C., 1964.

TSERETELI, K. G., *The Modern Assyrian Language*, Moscow, 1978.

Türkçe Sözlük, Ankara, 1983.

VAN ESS, J., *Spoken Arabic of Iraq*, 2nd ed., Oxford, 1938.

VOCKE, S.—WALDNER, W., *Der Wortschatz des anatolischen Arabisch*, Erlangen, 1982.

WAHBY, T.—EDMONDS, C. J., *A Kurdish-English Dictionary*, Oxford, 1966.

WEHR, H., *A Dictionary of Modern Written Arabic*, Ithaca, 1966.

WEIMAN, R., *Native and Foreign Elements in a Language, a Study in General Linguistics Applied to Modern Hebrew*, Philadelphia, 1950.

WOODHEAD, D. R.—BEENE, W., *A Dictionary of Iraqi Arabic: Arabic-English*, Washington, D.C., 1967.

YUSHMANOV, N. V., *The Structure of the Arabic Language*, Washington, D.C., 1961.

Appendix: General European Words in the Jewish Neo-Aramaic Dialects of Azerbaijan (gleaned from Garbell, *Glossary*, pp. 295-342)

adres f. K/T<R "address"
ADYAL m. R "coarse blanket used as bed cover"
afiser m. K/T<R "officer"
ALMANI K<A<Fr. "German (language)"; cf. *germani*
ALMANNA m./f. K<A<Fr. "German (person)"; cf. *germanna*
AQIŠQA f. K/T<R "window"
blita f. R "ticket"
BRILYAND m. R "cut diamond"
ČAKET f. K<R<Fr. "jacket"
ČAYNIK f. K<R "tea-pot"
droga f. R. "cart"
droska f. R. "carriage"
ERPLAN f. R. "airplane"
faeton K/T<R<Fr. "light carriage"
fransawi A/T<It. "French (language)"
fransayna m./f. T<It. "French (person)"
gazeta f. T<It. "newspaper"
germani [modern H. ?] "German (language)"
germanna m./f. "German (person)"
inglizi A "English (language)'
inglizna m./f. "English (person)"
inglizula f. "England"
ISKAN, ISTIKAN f. K/T<R "drinking glass, tumbler"
IŠKAP f. K/T<R "cupboard"
JḠARA f. T/K<E "cigarette"
jiletqa f. K<R<Fr. "waistcoat, brassière"
kaliska, kaniska f. K<R "open carriage"
kampa f. E "camp"
kartopita, pl. *kartopye*, R ? "potato"
kek f. E "(Western style) cake"
killisa f. K/T/P<Gr. "church"
LOTKA f. K/T<R "boat, barge"
MANAT m. K/T<R [*monyeta* "coin"] "rouble"
MAŠIN, MAŠINA K<R "machine, engine; mechanically propelled vehicle"
mistuk f. T/K<R "cigarette-holder"
OTMABEL f. K/T<R<Fr. "automobile, motor car"
paket f. K/R<R ?<E "packet, package"
PALTON f. K/T<R<Fr. "overcoat, topcoat"
pansil m. En "pencil"
PARTRON m. K<R ?<Fr. "European style trousers"
PRAXOD f. R "steamer, train engine"

put m. P<R "pud, about 40 lbs."

PYALA m. K/T/P<Gr. "goblet, tumbler"

PYAN, PYANCI R "drunkard"

QONSOL m. T<It. "consul"

RUNGA f. R. "small liquor-glass"

RUSI, URUSI K<P<R "Russian (language)"

RUSNA, URUSNA m./f. "Russian (person)"

RUSYA, URUSYA "Russia"

SALDAT m. K/T<R "soldier"

SAMAWAR f. K/T<R "samovar, tea-urn"

santin m. A<Fr. "centimeter"

sinama f. K/T<Fr. "cinema"

STANSYA f. R "station, landing place"

STOL m. K<R "table; chair"

SUP f. T<R<Fr. "soup"

šamandafer f. Fr. "railway, train"

špital f. R<Ger. "hospital"

YUBQA f. K/T<R "skirt, petticoat"

ZONDIG f. R. "umbrella"

IV. Comparative Studies

CLITICIZATION IN NEO-ARAMAIC

Samuel Ethan Fox

The verbal system of Neo-Aramaic (NA) is remarkable for both its complexity and its regularity. One of the best-known aspects of NA verbal inflection is that the subject and object markers of the preterite tense are essentially identical to the object and subject markers, respectively, of the tenses formed from the jussive (J) stem. The present study, however, is concerned with the suffixes of the continuous (C) stem and their relationship to those of the J stem. We will examine historical and comparative evidence which suggests that the J stem can help in understanding the origins and current status of the C stem and its suffixes. A comparison of the two tenses will point to some of the forces which have shaped and continue to shape the language. Our discussion will be concerned principally with the subject markers.

The suffixes which we will be considering belong to three sets, which we will label x, y, and z. The x series is used with the J stem in the formation of the present habitual and future tenses. The y series is added to the P stem to produce the preterite. The z series is added to the C stem to form the continuous present. Representative forms for the verb *tpəqle* "visit" are given for Iraqi Koine in table 1. Certain similarities between the three paradigms are immediately apparent. *a* marks feminine forms, as opposed to another vowel or no vowel at all for masculines: y series *-lux/-lax, -le/la*; x series *-ən/-an, -ət/-at, ·φ/-a*; z series *-wən/-wan, -wət/-wat, -le/-la*. The third person singular suffixes *-le* and *-la* appear in both y and z. Several of the z series consist of their x counterparts preceded by *w*. Lastly, all three series have second person plural affixes which end in *-un*.

The forms of the three tenses which are exemplified here are not so comparable as the bare paradigms seem to suggest. To understand the differences, we will have to consider some other related forms. The first set which will be helpful are those which include the affix *-wa*. Forms with *-wa* express anteriority with respect to their counterparts without it. Added to the preterite, the affix forms a pluperfect. Added to the future, it is a future from a vantage point in the past. Added to the continuous, it is a past continuous. The relevant point for our discussion is the placement of *-wa*. In table 2 fragments of the *-wa*-form paradigms are given. *-wa* occupies the final

69

position when added to the future and to the continuous, but when added to the preterite it comes between y and the stem. This suggests that the y series is attached differently from the others.

Table 1

	preterite P + y	future bə + J+x	continuous bə + C + z
1m	tpəq - li	bə - tapq - ən	bə - tpaqa - wən
f	tpəq - li	bə - tapq - an	bə - tpaqa - wan
2m	tpəq - lux	bə - tapq - ət	bə - tpaqa - wət
f	tpəq - lax	bə - tapq - at	bə - tpaqa - wat
3m	tpəq - le	bə - tapəq	bə - tpaqa - le
f	tpəq - la	bə - tapq - a	bə - tpaqa - la
1p	tpəq - lan	bə - tapq - ax	bə - tpaqa - wax
2p	tpəq - loxun	bə - tapq - itun	bə - tpaqa - tun
3p	tpəq - lun	bə - tapq - i	bə - tpaqa - na

Table 2

	preterite + wa P + y	future + wa bə + J + x	continuous + wa bə + C + z
1m	tpəq - wa - li	bə - tapq - ən - wa	bə - tpaq - ənwa
f	tpəq - wa - li	bə - tapq - an - wa	bə - tpaq - anwa
2m	tpəq - wa - lux	bə - tapq - ət - wa	bə - tpaq - ətwa
f	tpəq - wa - lax	bə - tapq - at - wa	bə - tpaq - atwa

An additional piece of evidence is provided by the object suffixes. In some cases it is possible to mark the verb for object as well as subject. The extent of object marking varies considerably from dialect to dialect, ranging from full to highly restricted. Table 3 shows forms for a 3p ms subject and 3p fs object in Iraqi Koine. The J and C stem tenses add the object marker on the end, where we would expect to find it, but the object marker intervenes between the P stem and the y series affix. Again, the y series seems to be attached differently to the stem. Further, depending on the dialect, the preterite object markers are close to or identical to the subject markers of the J stem, and the preterite subject markers, the y series, tend quite strongly to be the same as the J stem object markers. The y series, then, always comes at the end of the word, whether it is serving to indicate the subject or object of the verb.

Table 3

preterite	future	continuous
tpiq - a - le	bə - tapəq - la	bə - tpaq - o - le
"he visited her"	"he will visit her"	"he is visiting her"

We have seen that there are reasons to think that the y series differs from x and z in the nature of its attachment to the verb stem. The z series also differs from the two others. The demonstration here is more straightforward. First, we should note that the z series is identical to the clitic version of the copula which we find in sentences like *atoraya-le* "He is Assyrian." The copula also has independent forms which begin with *i*. The full paradigm is given in table 4. The special status of the z series is reinforced by its ability, under some conditions, to detach itself from the verb and join to another word instead. In table 5 we find examples of the attachment of z to the interrogative *mudi* "what" and to the negative *le*. z forms special contractions with *le*. These special contracted forms are given in table 6.

Table 4

1m	iwən	-wən
f	iwan	-wan
2m	iwət	-wət
f	iwat	-wat
3m	ile	-le
f	ila	-la
1p	iwax	-wax
2p	itun	-tun
3p	ina	-na

Table 5

qrile xa ktawa	"He read a book."
la qrile ktawa	"He didn't read a book."
mut qrile	"What did he read?"
bəqrayale xa ktawa	"He's reading a book."
lele bəqraya ktawa	"He isn't reading a book."
mudile bəqraya	"What is he reading?"

Table 6

1	len
2	let
3m	lele
f	lela
1p	lex
2p	letun
3p	lena

The three degrees of attachment to the stem are now clear. x is most closely bound to the stem. No affix intervenes between it and the stem, and it is not detachable. y's attachment is a bit looser. Both -*wa* and the object markers can come between it and the stem, and it does not participate fully in the accentual unit of the word, as we will see later. On the other hand, though the position of y is peripheral—it is always the last element in the word—it is fixed, and cannot attach to another word. z is more loosely bound still. It can, unlike y, be followed by -wa but under some syntactic conditions it anchors itself elsewhere.

Classifying x and z is relatively simple. Klavans (1985) gives three rules which can be useful in distinguishing affixes from clitics. They are:

1. A clitic is generally less selective of its host.
2. Clitics often do not undergo rules of internal phonology.
3. Semantically, clitics are more word-like than affix-like.

x is highly selective of its host, attaching only to verbs. z is much less selective. It attaches not only to the C stem of the verb, but to interrogatives, the negative le, and to nouns and adjectives in its role as copula.

x and z behave differently with respect to rules of internal phonology as well. Stress in NA is primarily penultimate. x participates in this scheme: stress on the next-to-last syllable throughout the paradigm, with x counted as part of the word. z stands outside the word for the purpose of accentuation. The addition of z does not move the stress from the penultimate syllable of the naked C stem. The contrast between x and z is clear in the forms of table 7. The semantic criterion also divides sharply between x and z. x had no meaning outside of the word of which it forms a part. z is a verb in its own right, and is used as such elsewhere. The difference is similar to that between English "He reads" and "He is reading." The suffixed s of "reads" is the marker of the 3p singular in the present tense, but in itself it has no meaning. The word "is" of "is reading" can appear in other contexts and does have a meaning of its own on its own.

Table 7

bəqráyale	"He is reading."
lele bəqráya	"He is not reading."
bətáyawət	"You are coming."
let bətáya	"You are not coming."
bəpátəx	"He will open."
bəpátxət	"You will open."
bəpatxîtun	"You (pl.) will open."

On all three counts the status of x and z is clearly indicated. x is highly selective of its host, participates in rules of internal phonology, and has no word-like meaning. z is not very selective of its host, does not participate in rules of internal phonology, and has word-like meaning. The rules which Klavans gives us for telling an affix from a clitic are not ironclad. They are simply properties which are usually characteristic of the two classes and can be helpful in telling them apart. Though they are only guidelines, they speak in one voice here: the x series are affixes, and the z series are clitics.

When it comes to y the situation is not so clear. With regard to rules 1 and 3, y is like the x series affixes, while its phonological behavior suggests that it may be a clitic. y, like x, can only be attached to a verb. y, like x, has no independent meaning. It can only contribute to the meaning of another word. On the other hand, y, like z, is outside of the accentual unit of the word. The forms in table 8 show that the accent stays on the stem syllable, even when what follows is two or more syllables long. A further clitic-like characteristic of y is its consistent position on the periphery of the word. This is particularly striking when an object marker intervenes between the stem and y. I have elected to term y a closely-bound clitic, but, without really firm definitions of clitic and affix, we cannot be too sure about this.

Table 8

ptə́x - li

ptə́x - loxun

ptə́x - wa - li

ptə́x - wa - loxun

It is now time to turn back the clock and see where these three very different series of markers came from. By examining their origins, we may arrive at a clearer understanding of their structure and even some insights into other facets of the language.

NA is an Eastern Aramaic dialect, and, in trying to get an idea of its earlier stages, we must turn to those forms of Eastern Aramaic which are attested at earlier periods. None of these is the direct ancestor of NA, but both Syriac and the Aramaic of the Babylonian Talmud (BT) are close enough to be helpful. The features which concern us here were probably much the same in Syriac and proto-NA, and it is to Syriac that we will most often turn. We will want to see the precursors of x, y, and z and to understand their status in Syriac. For our basic information, as well as much of the theorizing about diachronic development, we can rely heavily on Nöldeke's two vital works, his *Syrische Grammatik* and his *Neusyrische Sprache*.

The striking feature of the NA verbal system is its abandonment of the inherited tense/aspect forms and replacement of them with a new edifice, founded on the participles. This process is already begun in Syriac, the ancestors of some of the modern forms existing alongside the old tenses. This is clearest with the modern future and preterite, less so with the copular formations.

We can best begin with the J stem and x series of affixes. The predecessor of the J stem is the Syriac active participle. In sound verbs of the peal binyan the active participle takes the form *qāṭel*. It is frequently followed by a personal pronoun in a special enclitic form. The normal forms of the first person pronoun are *enā* (singular) and *ḥnan* (plural). When they follow the participle we get -*nā* and -*nan* giving *qāṭelnā* and *qāṭlīnan*. It is quite clear that the pronouns in this construction are clitics, and they are traditionally referred to as such. The clear indication is the special forms they take when joined to the participles or another word.

The P stem is a development of the old passive participle, which takes the form *qṭīl* in the peal binyan. The y series affixes derive from the forms of the preposition *l-* combined with pronominal suffixes. The passive participle with *l-* formed a kind of preterite even in Syriac, though it is not so common as the regular perfect. This form is found in BT and in Mandaic as well. For Syriac Nöldeke (1880:193) cites *qrēn lāḵ kṯāḇē* "You have read books." In BT (Megillah 6a) we find *ḥazī lī* "I have seen." Macuch (1965:434) gives Mandaic *knišlia uzlihlia* "I swept and I cleaned."

It is not so easy to determine the status of these forms. The suffixed preposition *l-* seems to be quite firmly attached to the verb and does not move elsewhere in the sentence. On the other hand, there are no special forms, either of the passive participle or of the preposition, in this combination. The fixed nature of the construction argues for *l-* being a clitic, while its unchanged form suggests that it is an independent word. Regarding this construction, we will simply say that the preposition began as an independent word and may have already become a clitic at the period of the older dialects.

The third combination is C + z. The C stem of class I verbs in NA results from the regularization of an old noun pattern used largely for abstracts in Syriac. It replaces the old infinitive of the form *meqṭal* with a new one: *qṭālā*.

Though we have confined our discussion to class I (peal) verbs up to this point, it may be interesting to note the C stem of class II verbs *qatole/maqtole*. These infinitives correspond to the infinitives of pael and afel verbs in BT, rather than to the Syriac forms of the same verbs. This is one of the ways in which the modern dialects are closer to BT than to Syriac.

The z series does not have any obvious parallel in Syriac or BT. Nöldeke (1868:200-206) suggests a hybrid ancestry for these forms. One pattern is said to underlie the 3p singular, while another underlies all other forms. The 3p singular form *ile* "he is " and *ila* "she is" derive from *īṯleh* "he has" and *īṯlāh* "she has." The remaining forms are composed of three parts: *īṯ*, the active participle of *hwā* "be," and an enclitic pronoun. So, for example, Nöldeke suggests that *iwin* is a reduced form of *īṯ* + *hawe* + *nā*. The full range of base and derived forms is given in table 9. These derivations make sense, but we must regard them as a bit more tentative than the others. The source of the x and y series is immediately apparent from a comparison of Syriac and NA, while the z series has no clear parallel in Syriac. Nöldeke's suggestions are entirely reasonable, but not entirely compelling.

The status of these forms in Syriac is different from both y and x. z is not a single constituent in Syriac: it is a group of words which have not yet coalesced. The members of the z paradigm simply did not exist at the Syriac period. Further, the characteristic class I infinitive pattern *qṭālā* was not in

Table 9

īt - hāwē - enā	iwən
īt - hāwyā - enā	iwan
īt - hāwē - at	iwət
īt - hāwyā - at	iwat
īt - lēh	ile
īt - lāh	ila
īt - hāwī - aḥnan	iwax
īt - hāwī - aton	itun
īt - hāwī - enēn	ina

use as an infinitive in Syriac. Thus neither one of the elements in the C + z combination was in use in Syriac, at least in its modern form.

We have reason to believe that the combination C + z is the outcome of two successive developments: first, the creation of a new copula, and second, its attraction to a position after the verb. This evidence is provided by a comparison of the forms of the Iraqi Koine and other dialects. We have already seen in table 5 examples of cases where z is attached to words other than the verb. When a verb in the continuous tense is negated, z is attached to the negative particle rather than to the verb. The interrogatives like *mudi* "what" also take z in Iraqi Koine. Two other dialects which we will now consider provide very clear evidence for an origin of z in a site other than its present post-verbal position.

Krotkoff (1982) is a grammar of the dialect of Aradhin, a village in northern Iraq, ten miles from Amedia. In this dialect, C always follows the copular element, rather than preceding it. z is used only in relative and negative clauses, while in most cases a form of the copula which Krotkoff calls the emphatic takes its place. In table 10 we have examples of the use of the emphatic and simple copulas in the dialect of Aradhin, as well as the full paradigm of the emphatic copula.

Hoberman (1983) describes the dialect of the Jews of Amedia, a town just down the road from Krotkoff's Aradhin. This dialect uses cognates of z with the continuous to form the present tense, but, as in Aradhin, the copula precedes the verb. Table 11 shows two sentences in this dialect. The first person plural form *lax* is evidently unusual. The normal form is *(i)wax*, as in the other dialects. The parallel with the Koine dialect is particularly close here because the z series is used in both dialects, and the forms are quite close. Only the placement differs.

Jacobi (1973) describes a dialect now spoken by members of the Thuma tribe living in the Khabur valley in northeast Syria. According to the paradigm which she gives for the "durative present," z may either precede or follow the verb stem. When z follows the verb, it may be either enclitic or independent. When it precedes the verb it is, of course, an independent word. So *ile bəgrāša* "he is pulling" alternates with *bəgrāša-le* and *bəgrāša ile*.

Table 10

howin plaxa	"I am working"
hule dra:ya šarde	"He is making conditions"
lɛ:le qba:la babux	"Your father does not accept"
ti:le qya:ma ga:wɛ:hin	"Which he is performing"

1m	howin
f	howan
2m	howit
f	howat
3m	hule
f	hula
1p	howax
2p	hówutun
3p	hulɛ

Table 11

le bɨmyaθa ʔene lu bɨzwara mɨn kɨpna
"He is dying, his eyes are turning from hunger."

bédana lax bixala ṣaʿar ɨbbe
"Then we are eating (are full of) sorrow about him."

The absence of z from Syriac makes it clear that it is a later development. It has achieved its present status as copula and as person/gender/number marker of certain verb tenses during the same period that another marker receded. We have already noted that x is the descendant of the Syriac enclitic pronouns. These pronouns were not limited to appearance after participles. They were, in fact, the regular way of expressing the copula. They were commonly added to nouns and adjectives, as well as particles. A few examples from Goldenberg (1983) will give an idea of their use:

ṭalya - w	"He is a youth"
ḥakkīmē -nan	"We are wise"
mānā - nan	"What are we?"
ummānā - at ṭābā	"You are a good craftsman"
šemšā šrāgan - ū	"The sun is our lamp"

Now we are in a position to see the similarity between the Syriac enclitic pronouns and the NA z series. They share the same two related, but distinct, functions. On the one hand, they fasten to a variety of words, functioning as the normal copula in a nominal sentence. On the other hand, when appended to certain verb forms they produce new present tenses. These two functions together represent a distinctive niche, one which has endured even while its occupants have changed. The existence of this strong parallel between the syntactic and morphological structures of Syriac and NA is striking, but what is most striking is the lack of direct genetic connection between the old and new copulas and the old and new present tense stems. One wonders how such a turnover in material can take place without disturbing the pattern.

The very nature of the changes which took place sometimes makes it possible to determine their sequence. In other cases we cannot be certain of the order, but one may seem more plausible than another. Before we say anything at all about the timing, let us list the changes involved all together:
1. z formed
2. z becomes clitic copula
3. C becomes regular infinitive
4. C + z formation comes into use
5. enclitic pronouns disappear as copula
6. enclitic pronouns become x

It is clear that 1 > 2 > 4 and also that 3 > 4. The ordering of 5 and 6 is somewhat in doubt. One possibility is that the enclitic pronouns became the opaque affix series x when suffixed to the active participle and that the other cases of the enclitic pronouns were replaced with the new copula later. The other possibility is that the enclitic pronoun was replaced by z in all cases except after the participle, and only then did those remaining cases become x. Whether the enclitic pronoun following the active participle had become x yet or not, it must have been recognized as a special instance at the time of the general disappearance of the old enclitic pronoun copula in order to be spared from going the way of its morphological brethren. So while we do not know the exact timing, we can be sure that either 6 preceded 5 or was just begun when 5 started.

Another pair whose ordering we would like to determine is 2 and 5, the emergence of the new copula and death of the old. Here the question is old and familiar, but very difficult. Perhaps the disappearance of an old form created a vacuum into which was drawn a new one. On the other hand, the appearance of a new more highly marked form may have driven the old less highly marked one out of circulation. Our answer to this question must be, in the absence of evidence which bears directly on it, highly tentative. It seems reasonable to suppose that, if the language had a copula at the Syriac period and has one now, it did not lose the old one and then add the new one, but rather kept some sort of copula at all periods. This could be consistent with either ordering of 2 and 5, so long as there was some overlap. If the enclitic pronoun copula began to weaken, this could have led to the accelerated development of z, which would have gradually taken its place. If z came into use as a copula first, it would probably have co-existed with the enclitic pronoun copula for some time, only gradually supplanting it.

Table 12 gives a summary of the changes which we have been discussing and their timing. A single arrow indicates precedence, while a double arrow indicates overlap. The whole interlocking set of changes has taken place without seriously upsetting the pattern, a pattern which allots the copula a

special place in the verbal system. We have seen the strength of this pattern
and some of the mechanisms of its resiliency. The reasons for that strength
remain a topic for future investigation.

Table 12

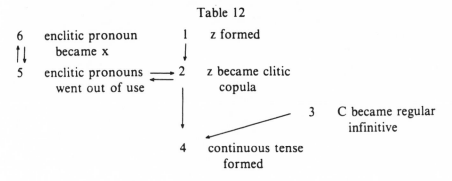

Bibliography

GOLDENBERG, Gideon, 1983. "On Syriac Sentence Structure" in *Arameans, Aramaic, and the Aramaic Literary Tradition*, ed. Michael Sokoloff, 97-140. Ramat Gan.

HETZRON, Robert, 1969. "The Morphology of the Verb in Modern Syriac," *JAOS* 89.112-127.

HOBERMAN, Robert D., 1983. "Verb Inflection in Modern Aramaic." University of Chicago Dissertation.

JACOBI, Heidi, 1973. *Grammatik des thumischen Neuaramäisch*. Wiesbaden.

KROTKOFF, Georg, 1982. *A Neo-Aramaic Dialect of Kurdistan. Texts, Grammar and Vocabulary*. New Haven.

KLAVANS, Judith, 1985. "The Independence of Syntax and Phonology in Cliticization," *Language* 61.1:95-120.

MACUCH, Rudolf, 1965. *Handbook of Classical and Modern Mandaic*. Berlin.

NÖLDEKE, Theodor, 1868. *Grammatik der Neusyrischen Sprache*. Leipzig.

NÖLDEKE, Theodor, 1880. *Kurzgefasste Syrische Grammatik*. Leipzig.

Reconstructng Pre-Modern Aramaic Morphology: The Independent Pronouns

Robert D. Hoberman

1 Introduction

Is work on the comparative grammar of Neo-Aramaic at this time justified? There are several reasons for answering that it is not. One might argue that we do not have precise enough information about a large enough variety of contemporary dialects for comparative work to be valid. Furthermore there exist unpublished Neo-Aramaic documents of several centuries ago which would add time-depth to comparison of the twentieth-century speech forms.[1] Since these are known to exist, one might say they may not be neglected: work on comparative Neo-Aramaic must be put off until after the analysis of these texts.

Another line of argument would say that, given the tenuous situation of Neo-Aramaic speakers today and the strong tendency toward the replacement of local dialects by koinē varieties, we are obligated to devote all our resources to collecting information on the existing spoken dialects before they disappear, and to set aside for some time any kind of library research on Neo-Aramaic. Georg Krotkoff has commented with justice that the "great chance" of Neo-Aramaic studies "is that they can still mine a living reservoir of language and thus provide a much needed supplement to Arabic dialectology. But time may be running out, and nobody in a position to contribute should delay doing to" (1985, 133). Personally I find this last argument very persuasive.

Nevertheless, there are benefits to be gained from pursuing comparative Neo-Aramaic at this time, using whatever material is at our disposal. This refers specifically to the comparison of dialects within Northeastern Neo-Aramaic (NENA), not comparison among the major Neo-Aramaic languages.[2]

---

[1]These are surveyed, and an important sample published, by Bruno Poizat in this volume.

[2]There are four extant Aramaic language groups. Tsereteli (1977) has labeled three of them "Western" (Maʻlula, etc.), "Central" (Ṭuroyo, to which Jastrow [1985b] has

79

Ma'lula Aramaic and neo-Mandaic are no more relevant, and in some ways much less, for the purpose of comparative reconstruction within NENA than the many varieties of earlier Aramaic, such as Palestinian, Babylonian, Syriac, etc. On the other hand, Ṭuroyo shares with NENA some innovations undergone since the old Aramaic stage, so comparison of these two indeed makes sense.

Two main benefits can result from even a sketchy attempt at comparison within NENA. First, it is a way of taking stock of the scope and accomplishments of NENA studies so far, by putting together our knowledge of the dialects that have been documented. We should be able to offer at least rudimentary answers to questions like these: how many major dialect groups are there within NENA, and what linguistic features delineate the groups? Maclean (1892, xii-xv) systematically characterizes the groups in his classification only according to the reflexes of old Aramaic θ and ð—what are the major morphological features of the dialects? Is there any overreaching dialectal split like Blanc's division of the Mesopotamian Arabic into *qeltu* and *gelet* dialects? Do the Jewish dialects fall into the same linguistic-geographical groupings as the Christian ones or not, and are there any features which characterize all the Jewish dialects as distinct from the Christian ones? And the most enigmatic question, but in some ways the most interesting: what can we conclude the language was like between the time of old Aramaic and the first recorded Neo-Aramaic?

The second kind of benefit of this work comes from the answers we find to these questions. We are not going to be able to compile voluminous grammars and dictionaries for all the dialects of NENA spoken today. That being the case, our work should be guided by an attempt to fill in the gaps in our knowledge and answer significant questions. For this we need an inventory of the existing information and some hypotheses about the most significant features of variation among the dialects.

The present essay takes only a single small step towards these goals, hardly more than to illustrate the method. I take morphological innovations in general to be more significant for classification and reconstruction than phonological changes. Unlike the vast majority of the vocabulary, which is loosely organized and has much borrowed material, the pronouns form a delimited and highly structured system and their origins in older Aramaic are

added Mlaḥsō), and "Eastern" (northern Iraq and adjacent parts of Iran and Turkey). A better name for this third group would be Northeastern Neo-Aramaic, for two reasons. The discovery of a fourth group, modern Mandaic in southwestern Iran, makes the term "Eastern" for the group in northern Iraq and Iran something of a misnomer, since Mandaic is located just as far to the east. Furthermore, "Eastern Neo-Aramaic" is liable to mislead since the term "Eastern Aramaic" conventionally takes in the older literary languages, Syriac, Babylonian Talmudic, and Mandaic, as well.

for the most part evident. For these reasons, clear conclusions can be drawn from them for the history nd classification of the NENA dialects. The object of this study, then, is to determine as nearly as possible what the pronouns were at the time of proto-NENA (PNENA); this is defined as the latest stage that was ancestral to all the NENA dialects (but to no other known varieties, such as Ṭuroyo). Anything attested in two or more NENA dialects of widely separated geographical areas is attributed to PNENA, except in a few cases where parallel analogical developments are assumed to have taken place later in more than one dialect separately. It is sometimes difficult to decide whether a particular analogical change took place before or since the PNENA stage, so in several instances two competing forms are reconstructed for PNENA, when both are widely attested in the NENA dialects. Evidence from other, older Aramaic languages is in principle irrelevant to the reconstruction of PNENA, but in fact has been brought in once or twice where the data from attested modern dialects are open to several conflicting interpretations. When there are two similar NENA forms, either of which could have given rise to the other, the one that is more like forms attested in older Aramaic is postulated for PNENA. This means that a form which may be attested only in one dialect or a group of closely related dialects may still be attributed to PNENA, if it is clearly a survival of an older Aramaic form. The historical changes that produced the PNENA pronouns from old Aramaic forms are discussed afterwards.

The reconstructions presented here are quite tentative because information is lacking for many dialects, of which two stand out: the Christian dialects of Turkey and the Jewish dialects of southern Kurdistan. The main NENA dialects used here, and the chief sources of information, are the following, listed in the order in which they appear in the tables:

U	Urmi—Christian (Maclean 1895, Marogulov 1976)
Az.	Azerbaijan—Jewish (Garbell 1965)
Al.	Villages in the plain of Moṣul (prominent among them being Alqosh)—Christian (Rhétoré 1912, Sachau 1895, Guidi 1883, Sabar 1978 and the sources referred to as Bart.)
Bart.	Barṭille—Christian (unpublished notes collected in 1976 from a speaker from the town, located about 10 miles east of Moṣul)
Mang.	Mangesh—Christian (Sara 1974)
Ar.	Aradhin—Christian (Krotkoff 1982)
NT	Nerwa Texts—Jewish (from seventeenth-century manuscripts edited by Sabar [1976])
Am.	Amadiya—Jewish (pronounced 'amɨdya) (Hoberman 1987)
Z	Zakho—Jewish (Polotsky MS)
Hart.	Härtəvən—Christian (Jastrow 1971)[3]

Other Abbreviations and Sources:

Tur.	Ṭuroyo (Jastrow 1985a)

OA   Old Aramaic (unless otherwise specified, examples are from
          Syriac, Nöldeke 1904, Mingana 1905)
NENA   Northeastern neo-Aramaic
PNENA   proto-Northeastern neo-Aramaic
Babylonian Talmudic Aramaic (Epstein 1960)
Mandaic (Nöldeke 1875)
Biblical Aramaic (Rosenthal 1974)
1., 2., 3. first, second, third person
sg.   singular
pl.   plural
masc.   masculine
fem.   feminine

For ease of comparison a fairly uniform set of phonetic symbols is used for
all the dialects, including older Aramaic. Because all the independent
pronouns in NENA begin with a glottal stop followed by a vowel, it is
convenient to omit an indication of the glottal stop in such word-initial
sequences. It is also possible to simplify the representation of vowel quantity,
because in all the dialects vowels are generally short in closed syllables, long in
open syllables (especially stressed ones). I have therefore indicated vowel
quantity only where it deviates from this pattern. For the Azerbaijan Jewish
dialect, however, the transcription of Garbell 1965 is retained, except that *y* is
used for Garbell's *j*. I have also retained the distinction between the vowels *i*
and *i̵*, which is lower, centralized, and always short, in those dialects for which
the published sources make such a distinction and in PNENA. The symbols *i̵*
also transcribes the Syriac vowel sign *zlama pšiqa* or *zlama zoga*.

2 Reconstruction of the PNENA Independent Pronouns

First and Second Person. The first and second person independent
pronouns are listed in Table 1. The first person singular form *ana* is identical
in all the dialects. The first person plural has two main forms, *axnan* and *axni*;
both are geographically widespread, and both very likely existed at the time of
PNENA. The form *axneni* occurs in those dialects in which the corresponding
possessive suffix has the alternate form *eni* in addition to the more general
an,[4] *an* is original, while the suffix *eni* arose through analogical processes
within NENA, along with the reshaping of other pronominal suffixes.

---

[3]Härtəvən is located in the Siirt Vilayet of Turkey. Although the published
information on the Härtəvən dialect consists only of two small texts and a few
grammatical notes, it is the NENA dialect most linguistically divergent and
geographically distant, and therefore is of great importance for reconstruction. I am
grateful to Otto Jastrow for allowing me to use Härtəvən data which he is publishing
for the first time in this volume. I have not discussed issues specific to Härtəvən in my
paper, since they are treated in detail by Jastrow.

[4]Polotsky 1961, 19-20 established a semantic difference between the two suffixes in
Urmi.

Table 1

Independent Pronouns, First and Second Persons

Dial.	1sg.	2sg.			1 pl.			2pl.	
		common	masc.	fem.					
U	ana	at(in)				axnan axneni	axni	axtun	axtoxun axnoxun
Az.	ana	at				axnan	axni	atxun axnxun	
Al.	ana	at	aʔit ayit ahit	ati ate	aʔat ayat ahat	axnan	axni	axtu(n)	
Bart.	ana		ait		ayat		axni		
Mang.	ana	at	ayit		ayat		axni	axnutin	
Ar.	ana		a(y)it	ati	ayat		axni	axtu(n)	
NT	ana		ahit		ahat		axni	axtun	
Am.	ana	(ăhit)	ahit		ahat		axni	axtun	
Z	ana		ahet		ahat	axnan axneni	axni	axtun	axtoxun axnoxun
Hart.	ana	ahet			aḥnaḥ			aḥniton	
PNENA	ana	at				axnan	axni	axtun	

For the second person singular, two widespread sets of forms exist: one, *at*, which does not indicate gender, and one which differentiates gender by means of the terminations masc. *it*, fem. *at* (usually with a hiatus-breaking glide ʾ, *y*, or *h*).[5] Gender-differentiating forms are found in all the dialects of Iraq, but not in Iran, while the common-gender *at* is geographically widespread. Therefore the gender-differentiating forms are an innovation of Iraqi NENA (on the analogy of the corresponding verbal suffixes, masc. **it*, fem.**at*), and PNENA had **at*.

The second person plural pronouns show a diversity of forms, but *axtun* is the most widespread and is reconstructed for PNENA; the other forms are explicable by a variety of analogical mechanisms within NENA: Az. *atxun* is the singular *at* plus the possessive suffix *(o)xun*, and Az. *axnxun* is the stem of 1.pl. *axn-an* with the same suffix. Essentially the same is Z. *axnoxun*, while Z. *axtoxun* has the stem of *axtun* with the same suffix. Mang. *axnutin* is the stem

---

[5] In addition two Iraqi Christian dialects have the feminine form *ati*, which, as suggested by a comment of Rhétoré (1912, 61), may be a hypercorrect classicism, based on classical Syriac *at* spelled ʾnty. I have no explanation for three other forms, Al. fem. *ate*, cited by Rhétoré on the same page, U *atin* (or perhaps *attin*), cited by Maclean (1895, 16) and Am. *ăhit*, which serves for both masculine and feminine, and seems to be derived from *ahit*.

of the first person plural with the verbal suffix *utin*. The final *n* is optional in Alqosh and Aradhin, as it frequently is in the Iraqi Christian dialects after the vowel *u*.

Table 2

Independent Pronouns, Third Person

Dialect	3sg.masc.		3sg.fem.				3pl.	
U	avun avɨn	ɵav	ayɨn		ay		aniy	
Az.		ɵ	ahi		(ɵ)			oyne une
Al.	ahu a(?)u	awa	ahi a(?)i	aya		anhi	ani	ane
Bart.	awun		ayɨn			ănɨn	ani	
Mang.		awa		aya	e		ani	
Ar.		awa		aya	ɵ		ani	
NT	ahun	awa	ahin			ahnun	ani	
Am.	ahu	awa	ahi	aya			ani	
Z		awa		aya			ani	
Hart.	ahu		ahi				aḥni	
PNENA	*ahu		*ahi			*anhi(n)	*ani	

Third Person. The third person independent pronouns are listed in Table 2. For the masculine singular pronoun there are two main types, *ahu* and *awa*. All the other forms are minor variants of *ahu*: *ahu* became *a'u* or *au* (bisyllabic), then *aw* (monosyllabic); from *aw* came U ɵav on one hand the *ɵ* on the other.[6] The source of the final *n* in *ahun, awun* and *avin* is unclear, and these forms must be set aside to await a specific explanation along with other as yet unexplained variations with loss or accretion of final *n* in various dialects.[7] The feminine forms show parallel developments. Az. fem. *ɵ* is the originally masculine pronoun generalized to both genders.

It remains to consider the relationship between the types *ahu, ahi* and *awa, aya*. I take the *ahu, ahi* type to be the more original and the *awa, aya* type to be derived from it, for two reasons. Note first that, although the forms *awa, aya*

---

[6]PNENA *w regularly becomes *v* in Urmi, and this *v* is apparently distinct from a separate phoneme *w* (Hetzron 1969, 113). The symbol ɵ indicates emphatic (flat, back, labialized) pronunciation; the emphatic character of U ɵav is perhaps the result of the back quality of the *a* in *aw* and the *w* itself.

[7] Several instances are cited by Sabar (1976, xxxiv) who observes, "The consonant *-n* [actually the syllable fragment *-in*] may be suffixed to preserve a preceding long vowel of a closed or open syllable."

appear only in Iraq, the forms *ahu(n), ahi(n)* are attested in Iran, Iraq, and Turkey (Härtəvən). Furthermore, we can see a route from the *ahu, ahi* type to *awa, aya* but not in the other direction. From *ahu* came the shortened form *aw*, as described in the preceding paragraph. To this was added a final vowel *a*, producing *awa*, on the model of the first person pronoun *ana*. The third person singular pronouns of PNENA were, therefore, **ahu, *ahi*, while *awa* and *aya* were innovations in Iraq.

In the plural pronoun, let us dispose of the more divergent forms first. The *e* ending in some dialects is very likely from the noun plural ending, as in *bate* 'houses.'[8] Az. *oyne* (which became *une* by a regular sound change in the northern subdialect) is a totally new formation; it has the ending of forms like NT *ane* and the stem vowel of the singular *o*, but the *y* is unexplained.

This leaves the widespread *ani* and two forms with *h*: Al. *anhi*, NT *ahnun*. The Barṭille form *änin* very likely comes from something like **anhin*, and this would explain the short *ă*. NT *ahnun* may be from **anhun*, though the metathesis is unexplained; the ending *un*, attested in this dialect only, was not present in this pronoun in PNENA but is influenced by the pronominal suffix *lu(n)*. The form *ani* could come from *anhi(n)*, if after the *h* disappeared giving *äni* the *ä* lengthened as is regular in open syllables. Therefore *anhi(n)* is older than *ani*. However, since *ani* is so nearly universal in NENA, it must have already been in existence at the PNENA stage, and so the reconstructed PNENA forms are **anhi(n)* and **ani*.

Table 3

The Reconstructed PNENA Independent Pronouns

Person	Masculine	Singular Common	Feminine	Plural
1.		ana		axnan, axni
2.		at		axtun
3.	ahu		ahi	anhi(n), ani

3 From Old Aramaic to PNENA

When we compare the forms that have been reconstructed for PNENA, listed in Table 3, with the corresponding forms in older Aramaic, the most striking innovation is the spread of the initial vowel *a* to the third person pronouns, and thus its presence throughout the paradigm of the independent pronouns.[9]

[8] Al. *anai*, attested only by Sachau (1895, 6), may be an erroneous transcription for what was actually *ane*, since PNENA **ay* became *e* in many dialects, including Alqosh.

[9] Scholars have offered individual explanations for the initial *a* in some of the forms (as when Nöldeke [1868, 75] suggests that the third person singular pronouns are from *hahu, hahi*) but none to my knowlege has noticed that this is a systematic feature of the paradigm.

In the older Aramaic ancestor of PNENA, initial *a* had been part of the second person pronouns (e.g., Syriac *at, atton, atten*) and probably also the first person (Biblical Aramaic *ăna, ănaḥna*, Babylonian Talmudic *ăna, ănan*, Mandaic *'n', 'nyn 'n'n*, Ṭuroyo: sg. *ono* (from *ana), pl. *aḥna*.[10] In view of the fact that initial *a* exists throughout the paradigm in PNENA, its presence in the individual third person forms is best explained not unitarily, taking each form separately, but holistically: the initial *a* was acquired in the third person forms by analogy with the first and second person, that is to say, *ahu* and *ahi* are the older Aramaic pronouns *hu* and *hi* amplified with initial *a*, the pronoun stem.

The reconstructed PNENA third person plural forms are *ani* and the more original *anhi(n)*. The most similar forms in older Aramaic are the Babylonian Talmudic feminine *inhi, inin*, along with the masculine *inho, inon*. Nöldeke (1875, 86) analyzes these as the deictic particle *(h)ēn* (which he translates with the Latin word "ecce," and which is perhaps related to Hebrew *hinnē* [Epstein 1960, 20]), to which are added the pronominal suffixes masc. *hōn*, fem. *hēn*. If pre-PNENA did have such forms beginning with the syllable *ēn* or *īn*, then the initial vowel must have become *a* along with the initials of the whole paradigm. On the other hand the particle *(h)ēn* may never have been part of the pre-PNENA form, and the initial *a* may simply have been added to the OA pronoun *(h)innōn, -ēn* by analogy with the first and second person, just as it was added to the third person singular pronouns. The apparent selection of the feminine *-ēn* rather than masculine *-ōn* is less surprising when we notice that the *i* termination of the first and third persons plural may have been influenced by the third plural verbal suffix (as in *kaθwi* 'they write'), itself from the OA noun plural suffix *īn*.

The only other significant innovation of PNENA with respect to OA is that the second person plural took on the stem shape of the first person, *ax-* (Nöldeke 1868, 74).[11]

4 Implications for Classification

The independent pronouns are altogether a small number of items, and cannot themselves furnish decisive criteria for classing dialects into genetic groups. Nevertheless the pronouns provide a few specific isoglosses which support groupings that are plausible on other grounds

The dialect of Härtəvən was referred to by Otto Jastrow (1971, 216)[12] as

---

[10]The Syriac forms *ina, ḥnan* are thus innovations of Syriac itself, and there is no need to consider them in relation to PNENA However even if the first person pronouns in PNENA should have been like those in Syriac, the initial *a* of the paradigm would still have a source in the second person pronouns. On the long initial vowel in PNENA *ana* see Nöldeke 1868, 73.

[11]OA *ḥ* regularly becomes *x* in PNENA except Härtəvən.

[12]Tsereteli (1977, 251) follows Jastrow in this.

Eastern Neo-Aramaic, i.e., NENA as distinct from Ṭuroyo, and although the data are scant the pronoun facts bear this out. Two innovations are shared by Härtəvən and NENA, but absent from Ṭuroyo:

(1) the spread of initial *a* to the third person pronouns: PNENA **ahu, *ahi, *ani*, Hart. *ahu/awa, ahi/aya, aḥni/ani*;

(2) the addition of final *i* to the third person plural pronoun, PNENA *ani* and Hart. *aḥni/ani*.

These two innovations clearly support the view of Härtəvən and NENA as one group, despite the striking differences between them.

The dialects of Iraq examined here, both Christian and Jewish, share two innovations:

(1) the differentiation of gender in the second person singular pronouns by means of the terminations masc. *it*, fem. *at*;

(2) the addition of final *a* in the third person singular, *awa, aya*.[13]

These two shared innovations, along with others, provide evidence for considering these dialects of Iraq as a linguistically valid subdivision of NENA.

References

JAOS - Journal of the American Oriental Society

ZDMG - Zeitschrift der Deutschen Morgenländischen Gesellschaft

Epstein, Ya'aḳov Naḥum Ha-Levi. 1960. *Diḳduḳ Aramit Bavlit.* (English title page: *A Grammar of Babylonian Aramaic*, by J. N. Epstein.) Ed. by 'Ezra' Tsiyon Melamed. Jerusalem: Magnes; Tel-Aviv: Dvir.

Garbell, Irene. 1965. *The Jewish Neo-Aramaic Dialect of Persian Azerbaijan: Linguistic Analysis and Folkloristic Texts.* (Janua Linguarum, Series Practica, 3.) The Hague: Mouton.

Hetzron, Robert. 1969. "The Morphology of the Verb in Modern Syriac (Christian Colloquial of Urmi)." JAOS 89: 112-127.

Hoberman, Robert D. 1989. *The Syntax and Semantics of Verb Morphology in Modern Aramaic: A Jewish Dialect of Iraqi Kurdistan.* (American Oriental Series.) New Haven: American Oriental Society.

Jastrow, Otto. 1971. "Ein neuaramäischer Dialekt aus dem Vilayet Siirt (Ostanatolien)." ZDMG 121: 215-222.

————. 1985a. *Laut- und Formenlehre des neuaramäischen Dialekts von Midin im Ṭūr 'Abdīn.* 3rd ed. Wiesbaden: Harrassowitz.

————. 1985b. "Mlaḥsō: An Unknown Neo-Aramaic Language of Turkey," *Journal of Semitic Studies* 30: 265-270.

[13]The same change has taken place in Härtəvən as well, where *awa, aya* function as demonstratives.

Krotkoff, Georg. 1982. *A Neo-Aramaic Dialect of Kurdistan: Texts, Grammar, and Vocabulary.* (American Oriental Series, 64.) New Haven: American Oriental Society.

————. 1985. "Studies in Neo-Aramaic Lexicology." *Biblical and Related Studies Presented to Samuel Iwry.* Winona Lake, Indiana: Eisenbrauns. 123-134.

Maclean, Arthur John. 1895. *Grammar of the Dialects of Vernacular Syriac.* Cambridge: The University Press. Repr. Amsterdam: Philo, 1971.

Marogulov, Q. I. 1976. *Grammaire néo-syriaque pour écoles d'adultes (dialecte d'Urmia).* Tr. Olga Kapeliuk. (Comptes Rendus du Groupe Linguistique d'Etudes Chamito-Sémitiques—G.L.E.C.S., Supplément 5.) Paris: Geuthner.

Mingana, Alphonse. 1905. *Clef de la langue araméenne ou Grammaire complète et pratique des deux dialectes syriaques occidental et oriental.* Mosul: Imprimerie des Pères Dominicains.

Nöldeke, Theodor. 1868. *Grammatik der neusyrischen Sprache am Urmi-See und in Kurdistan.* Leipzig: Weigel. Repr. Hildesheim: Olms, 1974.

————. 1875. *Mandäische Grammatik.* Halle. Repr. Darmstadt: Wissenschaftliche Buchgesellschaft, 1964.

————. 1904. *Compendious Syriac Grammar.* Tr. by James A. Crichton. London: Williams & Norgate. Repr. Tel-Aviv: Zion, n.d.

Polotsky, H. J. 1961. "Studies in Modern Syriac." *Journal of Semitic Studies* 6: 1-32.

————. MS. Notes on Neo-Aramaic grammar, Zakho dialect. Department of Linguistics, The Hebrew University of Jerusalem.

Rhétoré, J. 1912. *Grammaire de la langue Soureth.* Mosul: Imprimerie des Pères Dominicains.

Rosenthal, Franz. 1974. *A Grammar of Biblical Aramaic.* (Porta Linguarum Orientalium, n.s., 5.) Wiesbaden: Harrassowitz.

Sabar, Yona. 1976. *Pəšaṭ Wayəhi Bəšallaḥ: A Neo-Aramaic Midrash on Beshallaḥ (Exodus).* Wiesbaden: Harrassowitz.

————. 1978. "From Tel-Kēpe ('A Pile of Stones') in Iraqi Kurdistan to Providence, Rhode Island: The Story of a Chaldean Immigrant to the United States of America in 1927." JAOS 98: 410-415.

Sachau, Eduard, 1895. *Skizze des Fellichi-Dialekts von Mosul.* Berlin: Königliche Akademie der Wissenschaften; Reimer.

Sara, Solomon. 1974. *A Description of Modern Chaldean.* (Janua Linguarum, Series Practica, 213.) The Hague: Mouton.

Tsereteli, Konstantin. 1977. "Zur Frage der Klassifikation der neuaramäischen Dialekte." ZDMG 127: 244-253.

PERSONAL AND DEMONSTRATIVE PRONOUNS
IN CENTRAL NEO-ARAMAIC

A Comparative and Diachronic Discussion Based on Ṭūrōyo
and the Eastern Neo-Aramaic Dialect of Hertevin

Otto Jastrow

1. Introduction

In his seminal paper on the comparative grammar of Northeastern Neo-Aramaic, Robert HOBERMAN (1985) argues for the need of comparative studies even in the present situation in which we still lack reliable information on many individual Neo-Aramaic dialects and where, moreover, many of them are threatened with extinction which makes it seem more imperative to continue with purely descriptive work for as long as we can. Hoberman argues that only comparative work can help us to establish a classification of the existing dialects which, in turn, will tell us what dialects should be given priority in field work and documentation and, on the level of language structure, which features should be investigated first and foremost since "we are not going to be able to compile voluminous grammars and dictionaries for all the dialects."[1]

Comparative work is also the first step for any kind of diachronic investigation because only the combined evidence from a number of dialects will ensure a sound basis for linguistic reconstruction. This conception, of course, is not a recent discovery. In his review of the collection of Ṭūrōyo texts by Eugen PRYM and Albert SOCIN (1881) Theodor NÖLDEKE confesses: "Begreiflicherweise hat mich das Studium dieses Dialects auch sonst wieder auf einige Irrthümer in meiner neusyr. Grammatik aufmerksam gemacht."[2] The reference is, of course, to his famous *Grammatik der neusyrischen Sprache am Urmia-See und in Kurdistan* (1868); in other words, had the Ṭūrōyo data been available to him at the time he wrote his grammar of the Eastern dialects he would have avoided a number of misjudgments.

The present paper is a modest contribution to the comparative study and internal reconstruction of Ṭūrōyo and Eastern Neo-Aramaic (ENA).

---

[1] Hoberman 1985, p. 2.
[2] Nöldeke 1881, p. 232, n. 3.

Although Ṭūrōyo is separated from ENA by a number of important differences on all levels of language structure and therefore cannot be considered as a subdialect of ENA, it nevertheless shares with ENA a number of common innovations which make it its closest congener. This is corroborated by its geographical proximity to the ENA area, whereas the remaining two Neo-Aramaic languages, Ma'lūla Aramaic and Neo-Mandaic, are both structurally and geographically at a much greater distance from ENA. Thus while one may speak of four different Neo-Aramaic languages or groups of languages, it may be helpful, in certain contexts, to treat Ṭūrōyo and ENA as a single unit for which I would like to propose the designation *Central Neo-Aramaic* (CNA).[3] The suggested classification is summarized in the following table:

(1)   The Neo-Aramaic Languages

Central Neo-Aramaic

Ma'lūla Aramaic   Ṭūrōyo   ENA   Neo-Mandaic

The following discussion is based on two varieties of Neo-Aramaic with which the author is acquainted through his own fieldwork, viz. Ṭūrōyo and the ENA dialect of Hertevin. The data from these two languages are contrasted with Old Syriac, not because the literary language of Edessa is considered to be the direct ancestor of either or both varieties but rather because this well-documented language is relatively close to the presumed proto-language(s) of CNA. The transcription used for Old Syriac is somewhat archaizing and tries to capture the state of the language prior to its split into the Jacobite and Nestorian traditions.

2. Hertevin vs. Ṭūrōyo

Ṭūrōyo has been known fairly well for over a hundred years, starting with the above-mentioned collection of texts by PRYM and SOCIN (1881). For a short introduction to the Ṭūrōyo language area and the relevant literature see JASTROW [3]1985, XV-XXV. Our data are based on the dialect of Midin (mīdən) described in the same book; in a few instances we give additional data from the dialect of Midyat (miḏyaḏ), based on more recent fieldwork of the author.

The ENA dialect of Hertevin was discovered in 1970 and first described in a short paper two years later.[4] Recently the present author has resumed his work on this dialect and prepared a monograph which contains a grammatical description, a sizeable collection of texts with translation and a glossary.[5] The importance of Hertevin Neo-Aramaic lies, among other things, in its unique geographical position: it is the northwesternmost ENA dialect

---

[3]This terminology differs from Tsereteli 1977 who proposes the terms "Zentral-Aramäisch" for Ṭūrōyo and "Ost-Aramäisch" for ENA.

[4]Jastrow 1971; the actual year of publication was 1972.

[5]The book is expected to be published by Otto Harrassowitz in early 1988.

still encountered *in situ* after the combined catastrophes of the Armenian genocide and the expulsion of the Nestorian tribes which led to an almost complete evacuation of the vast ENA-speaking area of Eastern Turkey. The village of Hertevin[6] is situated near the district town of Pervari in Siirt province; the other ENA villages still extant are situated much farther south and/or east and hence much closer to the Iraqi border.[7]

As mentioned earlier, the Ṭūrōyo and ENA language areas are in close geographical proximity. It is, in fact, the river Tigris which, north of the Turkish border, separates the two linguistic areas: west of the Tigris lies the small and compact Ṭūrōyo-speaking area which extends between the district towns of Midyat and Idil,[8] east of the Tigris begins the vast ENA area which stretches all through southeastern Turkey, northern Iraq and way into Iran. Being situated on the western fringes of the ENA area, Hertevin quite expectedly shows a number of affinities to Ṭūrōyo; nevertheless, its affiliation with ENA remains unchallenged. Thus, e.g., Hertevin has a pharyngeal pronunciation [ḥ] of older *ḥ. This falls into line with Ṭūrōyo pronunciation, whereas most ENA dialects have a (post-)velar pronunciation [x]. However, Ṭūrōyo has kept distinct the reflexes of *ḥ and *k̲ (the spirant reflex of *k) whereas Hertevin has followed ENA in collapsing them, e.g.,

(2)	*Ṭūrōyo*	*Hertevin*	*ENA*
*k̲	x	ḥ	x
*ḥ	ḥ	ḥ	x

Similarly, Hertevin follows ENA in reshuffling initial CC- clusters in a number of non-verbal forms into CiCC- whereas Ṭūrōyo has retained the cluster and prefixed an anaptyctic vowel; notice, however, that in the last four examples Hertevin is closer to Ṭūrōyo word structure, e.g.,[9]

[6]In the forthcoming monograph I have chosen this conventional spelling for the name which is Härtəvən (transcribed) in Kurdish and Hertevinler (with the Turkish plural suffix) in Turkish.

[7]For a statement of the geographical position of these villages see Poizat 1982, appendix.

[8]Idil, natively called Āzəx, is Arabic speaking; see Jastrow 1978, p. 15 and 1981, p. 161ff.

[9]The transcription used for Ṭūrōyo and Hertevin is the same as in Jastrow [3]1985 (for Ṭūrōyo) and Jastrow 1971 and the forthcoming monograph (for Hertevin). However, in order to facilitate interdialectal and diachronic comparison, phonetically and/or phonemically long vowels have always been marked by a macron.

(3)	*Ṭūrōyo*	*Hertevin*	*ENA*	
*dmā	ʔadmo	demma	dĭmma	"blood"
*šmā	ʔəšmo	šemma	šĭmma	"name"
*šnayyā	ʔəšne	šenne	šĭnne	"years"
*mā	mō	mā	ĭmma	"hundred"
*kmā	kmō	kmā	kĭmma	"how many?"
*ʔeṭmāl	ʔaṭməl	ʔeṭmal	tĭmmal	"yesterday"
*brā	ʔabro	ʔebra	brōna	"son"

3. Personal Pronouns

Ṭūrōyo has the following set of free personal pronouns which is given in the urban variety of Midyat:

				Ṭūrōyo (Midyat)
(4)	3. person	sg. m.		hūwe
		f.		hīya
		pl. c.		hinne
	2. person	sg.		hat
		pl.		hātu
	1. person	sg.		ʔuno
		pl.		ʔaḥna

The villages have an identical set of forms, with two exceptions: the 3. person sg. m. tends to be /hīye/ rather than /hūwe/, and the 1. person sg. is /ʔōno/. The 3. person pl., although phonetically close to the Midyat form, would preferably be written as /ḥənne/ since most villages have a different inventory of short vowels (Midyat i, u → villages ə). The Ṭūrōyo paradigm thus is still fairly close to the forms of the proto-language, as can be shown by means of the corresponding Old Syriac forms:

			Old Syriac
(5)	3. person	sg. m.	hū
		f.	hī
		pl. m.	hennōn
		f.	hennēn
	2. person	sg. m.	ʔatt
		f.	ʔatt(ī)
		pl. m.	ʔattōn
		f.	ʔattēn
	1. person	sg.	ʔenā
		pl.	ḥnan

The first thing which differentiates between the two sets of data (4) and (5) above is the loss of gender distinction in the plural and in the 2. person sg., through which the Ṭūrōyo personal pronouns have been reduced to seven. The remaining forms relate fairly well to the corresponding Old Syriac forms although a few seemingly irregular changes need explanation.

The forms which are easiest to explain are /hat/ "you" and /hātu/ "you (pl.)." The initial h no doubt has been carried over from the 3. person pronouns. The final -n of /ʔattōn/[10] has been dropped, as has been the case in the remaining plural forms (/hinne/, /ʔahna/); this reflects a general trend in Ṭūrōyo which has also affected the inflected forms of the present tense: /(kō)gəršīna/ "we pull," /(kō)gəršūtu/ "you (pl.) pull," /(kō)gərši/ "they pull."[11] In Ṭūrōyo inherited consonant gemination has been abandoned, the preceding vowel being lengthened in compensation, thus /hātu ‹- •hattu.[12]

In the 1. person, /ʔōno/ of the villages is reminiscent of ENA /ʔāna/ and leads one to postulate a proto-form /*ʔānā/ rather than /*ʔenā/ ; however, Midyat has a short vowel in the first syllable: /ʔuno/. The initial vowel of /ʔahna/ "we" no doubt results from an anaptyctic vowel inserted before the word-initial cluster—note that beside /ʔahna/ there is also a variant /ʔihna/.

The 3. person pronouns are a lot more difficult to explain. Referring to /hūwe/, /hīya/ Nöldeke remarks that, although they look very archaic (that is, dissyllabic as opposed to the Old Syriac monosyllabic /hū/ and /hī/) they cannot possibly be explained as archaisms.[13] He instead suggests that /*hū/ and /*hī/ have been expanded to dissyllabics by adding the corresponding pronominal suffixes, sg. m. -e (‹ *-eh) and sg. f. -a (‹ *-āh); cf. Ṭūrōyo /bayto/ "house," /bayte/ "his house," /bayta/ "her house." This certainly is a very convincing argument which is further corroborated by the village variants (sg. m. /hīye/, f. /hīya/) which were not known to Nöldeke: if /hūwe/ and /hīya/ are interpreted as containing the pronominal suffixes -e and -a, greater regularity can be achieved by suffixing them to a unified base, /*hī(y)-/ .[14] The village variants would thus be viewed as a later development starting from the forms still preserved in Midyat.

There is yet another aspect to this problem which was not mentioned by Nöldeke. To the west, Midyat borders immediately on the large Arabic-speaking area of Mardin province. The closest Arabic-speaking village is Astal, which is situated only 3 kms from Midyat and administratively forms part of the town of Midyat. The Arabic area continues all the way to Mardin which is also Arabic speaking. All the dialects spoken in this area belong to the Mardin group of Anatolian qəltu Arabic.[15] Most people in Midyat are

---

[10]Given the final vowel of hātu it can be assumed that the proto-form was pronounced as *ʔattūn, that is, according to the Jacobite tradition of Old Syriac.

[11]‹ *garsin + (h)nan, *gāršīn + (ʔa)ttūn and *gāršīn, all preceded by the present tense marker kō-.

[12]Cf. gēlo "grass" ‹ *gellā, sāmo "poison" ‹ *sammā, etc.

[13]Nöldeke 1881, p. 225.

[14]Similarly, in Mossul Arabic the 3. person pronouns are m. hīnu, f. hīya and pl. c. hīyəm, that is, a basis hī(y)- to which the corresponding pronominal suffixes have been added; cf. Jastrow 1979, p. 42.

[15]Cf. Jastrow 1978, p. 5ff., and especially p. 12.

fluent in Arabic, and there is a conspicuously larger percentage of Arabic loans in Midyat Ṭūrōyo than in the village dialects. Now, the 3. person pronouns in Midyat Ṭūrōyo and in the Arabic dialects of Mardin province are almost identical, cf.

(6)   *Mardin Arabic*
        3. person   sg. m.   hūwe
                        f.   hīye
                        pl. c.   hənne

One therefore gets the impression that /hūwe/ and /hīya/ in Midyat Ṭūrōyo (as opposed to /hīye/, /hīya/ of the villages) were probably preserved thanks to the strong Arabic influence. On the other hand, the plural hinne (villages: /hənne/) "they" looks like a direct loan from Arabic in the whole Ṭūrōyo area. It is very difficult to relate hinne/hənne to such older forms as Old Syriac hennōn/hennēn since they would have yielded *hēnu/hēne rather than hənne. In particular the geminated -nn- in hənne cannot adequately be explained in terms of diachronic development because geminated consonants in inherited words have invariably been reduced and compensated for by vowel lengthening (see n. 12 above).[16]

Let us now turn to Hertevin which has the following set of free personal pronouns:

(7)   *Hertevin*
        3. person   sg. m.   ʔāhu
                        f.   ʔāhi
                        pl. c.   ʔaḥni
        2. person   sg.   ʔāhet
                        pl.   ʔaḥnīton
        1. person   sg.   ʔāna
                        pl.   ʔaḥnaḥ

Just like Ṭūrōyo, Hertevin has abandoned gender distinction in the plural and the 2. person sg., arriving at an exactly parallel set of pronouns. These pronouns do display, as in the case of Ṭūrōyo, an unmistakable relationship to the forms of the proto-language, although the changes that occurred are

[16]The geminated consonants found in present-day Ṭūrōyo always cut across morpheme boundaries; they do not go back to geminated consonants in the proto-language but derive from assimilation, e.g. Ṭūrōyo grəšše "they pulled" (< *griš + lhōn/lhēn). In Ṭūrōyo verb morphology consonant gemination is a productive device to express plurality of the verbal agent, e.g. grəšle "he pulled" vs. grəšše "they pulled." The only other possible explanation for hənne (beside its being an Arabic loan) would be its association with plural agent and/or object pronouns in verb morphology. In particular one could cite the form grīšənne "they pulled them" (< *grīšin + lhōn/lhēn) where -ənne is a portmanteau morph containing both the plural agent and the plural object suffixes.

somewhat more drastic than in Ṭūroyo. Without delving too much into the details, they can be summarized as follows.

Starting from *ʔatt, *ʔattōn/ʔattēn and probably *ʔānā, word-initial *ʔa- was spread throughout the remaining forms.[17] By this process *hū and *hī became dissylabic (> ʔāhu, ʔāhi); *ʔatt was in turn rendered dissyllabic by restructuring it according to ʔāhu, ʔāhi (> ʔāhet); the vowel e of the second syllable has been chosen to match that of the corresponding masculine verbal form (m. napqet, f. napqat "you come out"). The prefixation of *ʔa- to *hennōn/hennēn must have yielded an intermediate form *ʔahnun/ʔahnin whose h was shifted to ḥ by analogy with the other two plural forms (ʔaḥnīton, ʔaḥnaḥ); the ending was then replaced by -i in analogy to the corresponding verbal form (3. person pl. of the present tense), thus ʔaḥni napqi "they come out." Similarly, *ḥnan became *ʔaḥnan and was subsequently changed to ʔaḥnaḥ by analogy to the present tense ending -aḥ of the 1. person pl., thus ʔaḥnaḥ napqaḥ "we come out." *ʔattōn/ʔattēn first was subjected to the analogy of *ʔaḥnan, arriving at *ʔaḥtun/ ʔaḥtin; the restructuring did not stop at that, however, but eventually arrived at the form ʔaḥnīton which shows the same initial sequence ʔaḥn- as the two other plural pronouns (ʔaḥnaḥ, ʔaḥni) whereas its ending has been restructured to match the corresponding verbal form (napqīton[18]).

The system of free personal pronouns which results from these complex changes displays a remarkable symmetry: all forms are dissyllabic, except the 2. person pl. which, however, corresponds to an equally trisyllabic verbal form. All pronouns have an initial ʔa-/ʔā-, the singular forms beginning with ʔā- and the plural forms with ʔaḥn-. Furthermore the plural forms correspond to the respective endings of the present tense.

Seen from a comparative point of view, the Hertevin system of personal pronouns is interesting in two respects. The two forms ʔaḥnīton and ʔaḥnaḥ are rather progressive because, as was shown above, they were arrived at by subjecting the reconstructed intermediate forms *ʔaḥtun/ʔaḥtin and *ʔaḥnan to a second process of analogical restructuring. A number of ENA dialects have retained the intermediate forms, e.g. Urmi axtun "you (pl.)," axnan "we."[19] On the other hand, Hertevin seems to be unique among ENA dialects in preserving the 3. person pronouns (ʔāhu, ʔāhi, ʔaḥni) as distinct from the demonstratives (ʔāwa, ʔāya, ʔāni—see following paragraph). Most—if not all—ENA dialects have lost the older 3. person pronouns and replaced them by the demonstratives. As a consequence the opposition between "he came" and "that one came" has not been maintained. Thus Urmi aị tīlä lbēto ğäldi "sie ging schnell nach Hause"[20] can also be translated "that one went home

---

[17]See Hoberman 1985, p. 6.

[18]napqīton is derived from *nāpqīn + (ʔa)ttōn, cf. Old Syriac nāpqīttōn.

[19]Tsereteli 1978, p. 59.

[20]Tsereteli 1978, p. 63.

quickly"; Hertevin, however, would differentiate between ʔāhi tēla "she came" and ʔāya tēla "that one came."

4. Demonstrative pronouns

Contrary to most ENA dialects Ṭūrōyo has two sets of demonstrative pronouns, denoting closeness and remoteness respectively.

(8) *Ṭūrōyo*

a) close	sg. m.	hāno	"this"
	f.	hāṭe	
	pl. c.	hāni	
b) remote	sg. m.	hāwo	"that"
	f.	hāyo	
	pl. c.	hānək	

These forms reflect, with a few irregularities, the demonstrative pronouns of the proto-language, compare, e.g.,

(9) *Old Syriac*

a) close	sg. m.	hānā	"this"
	f.	hāḏē	
	pl. c.	hālēn	
b) remote	sg. m.	haw	"that"
	f.	hāy	
	pl. m.	hānōn	
	f.	hānēn	

The diachronic interpretation of the Ṭūrōyo demonstratives is best started with hāwo and hāyo which have become dissyllabic by suffixing a deictic element *-hā to the corresponding proto-forms, e.g. *haw-hā > *hawwā > hāwo, *hāy-hā > *hayyā > hāyo—an explanation already proposed by Theodor Nöldeke.[21] The plural hānək is related by Nöldeke (same place) to a rare Syriac form ⟨hnwk⟩—presumably *hānnōk—or a corresponding, though unattested, feminine *hānnēk. From hānək has obviously been derived the plural hāni for the close demonstrative, thus discontinuing older *hālēn.

The singular forms hāno (m.) and hāṭe (f.) are, at first glance, somewhat irregular since one would expect something like *hōno, *hōḏe. It is likely, however, that the proto-form of the masculine was not *hānā but rather *hānnā, since it is derived from *hā- + dənā;[22] *hānnā > *hannā > hāno would be a regular derivation.[23] The first vowel of the feminine hāṭe (instead of

---

[21]Nöldeke 1881, p. 226.

[22]Nöldeke ²1898, p. 46.

[23]This assumption is corroborated by Maʻlūla hanna "this."—Similarly, Old Syriac hānōn, hānēn may be read as *hānnōn, *hānnēn since they derive from *hā- + hennōn, hennēn (Nöldeke ²1898, p. 46).

*hōde) is best explained as an analogy to the masculine and plural, but the voiceless t̲ still remains puzzling.

As opposed to Ṭūrōyo, ENA dialects have preserved only a single set of demonstratives with a straightforward genetic relation to the proto-language; it corresponds to set b) of the preceding Ṭūrōyo (8) and Old Syriac (9) forms.

(10)   *Hertevin*

sg. m.	ʔāwa	"this, that"
f.	ʔāya	
pl. c.	ʔāni	

ʔāni is, of course, descended directly from older *hānnōn/hānnēn, unlike Ṭūrōyo hāni which has been reconstructed from hānɔk to denote closeness. The main irregularity in the Hertevin forms is the substitution of ʔ for initial h; this may be seen as an analogy to the personal pronouns.

The Hertevin demonstratives given in (10) above are typical of a large majority of ENA dialects. They are used as unspecific demonstratives not implying any particular closeness or remoteness.[24] However, Hertevin has derived from the above pronouns a second set of demonstratives with a strong deictic quality, denoting objects close by:

(11)   *Hertevin*

sg. m.	ʔōhá	"this one right here"
f.	ʔēhá	
pl.c.	ʔanhí	

As can be readily seen these pronouns consist of the shortened forms of the unmarked demonstratives (ʔō, ʔē, ʔan for ʔāwa, ʔāya, ʔāni) plus a deictic element *-hā which carries the stress; in the plural -hā has been changed to -hī by analogy to the unmarked demonstrative ʔāni.

5. Attributive demonstratives and the definite article

In Hertevin, both the ʔāwa set (10) and the ʔōhá set (11) are only used in the function of substantives. When used in attributive function, that is, in connection with a noun, the ʔāwa set is replaced by the following shortened allomorphs:

(12)   *Hertevin*

	substantival	*attributive*
sg. m.	ʔāwa	ʔō
f.	ʔāya	ʔē
pl. c.	ʔāni	ʔan

---

[24]This reminds the author of his native German where nowadays only "dieser" is employed and "jener" has fallen in complete disuse; as a consequence "dieser" has become an unspecific demonstrative without any reference to distance.

Thus, in Hertevin one says ʔāwa tēle "that one came" but ʔō kalba tēle "that dog came." However, in connection with nouns the attributive demonstrative is more often used as a kind of determination marker rather than a demonstrative proper. This has been remarked upon, among others, by TSERETELI for Urmi: "Es macht sich eine Tendenz zum Gebrauch der Demonstrativpronomen o und e als Artikel bemerkbar";[25] similarly KROTKOFF on Aradhin.[26] What is a "tendency" in ENA has, in Ṭūrōyo, led to the development of a full-fledged definite article, i.e.,

(13)   Ṭūrōyo
    sg. m.   ʔū-   (definite article)
    f.   ʔī-
    pl. c.   ʔan(n)-

The Ṭūrōyo definite article is prefixed to the noun and carries the main stress, e.g.,

(14)   Ṭūrōyo
        ʔú-malko   "the king"
        ʔí-barṭo   "the daughter"
        ʔám-malke   "the kings"
        ʔá-bnōṭe   "the daughters"
        ʔánn-abne   "the sons"

As can be inferred from the last three examples, the plural of the Ṭūrōyo definite article has several allomorphs:[27]

a) preceding initial clusters it is simply ʔá-,

b) preceding a single consonant it is ʔáC-, that is, ʔá- plus the gemination of the initial consonant,

c) only before initial vowels appears the presumed original form *ʔan-[28].

It is important to point out that, in Ṭūrōyo, the definite article is by no means identical with the attributive demonstrative. Quite to the contrary, the demonstrative pronouns are suffixed to the noun which must be preceded by the definite article, e.g.,

(15)   Ṭūrōyo
        ʔú-malko   "the king"
        ʔú-malkáno   "this king"
        ʔú-malkáwo   "that king"

[25]Tsereteli 1978, p. 63.

[26]Krotkoff 1982, p. 21f.

[27]Cf. Jastrow ³1985, p. 36f.

[28]It is obvious that ʔann- (with a secondary gemination of n before the following vowel) represents the original shape of this morpheme. The final n has been assimilated to the following consonant, e.g. *ʔán-kalbe > ʔák-kalbe "the dogs," etc.

ʔí-barṭo	"the daughter"
ʔí-barṭáṭe	"this daughter"
ʔí-barṭáyo	"that daughter"
ʔám-malke	"the kings"
ʔám-malkáni	"these kings"
ʔám-malkánǝk	"those kings"

In this construction, the definite article and the suffixed demonstrative both carry primary stress; the final vowel of the noun and the initial h of the demonstrative are elided.

The above examples amply demonstrate that the Ṭúróyo definite article functions quite differently from the ENA attributive demonstratives ʔó, ʔé, ʔan. Nevertheless, the two sets of forms are close enough phonetically to be suspected of a common origin. Nöldeke, in fact, derives the Ṭúróyo "Determinativartikel" from the Old Syriac remote demonstratives haw, hãy, hãnón/ hãnén—see (9) b) above—and explicitly rules out the possibility of its harking back to the personal pronouns hū, hī, hennón/ hennén—see (5) above—although, as he admits, "dieser Gebrauch liesse sich syntactisch wohl erklären."[29] This explanation, however, does not take care of the vowel quality of ʔū- and ʔí-. If harking back to *ʔaw and *ʔay the forms should have been retained as such because diphthongs are generally preserved in Ṭúróyo; if the forms had been subjected to an irregular monophthongization they should, nevertheless, be ʔó-, ʔé- rather than ʔū-, ʔí-. I am therefore inclined to think that, contrary to Nöldeke's opinion, the definite article might well hark back to the personal pronouns of the proto-language. This is also true for the plural ʔan(n)- which could just as well be derived from *hennón/ hennén as from *hãnnón/ hãnnén.[30]

There remains one important hypothetical question: if Ṭúróyo has developed a definite article, why didn't ENA, given the strong tendency mentioned by the authors? The explanation probably lies in a syntactic device called "object conjugation" by Krotkoff[31] which is widespread throughout ENA. In Hertevin, e.g., the definiteness of a noun functioning as a verbal object is not marked on the noun itself but on the preceding verb which receives a pronominal object suffix, e.g.,

(16)   *Hertevin*
       ḥázen (ḥá) ʔarnowwa   "I see a hare"
       ḥázenna ʔarnowwa   "I see the hare"

---

[29]Nöldeke 1881, p. 226.

[30]Stressed *e in closed syllables was shifted to a in Ṭúróyo, e.g. baṣro "meat" < *besrã, ʔaḏno "ear" < *ʔeḏnã, etc.

[31]Krotkoff 1982, p. 28.

móqemle (ḥā) ʔarnowwa   "he roused a hare"
móqémlēla ʔarnowwa   "he roused the hare"

In the above examples, the pronominal object suffix -la (3. person sg. f.)[32] is added to the ınflected verb to express the definiteness of the object noun, literally: "I see her, hare" = "I see *the* hare." Definiteness in a noun is thus expressed by different means depending on whether it functions as an object or a subject; only in the *subject* noun is definiteness expessed by the shortened demonstrative pronouns ʔō, ʔē, ʔan, e.g.,

(17)   *Hertevin*
        tēla ḥā ʔarnowwa   "a hare came"
        tēla ʔō ʔarnowwa   "the/that hare came"

In Ṭūrōyo, on the other hand, definiteness of the noun is always expressed by means of the definite article, regardless of its syntactic function. The examples given in (16) and (17) above would read in Ṭūrōyo as follows:

(18)   *Ṭūrōyo*
        kōḥōzēno (ḥā) ʔarnūwo   "I see a hare"
        kōḥōzēno ʔū-arnūwo[33]   "I see the hare"

        māqəmle (ḥā) ʔarnūwo   "he roused a hare"
        māqəmle ʔū-arnūwo   "he roused the hare"

        ʔāṭi (ḥā) ʔarnūwo   "a hare came"
        ʔāṭi ʔū-arnūwo   "the hare came"

The development of a full-fledged definite article in ENA thus was blocked by the syntactic device of marking the definiteness of an object noun on the verb form rather than on the noun itself.

6. The Hertevin ʔōhá series in attributive function

Paragraphs 4 and 5 above have treated of the Hertevin demonstrative pronouns ʔāwa, ʔāya, ʔāni and their attributive allomorphs ʔō, ʔē, ʔan. What remains to describe are the attributive allomorphs of the ʔōhā set which point to an object close by. In this case, however, the attributive allomorphs are conspicuously different from the ones used as substantives, e.g.,

(19)   *Hertevin*
                substantival   *attributive*
    sg. m.   ʔōhá   ʔád- ... -ha
        f.   ʔēhá   ʔád- ... -ha
    pl. c.   ʔanhí   ʔán- ... -ha

---

[32]ʔarnowwa "hare" is feminine. The initial l of the suffix is regularly assimilated to n, thus *ḥāzen + -la → ḥāzenna "I see her."

[33]Contrary to its Hertevin cognate, Ṭūrōyo ʔarnūwo is masculine.

The attributive allomorphs thus might be described as circumfixed morphemes whose two discontinuous elements encase the noun, e.g.,

(20) *Hertevin*

ʔád-nāšā-ha	"this man here"
ʔál-laḥmā-ha	"this bread here"
ʔád-ʔōdā-ha	"this room here"
ʔán-kēsē-ha	"these pieces of wood here"[34]

However, the deictic element -ha may also be omitted from the construction without any apparent change in meaning, e.g. ʔál-laḥma "this bread here," ʔád-ʔōda "this room here."[35] If we start from the fact that ʔōhā consists of the shortened form of the demonstrative ʔāwa plus an additional deictic element -ha, it is not difficult to see why, in the corresponding attributive form, the deictic -ha is suffixed to the noun, thus splitting the demonstrative into two discontinuous elements. It is precisely the deictic quality of -ha which calls for its position at the end of the construction. What is puzzling, however, is the shape of the first element. By simply splitting ʔōhā, ʔēhā we should arrive at *ʔō- ... -ha, *ʔē- ... -ha; however, the first element is a completely different morpheme, ʔád-, and only in the plural do we find the expected ʔán-. The prefix ʔád- may be interpreted as going back to *hā-d-, that is, the same combination of two old demonstrative elements which is also at the basis of Old Syriac hānā (< *hā- + dənā), hādē "this (m./f.)," see paragraph 4 above. In many ENA dialects there are traces of this old demonstrative prefix which appear, e.g., in the word for "today," cf. Urmi udyu,[36] Txuma ədyu(m),[37] Jewish Azerbaijani Aramaic ïdyo(m),[38] Hertevin ʔeǧǧu (< *ʔedyu). Some dialects also have a corresponding word for "tonight," e.g. Urmi ädlēli,[39] Jewish Azerbaijani Aramaic ïdlel.[40] Ṭūrōyo, on the other hand, has a whole series of adverbs formed with the prefix ʔád-. The following, mostly quite common, adverbs can be found in Ritter's dictionary (RITTER 1979):[41]

---

[34]The final consonant of ʔád- tends to become assimilated to the following consonant. ʔád- always carries primary stress, a secondary stress may fall on the last syllable of the noun to which vowel length is restored.

[35]In the plural, however, omission of -ha would remove the opposition between the ʔāwa and ʔōhā series.

[36]Tsereteli 1978, p. 125.

[37]Jacobi 1973, p. 235.

[38]Garbell 1965, p. 310.

[39]Tsereteli 1978, p. 125.

[40]Garbell 1965, p. 310.

[41]The transcription has been adapted to the one used in this paper.

(21)

	Ṭūrōyo
ʔádyawma	"today"
ʔádlalyo	"tonight"
ʔádṣafro	"this morning"
ʔádšāto	"this year"
ʔádʔaṣrīye	"this afternoon"
ʔáḍḍarbo	"this time"
ʔánnaqla	"this time, now"
ʔámmarǧa?	"again"

Note that in Ṭūrōyo, as in Hertevin, the prefix ʔád- is always stressed. Since only the first four adverbs are formed from nouns of Aramaic origin, the demonstrative element ʔád- can be considered still productive in the formation of a certain type of adverb. Hertevin ʔád- (... -ha), on the other hand, is functioning as a normal morpheme in the contemporary stage of the language. ʔád- thus has been best preserved in Hertevin and, on a limited scale, in Ṭūrōyo, whereas in the majority of ENA dialects it survives only in one or two fossilized lexical items. It is worth noting that the word for "today" in Hertevin belongs to this general ENA stratum since, synchronically, it does not contain the Hertevin demonstrative prefix ʔád-.

Works cited

Garbell 1965 — Irene GARBELL: *The Jewish Neo-Aramaic Dialect of Persian Azerbaijan*. The Hague.

Hoberman 1985 — Robert D. HOBERMAN: "An Outline Comparative Grammar of Northeastern Neo-Aramaic." Paper, MESA meeting

Jacobi 1973 — Heidi JACOBI: *Grammatik des Thumischen Neuaramäisch (Nordostsyrien)*. Wiesbaden.

Jastrow 1971 — Otto JASTROW: "Ein neuaramäischer Dialekt aus dem Vilayet Siirt (Ostanatolien)," *ZDMG* 121, 2 (pub. 1972) p. 215-222.

Jastrow 1978 — Otto JASTROW: *Die mesopotamisch-arabischen qəltu-Dialekte. Band I: Phonologie und Morphologie*. Wiesbaden

Jastrow 1979 — Otto JASTROW: "Zur arabischen Mundart von Mossul," *ZAL* 2, p. 36-75.

Jastrow 1981 — Otto JASTROW: *Die mesopotamisch-arabischen qəltu-Dialekte. Band II: Volkskundliche Texte in elf Dialekten*. Wiesbaden.

Jastrow ³1985 — Otto JASTROW: *Laut- und Formenlehre des neuaramäischen Dialekts von Mīdin im Ṭūr ʿAbdin*. 3., ergänzte Auflage, Wiesbaden.

Jastrow 1988 — Otto JASTROW: *Der neuaramäische Dialekt von Hertevin (Vilayet Siirt)*. Wiesbaden.

Krotkoff 1982 — Georg KROTKOFF: *A Neo-Aramaic Dialect of Kurdistan. Texts, Grammar and Vocabulary.* New Haven.

Poizat 1981 — Bruno POIZAT: "Une bibliographie commentée pour le Néo-Araméen," *GLECS* XVIII-XIII, p. 347-414.

Prym/Socin 1881 — Eugen PRYM und Albert SOCIN: *Der neu-aramäische Dialekt des Ṭûr 'Abdin.* 2 Teile. Göttingen.

Nöldeke 1868 — Theodor NÖLDEKE: *Grammatik der neusyrischen Sprache am Urmia-See und in Kurdistan.* Leipzig.

Nöldeke 1881 — Theodor NÖLDEKE: Review of Prym/Socin 1881. *ZDMG* 35, p. 218-235.

Nöldeke ²1898 — Theodor NÖLDEKE: *Kurzgefasste syrische Grammatik.* Leipzig.

Ritter 1979 — Hellmut RITTER: *Ṭûrôyo. Die Volkssprache der syrischen Christen des Ṭûr 'Abdin. B: Wörterbuch.* Beirut.

Tsereteli 1977 — Konstantin TSERETELI: "Zur Frage der Klassifikation der neuaramäischen Dialekte," *ZDMG* 127, 2, p. 244-253.

Tsereteli 1978 — Konstantin TSERETELI: *Grammatik der modernen assyrischen Sprache (Neuostaramäisch).* Leipzig.

V. New Fieldwork

ON THE SENAYA DIALECT

Estiphan Panoussi

Senāya is a dialect of Eastern Neo-Aramaic[1] spoken in Iran by fewer than one hundred families. In Sanandaj (Persian Kurdistan) where the dialect originated, there are no longer any speakers of Senāya left, because when the Chaldean Diocese of Senna (= Sanandaj) was moved to Tehran about forty years ago the few remaining Christians of the ancient Persian church who had lived there for centuries also moved to Tehran. There they gradually lost their identity amongst the other Sūrāye and the Persians. During the last few years a considerable number of Senāye, as they call themselves, emigrated to foreign countries, from Turkey to Australia, many also to Europe, America, and even Africa. In the diaspora, as already in Tehran, they are mostly absorbed by the Urmežnāya-speaking, predominantly Nestorian, Assyrians. In the United States they are concentrated in California.

The following is the first attempt to compile a sketch of the phonological and morphological data of this dialect. This will be followed by a number of text specimens. An extensive grammatical and lexical treatment of this dialect will be relegated to a later date.

I. The Sounds of Senāya in Comparison to Ancient Syriac (AS)

A. Labials

Plosive /b/ is usully retained, unless it is devoiced in contact with a voiceless consonant as in:

ptolta "virgin," AS bṭūltā
pxi "weep!" AS bk̲ī
pšāla "cooked food, dish," AS buššālā
rapsa "big (fem.)," AS rabbṭā

Fricative /b̲/ becomes /w/ which coalesces with a preceding /e/ into /u/ and with a preceding /a/ into /o/:

lāweš "he puts on (clothes)," AS lāb̲eš

---

[1][Or, more narrowly, Eastern Neo-Syriac, as the dialect described here is spoken by Christians.]   Notes in brackets are the editor's.

107

dēwa "wolf," AS dēḇā
dēwa "gold," AS dahḇā
ganāwa "thief," AS gannāḇā
kāsū "he writes," AS kāṭeḇ
qōra "grave," AS qaḇrā
Cf., however:
xpāqa "embrace," AS ḥḇāqā
Plosive / p/ is usually retained. Cf. however:
frāge "crockery," AS paḥḥārā "clay" (?)
Fricative / p̄/ (= /f/) is despirantized:
sepsa "lip," AS sep̄ṭā
nāpel "he falls," AS nāp̄el
Sporadic sound changes:
smelta "ladder," AS sebbelṭā
šošwāna "ant," AS šawšmānā
qū "rise!" AS qūm

B. Dentals

Fricative / ṯ/ normally becomes / s/:[2]
moxwās "like," AS men aḵwāṯ
tlās "because of, for," AS meṭṭūlāṯ-
īsen "there is," AS īṯ + ?
xēs "below," AS ṯḥēṯ
īsoqsa "ring," AS ʿezaqṯā
šensa "sleep," AS šenṯā
duksa "place," AS dukkṯā
In the following cases this / s/ has become an emphatic / ṣ/ by assimilation to
a velar environment:
baṣra "behind," cf. AS bāṭar
peṣqarwāse "graveyard," < *bēṯ qaḇrawwāṯā[3]
The / s/ is irregular in:
mdīsa "city," cf. AS mḏīttā
Cf. the regular equivalences in:
šāta "year," AS šattā
skinta "knife," < *sakkīntā, cf. AS sakkīnā
An unexpected despirantization occurs in:
latemal "the day before yesterday," cf. AS mnāṯmāl[4]

---

[2]In the Jewish Neo-Aramaic dialect of Senna it becomes / l/.

[3]In addition to the st. cstr. bēṯ reflected here there is the alternative form bī meaning
"the house, family, clan of...," e.g., Bī Pānōs "the Panoussis," Bī Adār "the Adaris."

[4][Most likely due to the influence of ṭəmal "yesterday".]

Sporadic sound changes:

kodyom "daily, every day," AS kol yōm[5]

ṭōma "there," cf. AS tammān, Urm. tāma

C. Velars and Laryngeals

Fricative /ḡ/ between vowels is weakened to a glide:[6]

črāya "lamp," AS šrāḡā, Pers. čerāg

An original /'/ usually vanishes, sometimes with changes in the adjacent vowels. Occasionally it is represented by /'/, and sporadically by /g/:

šāme "he hears," AS šāme'

šama "she hears," AS šām'ā

šmēli "I have heard," AS šmī' lī

ṭēna "load, burden," AS ṭa'nā

ṣā'er "he upbraids," AS mṣa"ar

ṣāra "she upbraids," AS mṣa"rā

bēli "I have wanted," AS b'ē lī

berga "hole," AS pa'rā with metathesis (?)

II. Syllabification

Initial clusters of two consonants are possible in Senāya:

blēl "up," AS b plus l'el

brōna "little son," AS ditto.[7]

ksūta "book," AS kṭībtā

ksāwa "letter," AS kṭābā

ksīsa "hat," AS kōsīṭā

šwīsa "bed," AS tešwīṭā

ṣlōṣa "prayer," AS ṣlōṭā

xmāsa "mother-in-law," AS ḥmāṭā

qdīla "key," AS qlīḍā with metathesis

ksēsa "chicken," AS akkḍaytā[8]

pšāqa "interpretation," AS puššāqā

tlānisa "shadow," AS ṭellānīṭā

Doubled consonants in medial position have been simplified without compensatory lengthening of the preceding vowel in:

---

[5]The sound shift l>d and d>l occurs sporadically also in other languages; cf. e.g., Pers. gosīd for gosīl "mission," nemaklān for nemakdān "salt container," Kurd. xolāy vs. Pers. xodāy, Arab. almās from Greek adamas "diamond," Lat. lacrima vs. Greek dakru "tear" (and several other pairs of this type for which see C. D. Buck: Comparative Grammar of Greek and Latin [Chicago, 1959], p. 123). In Neo-Syriac also xelmat from Pers. xedmat "service."

[6][See the contribution by K. Tsereteli in this volume.]

[7]Along with ebra "son."

[8][Some varieties of Aramaic, but not AS, have spirants after diphthongs (cf. Bibl. Aram. bayṭā vs. AS baytā) and so apparently did the precursor of Senāya.]

dema "blood," Urm. demma, AS dmā
šema "name," Urm. šemma, AS šmā
ḥoba "love," AS ḥubbā
leba "heart," AS lebbā
rakīxa "soft," AS rakkīḵā
šapīra "pretty," AS šappīrā
marīla "bitter," AS marrīrā
tanūra "oven," AS tannūrā
xaṭāya "sinner," AS ḥaṭṭāyā

III. Loss of initial consonants or syllables

šāna "tongue, language," AS leššānā
pōqa "nose," < *mappōqā (root n-p-q) "place of egress" of the breath (?)
pelle "he fell," < *npīl leh
šekyāse "testicles," AS sg. ešḵṭā
šāsa "fever," AS eššāṭā
gāre "roof," AS eggārā[9]
pyāye "bare-footed," AS ḥepyāy
kēle "where is he?" < aykā plus ile
šwīsa "bed," AS tešwīṭā
mar "say!" AS emar[10]
wāya "becoming, genesis," AS hwāya
wāda "doing (noun)," AS 'ḇāḏā[11]
rahmāna "merciful," AS mraḥḥmānā

IV. Loss of medial or final consonants with compensatory lengthening of vowels

xāsa "back (part of body)," AS ḥarṣā
kāsa "belly," AS karsā
kāka "tooth," AS kakkā (see A. J. Maclean: *Dictionary of the Dialects of Vernacular Syriac*, s.v.)
yāla "child," AS yaldā
āla "God," AS allāhā
šetqā "last year," AS eštqaḏ(y)
āxa "here," AS hārkā (the precursor dialect of Senāya may have had *harḵā)

Also under this heading may belong:

qū "rise!" AS qūm, but Urm. qum
edyū "today," < *hāḏ yōm, but Txumi 'ədyum

---

[9]It is thus a homonym of *gāre* "he shaves" (root *g-r-'*) and *gāre* "he holds" (root *'-r-y*).
[10]An alternative form in Senāya is *īmor*.
[11]Thus a homonym of *wāda* "belongings," of uncertain etymology.

V. Metathesis

Cf. the following cases:

frāge "crockery," AS paḥḥārē (?)—qdila "key," AS qlīḏā—berga "hole,"
AS paʻrā (via berʻa?)

VI. Morphology

A. Interjections and related utterances

Senāya is particularly rich in interjections, some of which are the following:

āy; hāy; ey; aha "hey! why! well now!"
dayday "go on"
ʻah "oh!" (rejecting s.th.)
axāy "lucky me!"
aywāy "woe to me! poor me!"
wes "pst!"
truṣṭā "truly!"
ḥaqqā "truly!"
taḥobʼāla "for the love of God!"
ayhāwār "O God!"
yalla "let's go! on with it!"
būʼāla "really!"
ulahā "there it is!"
pxāyox "honest to God!"

B. Pronouns

1. Independent personal pronouns:

	sg.	pl.
1p c.	āna	c. axni
2p m.	āyet	c. axtōxən
2p f.	āyat	
3p m.	āwa	c. āni
3p f.	ōya	

2. Pronominal suffixes

a. Possessive suffixes

1p sg. c. -i	ebri	"my son"
2p sg. m. -ox	ebrox	"your (m) son"
2p sg. f. -ax	ebrax	"your (f) son"
3p sg. c. -e	ebre	"his/ her son"
1p pl. c. -an	ebran	"our son"
2p pl. c. -oxən	ebroxən	"your (pl) son"
3p pl. c. -ū	ebrū	"their son"

b. Object suffixes

They express the direct as well as the indirect object. Cf. gāzēli "he sees me"
and kēwelli "he gives me (s.th.)."

1p sg. c. -li	1p pl. c. -lan
2p sg. m. -lox	2p pl. c. -loxən

2p sg. f. -lax
3p sg. m. -le   3p pl. c. -lū
3p sg. f. -la

c. Copulative suffixes

1p sg. m. -yen	ānayen	"it is I"
1p sg. f. -yan	ānayan	"it is I (f)"
2p sg. m. -yet	āyetyet	"it is you (m)"
2p sg. f. -yat	āyatyat	"it is you (f)"
3p sg. m. -le	āwale	"it is he"
3p sg. f. -la	ōyala	"it is she"
1p pl. c. -yox	axnīyox	"it is we"
2p pl. c. -īton	axtōxənīton	"it is you (pl)"
3p pl. c. -ilū	ānīyīlū/ānīlū	"it is they"

3. Independent demonstrative pronouns:

Near deixis   Far deixis
sg. m. aya or iya f. aya or iya   sg. m. āwa f. ōya
    pl. c. āni   pl. c. ōni

The same forms for the intensive demonstrative pronoun:
sg. c. ayanān or iyanān   sg. m. āwanān f. ōyanān
    pl. c. āninān   pl. c. ōninān

4. Proclitic demonstrative pronouns:

Near deixis   Far deixis
sg. m. ay f. ay   sg. m. ō f. ō
    pl. c. ān   pl. c. ōn

Examples:
   ay gōra "this man"   ō gōra "that man"
   ay baxta "this woman"   ō baxtā "that woman"
   ān yāle "these children"   ōn gōre "those men"
   ān bnāse "these daughters"   ōn ešenyāse "those women"

C. Nouns

1. Noun patterns

a. Biradical nouns
   kema "mouth," st. cst. kem (as in the term of abuse: gāw kem bābake
   bābox)
   šema "name," st. cst. šem (as in šemi "my name")
   ebra "son," st. cstr. ebr- before pron. suffixes (as in ebrox "your [m.sg.]
   son"), otherwise ber (as in kalba ber kalba), var. brōna, pl. bnōne
   brāta "daughter," st. cstr. brāt (as in kalepsa brāt kalepsa), pl. bnāse
   īda "hand," st. cstr. īd- (as in īdax "your [fem.sg.] hand"), pl. īdāse
   šāta "year," st. cstr. šāt (as in reš šāt tāza "beginning of the New Year"), pl.
   šene

sepsa "lip," st. cstr. seps (as in seps ḥōda "the rim of the basin"), pl. sepwāse

b. Nouns corresponding to the AS pattern qatlā

laxma "bread"	malka "king"
yarxa "month"	qalpa "rind"
zāga "bell," AS zaggā	kāka "tooth," AS kakkā
ara "earth," AS ar'ā,	gōra "husband," AS gaḇrā,
pl. arawāse	pl. gurāne
qōra "grave," AS qaḇrā,	zōna "time,"AS zaḇnā
pl. qorawāse	
bēsa "house," AS baytā	ēna "eye," AS 'aynā
gōza "walnut," AS gawzā	pōxa "wind," AS pawḥā
yōma "day," AS yawmā	danwa "tail," AS dunbā[12]

Special cases:

tawerta "cow," AS tōrtā	arxē "mill," AS raḥyā[13]
< *tawr-at-ā	
ṣīya "thirsty," AS ṣahyā	gomla "camel," AS gamlā
ṣlōṣa "prayer," AS ṣlōṭā	txīsa "pure (fem.)," AS dk̲ī̲ṭā
< *ṣalaw-at-ā	< *daky-a-tā

In some cases the precursor dialect of Senāya seems to have had the form qetlā where AS has qatlā:

xesna "bridegroom," AS ḥaṭnā	depna "side," AS dapnā
kepna "hunger," AS kapnā	gēba "side," AS gabbā
setwa "winter," AS satwā	

c. Nouns corresponding to the AS pattern qetla

meṭra "rain"	xelma "dream," AS ḥelmā
xeška "darkness," AS ḥeškā	qeṭra "knot"
mesta "hair," AS mezzṭā	bēra "well"
dēwa "wolf," AS dēḇā	dūša "honey," AS deḇšā
yema "mother," AS emmā[14]	leba "heart," AS lebbā
pl. yemawāse	

[12][The Senāya form seems to represent an original *danḇa < *danabā which would explain the /-w-/.]

[13][The Senāya form which is also common in related dialects probably represents a st. abs. *rḥē (not attested in AS) > *arḥē/arxe; for the prosthetic vowel compare AS brā and Sen. ebra. Similarly, the word xūwe "snake" is best explained as an original st. abs. of AS ḥewyā, i.e., *ḥwē which, in analogy to AS šmā > East. Neo-Aram. (not all dialects) šəmma, would be restructured as *ḥawwē/xəwwe > xūwe; for this latter sound change, cf. Sen. *kāsəw > kāsu "he writes."]

[14][Biradical words like AS šmā, dmā, etc., have been "normalized" in various Eastern Neo-Aram. dialects to become šəmma, dəmma, etc. These forms undergo the same shortening of the doubled consonant, thus Sen. šema, dema.]

ezza "goat," AS ʿezzā   ṭīna "clay"

Special cases:
isoqsa "ring," AS ʿezqṭā/   dmēsa "tear," AS demʿṭā
ʿezaqṭā, pl. isoqyāse   pl. dmayāse
ṣpēsa "finger," AS ṣebʿā[15]   ṭpersa "fingernail," AS ṭeprā
pl. ṣepyāse   pl. ṭeperyāse
xūwe "snake," AS ḥewyā   urba "sheep," AS ʿerbā

d. Nouns corresponding to the AS pattern qutlā
orxa "way," AS urḥā   gūda "wall," AS guddā
ṭūra "mountain," AS ṭūrā   rōḥa "spirit," AS rūḥā
pl. ṭūrāne
duksa "place," AS dukkṭā   nunīsa "fish," < *nūhīṭā
                                         pl. nunyāse

In some cases the form qetlā occurs where AS has qutlā
berka "knee," AS burkā

e. Nouns corresponding to the AS pattern qtūlā/qtōlā
xlūla "wedding," AS ḥlūlā   zōra "small," AS zʿōrā

The color adjectives belong here:
smōqa "red," cf. AS summāqā   kōma "black," cf. AS ukkāmā

f. Nouns corresponding to the AS pattern qātōlā (nomen agentis)
saxōra "beggar," AS sāḥōrā
The feminine form of this pattern seems to yield nouns of instruments:
nasorta "saw,"   nāsōrtā   balōta "throat," < *bālōʿtā
"one (fem.) who saws"   "one (fem.) who swallows"

g. Nouns corresponding to the AS pattern qattūla
payūxa "fresh, cool," AS payyūḥā rahūqa "far," < *raḥḥūqā
qalūla "light (adj.)," AS qallūlā yaqūra "heavy," AS yaqqūrā
tanūra "oven," AS tannūrā

h. Nouns corresponding to the AS pattern qattīlā
qarīra "cold," AS qarrīrā   šaxīna "warm," AS šaḥḥīnā
marīla "bitter," AS marrīrā   daqīqa "small," AS daqqīqā
makīxa "humble," AS makkīḵā

i. Nouns corresponding to the AS pattern qattālā
ganāwa "thief," AS gannābā

---

[15][The precursor dialect of Sen. obviously had forms with the feminine ending, thus
*ṣebʿṭā and *ṭeprṭā which, like AS ʿezaqṭā, were restructured as ṣbaʿṭā/ṣpēsa and
ṭperṭā/ṭpersa. Thus also AS demʿṭā > *dmaʿṭā/dmēsa; for /-aʿ-/ > /-ē-/, cf. AS ṭaʿnā >
Sen. ṭēna "load," AS purṭaʿnā > Sen. perṭēna "flea."]

j. Various patterns with doubled second radical which, in addition to the gemination, also lose the first vowel, and sometimes the initial radical as well.

šāsa "fever," AS eššāṭā

šāna "tongue, language," AS leššānā

gāre "roof," AS eggārā

pšāla "cooked dish," AS buššālā

pšāya "noiseless breaking of wind," < *puššāyā

gzūra "pig," AS ḥazzūrā

smelta "ladder," AS sebbelṭā

xwāra "white," AS ḥewwārā

tnāna "smoke," AS tennānā

pšāqa "interpretation," AS puššāqā

skinta "knife," < *sakkīntā

k. Quadrilitral nouns

aqobra "mouse," AS ʿuqbrā

maregla "kettle, casserole"; cf. AS margalṭā, Arab. mirjal

xorṭmāne "chickpeas," AS ḥarṭmāne

prezla "iron," AS parzlā

pertxe "bread crumbs," AS prtkʾ (vowels unknown)

l. Suffixes for the derivation of nouns

1- -ān
  a- forms active participles of the IInd and IIIrd conjugation:
    raḥmāna "commiserating, merciful," AS mraḥḥmānā
  b- forms adjectives (obsolete):
    šmayāna "celestial, heavenly," AS šmayyānā
  c- forms abstract nouns, as part of a nominal pattern (obsolete):
    perqāna "salvation," AS purqānā
    senqāna "need," AS sunqānā
2- -ōn
  Originally a diminutive suffix.
  axōna "brother," AS aḥōnā "little brother"
  brōna "son," AS brōnā "little son"
3- -āy/-nāy forms *nisba* adjectives (productive):
    šelxāya "naked"
    gawāya "interior," AS gawwāya
    Senāya "belonging to Senna"
    farangāya "French"

    xepyāya "bare-footed," AS ḥepyāyā
    barāya "exterior," AS barrāyā
    englisnāya "English"
4- -ūt (Senāya -ūs) forms abstract nouns (productive):
    yālūsa "childhood," from yāla "child"
    snīqūsa "need"
    Also from foreign words:
    dežmenūsa "enmity," from dežmen (kurd.) "enemy"
    moxālefatūsa "opposition, transgression," from moxālefat (pers.) "dto"

2. Plural formation

a. Ms. pl.

Some nouns have -āne instead of the regular -e:

karma "vineyard," pl. karmāne   rūša "shoulder," pl. rūšāne
melka "possession," pl. melkāne   (AS rapšā)
duksa "place," pl. dūkāne   yōma "day," pl. yōmāne

b. Fem. pl.

The AS suffixes -āṭā, -wāṭā, -awwāṭā, and -yāṭā appear in Senāya as -āse, -wāse, -awāse, and -yāse.

1- -āse

īda "hand," pl. īdāse   aqla "foot," pl. aqlāse
depna "side," pl. depnāse   orxa "way," pl. orxāse
šwīsa "bed," pl. šuyāse/šwiyāse   kolīsa "kidney," pl. kelyāse
ksēsa "chicken," pl. kesyāse   ṣlōṣa "prayer," pl. ṣlawāse
ṣpēsa "finger," pl. ṣepyāse
(var. ṣobēsa, pl. ṣobāse)

2- -wāse

māsa "village," pl. maswāse   xāsa "sister," pl. xaswāse
axōna "brother," pl. axonwāse   sepsa "lip," pl. sepwāse
bēsa "house," pl. baswāse
(varr. bēsawāse and bāte)

3- -awāse

yema "mother," pl. yemawāse   bāba "father," pl. bābawāse
dēda "breast," pl. dēdawāse   ara "earth," pl. arawāse
qōra "grave," pl. qorawāse   aṣra "land, country," pl. aṣrawāse
gāre "roof," pl. gārawāse   ēda "feast," pl. ēdawāse
xōra "friend," pl. xorawāse

4- -yāse

Originating in cases where the sg. already has a suffix /-y-/ — as in nunīsa (< *nūn-y-tā) "fish," pl. nunyāse—this ending spread to many other nouns, because it allowed the preservation of the sg. vocalization in the pl. form:

ṣe'orta "scolding," pl. ṣe'oryāse
ṣorta "picture," pl. ṣoryāse
dawelta "government," pl. dawelyāse
ksūta "book," pl. kesyāse (also kusyāse and ksuyāse)
škīsa "testicle," pl. šekyāse "testicles"

Note: the pl. nesyāse "ears" seems to be a pl. in -yāse derived from an unused sg. *nāsa (*nēsa ?); cf. Aradhin nāṭa, pl. naṭwāṭa. The Senāya sg. is a back-formation from the pl.: nesyasta, with the strange variant ne/usyata.

D. Numerals

	Cardinal	Ordinal		Cardinal	Ordinal
1	xa	qamāya	17	šo'āsar	hefdahom
2	tre	dowom	18	tmanēsar	heždahom
3	tlāsa	sewom	19	teš'āsar	nōzdahom
4	arba	čwārom	20	esrī	bīstom
5	xamša	panǧom	21	esrīwxa	bīstoyakom
6	ešta	šešom	30	tlā'ī	siyom
7	šo'a	haftom	40	arbī	čelom
8	tmanya	haštom	50	xamšī	panǧahom
9	teš'a	nohom	60	eštī	šaṣṣom
10	esra	dahom	70	šo'ī	haftādom
11	gdēsar	yanzahom	80	tmāni	haštādom
12	trēsar	dwānzahom	90	teš'ī	nawadom
13	teltāsar	siyanzahom	100	emma	ṣadom
14	arbāsar	čwardahom	101	emmawxa	ṣadoyakom
15	xamšāsar	pānzahom	1000	alpa	hazārom
16	eštāsar	šānzahom			

Note: The ordinal numbers from "second" and up are Kurdish.

E. Adverbs

tawāw "completely" (root t-m-m) tākadā "up to now"
kabīra "very, much" īman "when"
bassa "enough" (pers. bas) hal īman "until when"
qīlax "little" (< *qalīl-ak ?) xardāwa "afterwards"
zōda "more" qamdāwa "before (that)"
aymēla "on this side" edyu "today"
ōmēla "on the far side" qōme xoška "early tomorrow"
āxa "here" hadax "the same way"
mendāxa "from here" ekma "how much"
ṭōma "there" ūla "there it is"
blēl "up there" 'aǧǧa "again"
dā "now" xakarat "once"
oqa "so much" menzūna "for a long time" (past)

F. Verbs

There are three conjugations derived from the AS verb stems Pᵗal, Paᵗᵗel, and Afᵗel. The first conjugation is the most frequently used, while the second and the third are of rather rare occurrence. It is sometimes difficult to distinguish between forms of the first and the second conjugation. E.g., *sāwe* may mean "he is/becomes satiated" (act. part. of the first conjugation, AS root s-b-ʻ) or else "he makes" (act. part. of the second conjugation, Arab. root s-w-y). Only a comparison of the tenses and moods of such verb pairs can show that they belong not only to different stems, but also to different roots.

The tenses are more simple in Senāya than they are in Urmežnāya.

Tense	Derived from act. part.
Present	qaṭlen "I kill" qaṭlan, etc.
Present durative	qaṭlenyen "I am killing" qaṭlanyan, etc.
Imperfect	qaṭlenwa "I killed" qaṭlanwa, etc.
Imperfect durative	qaṭlenwayāwa "I was killing" qaṭlanwayāwa, etc.
Perfect transitive[16]	temqaṭlenne/a "I have killed him/her" temqaṭlanne/a, etc.
	Derived from pass. part
Preterite stative	qṭelli "I have killed"
Preterite	gīqṭelli "I have killed, am a killer"
Pluperfect	qṭelwāli "I had killed"

No tense has been derived from the infinitive.

In what follows I give a table of selected strong and weak verbs in all three conjugations. The 3p sg. m. and f. of the present, the 3p sg. m. of the preterite, and the sg. m. and f. forms (unless identical) of the imperative are given. A = Arabic root.

First conjugation

AS root	meaning	present	pret.	imperative
g-ḥ-k	"laugh"	gāxek gaxka	kxekle	kxok
d-m-k	"sleep"	dāmex damxa	dmexle	dmox
š-q-l	"buy"	šāqel šaqla	šqelle	šqol
n-t-š	"snatch"	nāče načya (!)	nčēle	nčī nčē
ḥ-d-r	"go around"	gāder gadra	gdēre	gdor
n-p-l	"fall"	nāpel napla	pelle	pol
b-q-r	"ask"	bāqer baqra	pqēre	pqor
b-š-l	"cook"	bāšel bašla	pšelle	pšol
š-b-q	"leave, let"	šāweq šōqa	šweqle	šōq
y-b-š	"dry, be dry"	yāweš yōša	īwešle	īwoš or yoš
b-ʿ-y	"want"	kebe keba[17]	bēle	bī bē

---

[16][This tense is synonymous with the preterite and owes its existence to the fact that the latter cannot take object suffixes; cf. Krotkoff 1982, 27-28.]

[17]Pres. subj. bāye bāya.

b-k-y	"weep"	bāxe baxya	pxēle	pxī pxē
b-s-m	"be cured"	bāsem basma	psemle	psom
b-n-y	"build"	bāne banya	bnēle	bnī bnē
t-b-r	"break"	tāwer tōra	twēre	twor
g-b-r	"marry"	gāwer gōra	gwēre	gwor
l-b-š	"wear, don"	lāweš lōša	lwešle	lwoš
'-b-d	"do"	kāwed kōda[18]	wedle	wod
'-b-r	"enter"	yāwer yōra	wēre	wor
'-r-q	"run away"	'āreq 'arqa	(')reqle	(')roq
r-h-ṭ	"run away"	rāxeṭ raxṭa (!)	rxeṭle	rxoṭ
'-r-y	"hold"	gāre garya[19]	'rēle	'rī 'rē
g-r-'	"shave"	gāre garya	grēle	grī grē
d-'-k	"be extinguished"	dāyex dēxa	dexle	dox
d-'-ṣ	"push in"	dāyeṣ dēṣa	deṣle	doṣ
d-'-t	"sweat"	dāyes dēsa	desle	dos
d-'-r	"return"	dāyer dēra	dēre	dor
r-'-š	"wake up"	rāyeš rēša	rešle	roš
l-y-š	"knead"	lāyeš lēša	lešle	loš
t-y-n	"urinate"	tāyen tēna	tenne	ton
d-w-š	"step, tread"	dāyeš dēša	dešle	doš
p-w-š	"remain"	pāyeš pēša	pešle	poš
q-w-m	"rise"	qāyem qēma	qemle	qū
h-w-y	"become"	kāwe kōya[20]	yēle	wī wē
y-d-'	"know"	kīde kīda[21]	īdēle	īdī īdē
y-t-b	"sit"	yātū yatwa	ītūle	ītū
y-l-p	"learn"	yālep yalpa	īleple	īlop
y-h-b	"give"	kēwel kēwa[22]	īwelle	hal
y-m-y	"swear"	yāme yamya	īmēle	īmī īmē
d-q-q	"grind"	dāyeq dēqa	deqle	doq
g-n-b	"steal"	gānū ganwa	gnūle	gnū
k-t-b	"write"	kāsū kaswa	ksūle	ksū
'-m-r	"say"	kāmer kama[23]	(ī)mēre	īmor or mar
'-z-l	"go"	kāzel kāza[24]	īzelle	say
'-t-y	"come"	kāse kasya[25]	īsēle	hālox hālax

[18] Pres. subj. *hāwed hōda.*
[19] Pres. subj. *'āre 'arya.*
[20] Pres. subj. *hāwe hōya.*
[21] Pres. subj. *yāde yada.*
[22] Pres. subj. *hēwel hēwa;* by incorporation of the preposition /l/ the root for some forms has been restructured to become *h-w-l.*
[23] Pres. subj. *'āmer 'ama.*
[24] Pres. subj. *'āzel 'āza.* The masc. has a variant ind: *kāl,* subj. *'āl.*
[25] Pres. subj. *'āse 'asya.*

'-k-l	"eat"	kāxel kaxla[26]	īxelle	īxol
'-s-r	"bind"	yāṣer yaṣra	īṣēre	īṣor
š-m-ʿ	"hear"	šāme šama	šmēle	šmī šmē
s-b-ʿ	"be satiated"	sāwe sōya	swēle	swī swē
b-l-ʿ	"swallow"	bāle bala	blēle	blī blē
z-d-ʿ	"fear"	zāde zada	zdēle	zdī zdē
q-ṭ-ʿ	"cut"	qāṭe qaṭa	qṭēle	qṭī qṭē

Second conjugation

s-w-y (A)	"make"	sāwe sōya	meswēle	sāwī sāwē
ṣ-ʿ-r	"upbraid"	ṣāʾer ṣāre	meṣʾēre	ṣārī ṣārē
š-d-r	"send"	šāder šadra	meždēre	šādir šāder
ḥ-l-l	"wash"	xallel xalla	xellelle	xallel
p-l-g	"divide"	pallel palla (!)	pellelle	pallel
ǧ-w-b (A)	"answer"	ǧāweb ǧōba	ǧawāb welle	ǧawāb hal

Third conjugation

ḥ-l-p	"exchange"	maxlep maxelpa	mexleple	maxlep
r-ʿ-š	"wake s.o. up"	mareš marīša (!)	merešle	mareš
ḥ-w-y	"show"	maxwē maxwa	moxwēle	maxwī maxwē
m-ṭ-y	"bring"	manṭe manṭya	mṭēle	manṭī manṭē
'-t-y	"fetch"	mēse masya	msēle	mēsī mēsē
	"throw"	mande mandya	mdēle	mandī mandē

The subjunctive of the present is identical with the indicative except for the cases mentioned in the notes. The negative of the indicative is formed in the first conjugation with the prefix *lē-*, thus *lēgāxek*, that of the subjunctive with *la-*, thus *lagāxek*. In the second conjugation the prefixes are *lēm-* and *lam-*, thus *lēmsāwe* and *lamsāwe*.

Texts

Text no. 1

1. balé yā šamāša!
   xa yōmā - axnī gāw taudīsad mšīḥaitūsa gāw yom xōšāba lakāwə pálxox. drosīlē? bālé.
2. xā yōma xa nāšā gāw yōm xōšābā kāse bēsa raḥat hāwəd.
3. taṣmīm ayanānīle: kāmər, edyū xōšābale, āzən bēsa ráḥat hōdən bēsa.
4. kāzal bēsā, baxtè kamá qamxà latán, tame īsēlox bēsá? Say árxē! xəṭṭē manṭī tqə́nnū.
5. kāmm báxta xōšābale, dáx kāwə āna āzən arxē? iǧāza lēsən.
6. kamá daɣ mē hodòx, kpīnə lakāy pēšox.
7. mēre tlāsa gōrád bàxta táme təmàl lamērax?

26Pres. subj. *ʾāxel ʾaxla*.

8. mēra monšēlī.
9. mērə čāra máyle?
10. mēra čāra lēsən! gàrak āzət ta árxē.
11. mēre xmāra mēsonne.
12. xmāra tmaṭīnīle mən xəṭṭē, ṭēna, tmanṭēle āzəl arxē.
13. fətlē mən qāməd ōṭāqəd qāša, mēre: dāna 'ubūr konyən, kānyən tá arxē,
šod āzən ammən tá qāša īǧāẓa, rāxṣa, šáqlən mə̀nne. īǧāza šaqlən mənne āzən
tá arxē.
14. īzəle gēbəd qāša mērə yā qāša! īǧāza hàlan - edyū xöšābale, láxma látan -
ān ta àrxē həṭṭē qamxən, taqnən.
15. mērə lēsən əǧāza, xöšābale. magar lakīdət xöšābale edyū?
16. mēre bále kīdən xöšābale, wále xəṭṭē latánu qamxá latánu láxma látan,
kpīnəyox.
17. mērə lēsən əǧāza.
18. mērə āxər xmārī tmaṭīnənne, kəmšádrənne, tšádrənne mən qāma.
19. mērē 'ən xmārox kəmmaṭīnəte kəmšádrəte qāmā, xənà gēbī tamə gīsēlox?

Translation

1. Yes, deacon!
   One day - in the Christian faith we may not work on Sundays. Is it [not]
true? It is.
2. One day a man comes home on Sunday to rest.
3. The decision is this that he says: Today is Sunday, let me go home to rest at
home.
4. When he comes home, his wife says to him: We have no flour. Why have
you come home? Go to the mill, take the wheat there and grind it!
5. He says: Wife, it is Sunday. How might I go to the mill?! There is no
permission.
6. She says: So what! What shall we do? We should not stay hungry.
7. The husband of the woman said to her: Why did you not say [so] yesterday?
8. She said: I forgot.
9. He said: What is the way out?
10. She said: There is no way out. You must go to the mill!
11. He said: Fetch [pl.] the donkey!
12. After they had loaded the donkey with wheat, he took him to the mill.
13. [When] he walked by the front of the room of the priest, he said: I am
about to pass and go to the mill. Let me enter to ask the priest for permission,
for a dispensation. Let me get permission and [then] go to the mill.
14. He went to the priest and said: Priest, give me permission - today is
Sunday and we have no bread - to go to the mill to grind wheat.
15. He said: There is no permission. It is Sunday. Don't you know that today
is Sunday?
16. He said: Yes, I know it is Sunday, but we have no wheat and no flour and
no bread. We are hungry.

122 Estiphan Panoussi

17. He said: There is no permission.
18. He said: But I have already loaded my donkey and sent it off.
19. He said: If you have loaded your donkey and sent it off, why then have you come to me?!

Text no. 2

1. šamāša! kəbən xa ekma masale šān gyānan amənox.
2. mar!
3. basīmelū, magəxkānelū, ham masalalū, ham gāw wāqe' tarbyatilū, ma'na etū, ta'sīr etū.
4. xa gōra kāwe xa kalba kā'ēle, kabīra ay kalba kəbēle.
5. ḥamām kāwədle, kodyōma xallele gāw māya, motūle rēš sefra mən gyāne nahār kāxəl.
6. mən gyāne manṭēle dašta, ǧyāla ay mēlaw ō mēla.
7. gāw dō asrā xa āxū kāwe, albata taṣēq kōt ā āxūnd ǧəgre kāse mən kalba. - masalan gāw šaraḥte šar'ate islām kalba kamī seplotile.
8. ay nāšaze, čon kalbe 'alāqa kabīra eswāle gāwē, hamīša xedmat kāwədwā gāw kalbe.
9. īxāle qašang, pəṣra, īxāle: behtarīn īxāle kewəlwāle.
10. hīče! tā xa yōma kalbe məsle.
11. mārəd kalba kabīra pxēle ta kalba, kabīra xafat īxəle, kabīra nāraḥat yēle.
12. xar diya mēre čāra lēsən! kalbī məsle!
13. īzəle kalbe tmesēle, təmxallele gāw māya.
14. īzəle mōrī tmesēle, təmgādēle gāwew xa ṣanōqa təmsāwēlew təmdārēle gāw ṣanōqaw təmmanṭēlew kəmqāwēre.
15. nāšəd asrā xzēlū ay šōla tmāwədle gair šar'ate islāmīle.
16. īzəlū xabar wəlū ta āxū.
17. mērū xa nāša īsən hādax šōla wədle.
18. āwā ham asabānī yēlew kabīra mērew sagon ō nāša mēsone!
19. īsēlū šōn dō nāša, tamanṭəle gəb āxū.
20. mēre āyət iyā mē šolale tmodəte? tauhīn gīwədlox gāw barnāša.
21. barnāša garak hādax tašrīfāt tlāse qā'əl hāwe xallīlew qorīlew mōrī gadī gāwew dārīle gāw ṣanōqa.
22. āyət ta kalba hādax gīwədlox, īyā āyət tauhīn gīwədlox.
23. garak rağmoxlox, garak qaṭloxlox.
24. ō mār kalba ham īda drēle pxāya kabīra.
25. fəkər wədle čāra lēsən, xa čāra garak hāwəd ta gyāne waylā nābūd kōyīle qaṭlīle.
26. īda drēle pxāya kabīra.
27. ta āxūnd mēre yā āxū! en yadət kalbī mē kalbayāwa, mē dārāyūsaswāle, mē mōlkāneswāle! ānīnān kulū, āna ta dayanān bāxən.
28. gāw sā'atəd mōsē tlāsī waṣyat wədle, mēre ānī urbelū.
29. hal ta flān nāša uqaw ta flān uqa.
30. kul mendīye təmpālēle. tlāsoxze xa əma urbe gīšoqle.

31. qāzī xzēle ad maḥkēsa kabərta špēra elē, yāne psəmla elēw šəməd urbē msēle ta qāzī.
32. qāzī mēre šəməd dō marḥūm mayāwa?
33. xləṣle mən dawāyəd qāzī.
34. ō nāša īsēle rāḥat go bēse. xar ekma yomāsa qāzī bəspārayāwa urbē āsī ta qāzī mən tarafəd mārəd kalba.
35. xzēle xa xabar lesən. dməxla masala.
36. nāša mšodēre gēbəd mārəd kalba. mēre kēlū urbē? lamṭēlay.
37. hīč la ǧūwuble layzəle.
38. xardāwa kabīra fušār msēlu elē tmanṭīle gēbəd qāzī.
39. mēre yā qāzī mē kəbət?
40. mēre āyət mērox kalbī waṣyat gīwədle əmā erbē qa qāzī, ta qāzī, lagīmṭēlay.
41. āwu ham mēre tlāse, mēre yā qāzī dax kalba maḥke? kalba dax urbe əte? dax əte dārāyūsa? dax əte hādax məndyāne?
42. āna ō yōma kəbītonwa qaṭlītonwāli ay mendī kəmsāwəne tad xalṣən.

Translation

1. Deacon! I want to tell you a few stories in our own tongue.
2. Tell!
3. They are interesting and funny. They are stories as well as really educational. They have a meaning, they have a [good] influence.
4. There is a man who has a dog, he likes that dog very much.
5. He bathes him every day and washes him in water. He lets him sit at the table to dine [with him].
6. He takes him for outings and walks with him to and fro.
7. There is in this city an Akhund who - as you will certainly agree - is nauseated by dogs. [Because] in the interpretation of the Islamic law they say, e.g., that the dog is unclean.
8. This man, since the dog was very much attached to him, constantly spoiled his dog.
9. He used to give him good food, meat, the best kinds of food.
10. Well, until one day his dog died.
11. The dog's master wept a lot for the dog, he became very sad and totally unconsolable.
12. After that he said: There is no way out. My dog has died!
13. He went and fetched his dog to wash him with water.
14. He went and got silk in which he wrapped him, and he made a wooden chest for him in which he laid him. And he took him away and buried him.
15. The people of the town saw that what he had done was outside the law of Islam.
16. They went and informed the Akhund.
17. They said: There is a man who has done such a thing.
18. He became quite angry and said: Go and bring me that man!

19. They went to that man and brought him before the Akhund.
20. He said: You! What kind of a thing was that you have done?! You have offended mankind.
21. Such rites must be reserved for mankind: that they wash a man and bury him, that they wrap him in silk and place him in a wooden chest.
22. You have done such a thing for a dog. You have committed an offense.
23. We must stone you, we must kill you.
24. The master of the dog started to weep very much.
25. It became clear to him that he must find a way out for himself, otherwise they would annihilate him, kill him.
26. He started to weep very much.
27. To the Akhund he said: Akhund! If you knew what kind of dog my dog was! What riches he had and what land he owned! All these! That is why I weep.
28. In the hour of his death he made out a will for me. He said: These are the sheep.
29. Give to so-and-so such-and-such and to so-and-so such-and-such.
30. Everything he owned he divided up. For you, too, he left some sheep.
31. The judge saw that this story pleased him very much, because sheep for the judge were mentioned in it.
32. The judge said: What was the name of the deceased?
33. [By this] he had freed himself of the complaint of the judge.
34. The man went calmly home. After a few days the judge was expecting the sheep to come to him from the owner of the dog.
35. He saw that nothing happened. The affair rested.
36. He sent people to the owner of the dog and said: Where are the sheep? - They had not yet arrived.
37. He did not answer at all and did not go to him.
38. After that they exerted strong pressure on him and brought him before the judge.
39. He said: Judge, what do you want?
40. He said: You have said: My dog made out a will - a hundred sheep for the judge. They have not yet arrived.
41. He said to him: Judge, how can a dog talk? How can a dog have sheep? How can he have riches? How can he own such things?
42. I made this thing up on that day when you wanted to kill me in order to save myself.

Text no. 3

1. xa masala xərta.
2. qāša elīyas kītwāle dəqna xwāra?
3. bale! kīnwāle.
4. kabīra īlīpayāwa xa nāša xoš mašrab.
5. yoḥana bər 'amīze kītwa šoxībāzyāwa.

6. aya hamīša ṣōma rāba xamšī yomāsa ṣōma gāroxwa axnī kolan bogdāy.
7. yoḥana bər 'amī čon gāw bagdādyāwa īləpwāle ṣōma lāre hamīša peṣraw mešxa kāxəlwa nārahatyāwa.
8. aya mukrəzlū gāw ēta xamšī yōmē nāše garak peṣraw mešxa laxlī.
9. ay kabīra nārahat yēle.
10. īzəle dosūsa mdēle mən qāša elīyas.
11. kod yōma gaz mšāqəlwāle mən šūqa manṭēwa ta qāša elīyas tad āxəl.
12. qāša pqēre mənne mē masalala?
13. mē kəbət?
14. kāmər čəməndī rābī xōšī kāse āt lāsəm.
15. mēre lā xa məndī īsən čon ilīpayāwa qāša elīyas xəna.
16. xa yōma īsēle gēbe mēre rābī elīyas ān kolū gazē kəmaxletwālū tmēwənwālū tlāsox.
17. ānaze arbūšābēw rōtēw ṣōma kole tmaxlənne.
18. mēre magar əğāza šqəlwālox mənī rəxṣa šqəlwālox mənī?
19. mēre lā!
20. mēre xōb dā fətla dā ettan šo'āsar yōme šaqlənū mənox gāw maqa kēwətū tlāsī?
21. ha ha ha kxəklan kabīra.

Translation

1. Another story.
2. Did you know Priest Elias, the one with the white beard?
3. Yes! I knew him.
4. He was very learned [and] a humorous man.
5. My cousin John was also - you know [it] - funny.
6. We all fasted together during Lent for fifty days.
7. Since my cousin John had lived in Baghdad, he had become used to not fasting. He always ate meat and fat, [otherwise] he would have been unsatisfied.
8. One day they preached in the church that people must not eat meat nor fat during the fifty-day [fast].
9. He became very depressed.
10. He went to become friends with Priest Elias.
11. Every day he bought Turkish honey from the market and brought it to Priest Elias to eat.
12. The priest asked him: What is all this?!
13. What do you want?
14. He says: Nothing, Father! I only want that you stay in good health.
15. He said: No, there is something the matter! - since Priest Elias was after all clever.
16. One day he [the cousin] came to him and said: Father Elias! You have eaten all the Turkish honey that I had given you.
17. I, too, have not kept the whole fast on Wednesdays and Fridays.

18. He said: Did you get permission, a dispensation from me?
19. He said: No.
20. He said: Well, it has already happened. Now we have seventeen days [left] which I will buy from you. For how much would you sell them to me?
21. Ha, ha, ha! We laughed a lot.

Text no. 4

1. xa gōra kāwe trē išənyāse kāēle məšulmāna.
2. ay gōra məšulmāna trē išənyāse kāwēle uqa nāraḥat kāy gāw bēsaw yōmaw lēle har lagbē gāw bēsa pāyəš.
3. palgəd lēle pālətwa kālwa ta mezgəd.
4. ḥālī kāwət?
5. bale.
6. mən nāraḥatūs gyāne uqa nāraḥat kāwəwa.
7. ay baxte 'azyat kōdāwālew ō baxte 'azyat kōdāwāle kālwa ta mezgəd.
8. duksa laswa dāməxwa kālwa ta mezgəd dāməxwa.
9. ō gōraze xa xōra eswāle kol yōmaw lēle bogdāy kāwīwa.
10. ō xōre xəna trē tlā sāate xar dāwa kālwa mezgəd.
11. hamiša har iman kālwa mezgəd xāzēwa ay xōre gāw mezgəd itīwale.
12. iya moštāq yēle ekma šənē xa yōma mən qām dō gōra dax trē išənyāsəswāle āl ta mezgəd layəlābe.
13. xa yōma pqēre mənne mēre yā xōrī əya mē 'ağibūsala daxīle əya hādax āyət qam dīdī?
14. trē šənēle āna kəbən qam diyox palgəd sāat āsən mezgəd āyət qam dīdi kāwət.
15. mēre āyət xa baxta əttox āna trē išənyāse əttī trē baxtāte əttī.
16. xədmad kōdī tlāsī xayū ləbāsī ḥāzər kodīlū xayū kəstādī ḥāzər koyīlū xayū čāy maštīli qala mandīli urxa.
17. āyət xa baxta əttox lēbox pakar kāwət.
18. mēre pas hawēsala āna ham trē baxtāte hāwēlī.
19. mēre pkēfox.
20. āwa pəlle sabab dyanān īzəle xa baxta xərta msēle rēšəd baxte.
21. baxtəd awəl eswāla yāle whawaw raḥat zendgānusū īzəle xa baxta xərta msēle.
22. awəl yōma ō baxta kəmmēsēwāla ō bēsa pəšle ğahanam.
23. ō gōra uqa nāraḥat yēle uqa kəmmağzīle uqa nāraḥat tmodīle uqa təmqapxīle uqa təmmāxīle.
24. mēre mē galatyāwa wədlī mē šolayāwa msēli rēšəd gyāni?
25. īzəle har gāw mezgəd dməxle xzēle ō nāša xənā har xəna laisēle.
26. laisēle tā mauqə' gyāne īsēle āwa dūke kmārewāla.
27. mēre yā xōri tamē baḷa msēlox gāw rēši əya tamē hādax wədlox gāwi?
28. mēre ya xōri dā āyət mā etwālox mənī mē eswālox mənī? āna ta gyāni kāsənwa yatwənwa āyət mērox āna qam dīdox kəbən āsen.
29. agar hādax lāwəwa trē išənyāse lamēsətwa xədā eswālox.

30. āna ham nāraxatyənwa mən trē išənyāsəyāwa palṭīwāli nārahat kodīwāli 'ăğəzyənwa mən bēsake āsənwa mezgəd dūksa xərta xəna laswa.

31. dā āyət mē kāse gāw nazārox xa məndī mar!

Translation

1. There was [lit. is] a man who had two wives. [He was] a Muslim.

2. This Muslim man who had two wives was day and night so ill at ease at home that he did not want to stay home.

3. In the middle of the night he went out to the mosque.

4. Do you understand that?

5. Yes.

6. He was very discontent about his own discontentment.

7. One of his wives angered him here and the other there. So he went to the mosque.

8. [As] there was no place [for him] to sleep, he went to the mosque to sleep [there].

9. This man also had a friend. They were together night and day.

10. This friend of his used to go to the mosque two or three hours after him.

11. Each time he went to the mosque, he saw his frind sitting in the mosque.

12. For years he had wished to go to the mosque earlier than the man with the two women just once. He did not succeed.

13. One day he asked him: My friend! What miracle is this?! How is it possible for you to be [always] earlier than me?

14. For two years I have wanted to come to the mosque half an hour earlier than you, [but] you are [always] earlier than me.

15. He said: You have one wife, I have two women, two wives.

16. They attend to me. One of them prepares my clothes, the other my shoes, the other gives me tea to drink. Quickly they make me ready for the road.

17. You have [only] one wife, [thus] you can't [be there before me] and you are unhappy.

18. He said: It would thus be better if I too had two wives.

19. He said: Please yourself.

20. [So] he became the cause of that man to marry an additional wife.

21. [Although] the first wife had children and they were happy and led a peaceful life, he went and married another wife.

22. Right on the first day he had married that woman, the house became hell.

23. That man became so unhappy, they angered him so much and made him miserable, they hit him on the head and attacked him,

24. [so that] he said: What mistake have I made! Into what situation have I maneuvered myself!

25. So he went and slept in the mosque. He saw that the other man did no longer come.

26. He did not come, until one day he did [and saw] that the other man had taken his place.

27. The other said: O my friend, why did you bring [this] tribulation upon me? Why have you done such a thing to me?

28. He said: My friend, what did you expect from me? I used to come here and sit for myself. But you said: I want to come here before you.

29. If that had not been so, if you had not become married to two women, you would have one [wife and everything would be all right].

30. I also was miserable because of two wives who drove me away and made me miserable. I had no peace at home. So I came to the mosque having no longer any other place. -

31. Now you tell something - whatever comes to your mind.

Appendix

(Editor's note: During the process of editing Dr. Panoussi's article and translating it from the original German, a number of questions arose which I submitted to the author in a letter. His lengthy reply contained several valuable and important items of additional information which I did not want to withhold from the readers of this volume. Since the article already was more or less in its final stage of preparation for the press, I chose the form of an appendix fo present the additional information item by item. I apologize for any inconvenience.)

1. To be added to the introductory paragraph: In Urmežnāya the Senāye are called Sīnāye. - The Senāye do not want to be called "Assyrians," but, since they are such a small minority, they do not object to being subsumed under this label. - In addition to Christian speakers of Neo-Aramaic, there was also a Jewish community in Sanandaj whose dialect differed from that of the Christians (as in other Jewish Neo-Aramaic dialects to the north /t̲/ becomes /l/ rather than /s/; cf. Chr. mīsa "dead" vs. Jew. mīla, Chr. ksēsa "chicken" vs. Jew. klēla). The Jews migrated partly to Tehran and partly, before the Iranian Revolution, to Israel.

2. To be added to the section on "Sounds": (a) Dentals: Due to assimilation /t̲/ becomes /t/ rather than /s/; cf. etan "we have" < *ettan < *etlan < ī̲t-lan. The negative equivalent latan "we do not have" is derived by the author from lā + etan, not from the original (AS) layt-lan which, according to him, would have yielded *lētan/letan. - (b) Laryngals: The sound /'/ is preserved in loanwords from Arabic; cf. in the texts wāqe' (I,3), šar'ate (I,7), 'alāqa (I,8,15), 'azyat (IV,7), 'ağīb- (IV,13), mauqe' (IV, 95), and 'āğez (IV,30). However, /ḥ/ coalesces with /ḵ/, here transcribed as /x/, except in some religious words, such as mšīḥa "the Messiah," and in some Arabic roots, such as ḥ-k-y.

3. To be added to the section on "Syllabification": (a) Simplification of geminates may also affect secondary ones; cf. hali < *halli < AS haḇ-lī "give me!," etan < *ettan < AS īṭ-lan "we have," kemšadrete < *kemšadrette < *kemšadret-le "you (m.) sent him." - (b) Along with the truncated form pyāya "barefoot" the full form xepyāya is also used, both mostly in the plural form pyāye / xepyāye to agree with aqlāse "feet."

4. To be added to the section on plurals of nouns: (a) Plural formation by reduplication of the last radical with an intervening /ā/ is also attested in Senāya: berga "hole," pl. bergāge; berka "knee," pl. berkāke; pōqa "nose," pl. poqāqe. - (b) Some further irregular plural forms: xmāsa "mother-in-law," pl. xmāse; kestakta "shoe," pl. kestāge or kestāde (cf. IV,16); āla "God," pl. ālaye; baxta "woman," pl. ešenyāse or baxtāte.

5. To be added to the section on "Verbs": (a) The perfect transitive appears in the texts with the genuine Senāya prefix tem-/tm- as well as with the foreign prefix kem-/km- which is characteristic of the language of the priests coming from Iraq. - (b) The verb pelle "he fell" occurs also in the variant forms npelle and inpelle.

6. Due to the strong influence of other dialects, Senāya is to some extent a mixed dialect. Note in particular the following cases in the texts: I,1. The verb palxox is not genuine Senāya where it would be šola kōdox (cf. Pers. kār mīkonīm). - I,7. The form tlāsa instead of tlāse is by interference of a dialect that distinguishes gender in the third-person singular pronominal suffix. I,8. The verb monšēli is Urm. for genuine Senāya men bāli īzele (cf. Pers. az yādam raft). - II,31. The verb psəmla would mean "she was cured (from illness)." - II,34. The verb bə• spārayāwa is alien to Senāya both in form (a tense based on the infinitive!) and in root. - II,36. The verb mšodēre should be məždēre, lamṭēlay should be lamṭēlū. - II,37. The verb laǧūwuble should be ǧwāb lawēle. - II,41. The verb mahkē should be ḥākē. - IV,28. The form etwālox should be eswālox (as a matter of fact, the speaker corrects himself on this point).

New Materials on Western Neo-Aramaic

Werner Arnold

The three dialects of Western Neo-Aramaic, those of Ma'lūla, Baxʻa and Ǧubbʻadīn (henceforth M, B, Ǧ) have been known for more than a century. It was the lack of a complete phonology and morphology as well as the scarcity of texts from B and Ǧ together with the lack of more recent texts from M that induced me to undertake a two-year field trip to Syria,* from which, in addition to a wealth of directly elicited paradigms and wordlists, I also brought back nearly eighty hours of tape recordings. While the previously published texts stem almost exclusively from one single speaker, I have made a point of recording as many different speakers as possible, of both sexes and from different age groups and religious allegiances and on as diverse a variety of themes as possible.

From among the many recordings in which the informants describe religious celebrations, I should like to present here three texts concerning weddings, one from each of the three villages. All three texts were told by Muslims and describe Muslim wedding celebrations. This is the first time that a text of a Muslim woman from M has been published and the first time also that a text told by a woman from B has appeared in print.

The following does not offer an exact description of the three dialects but is simply meant to point out the most important linguistic differences as they appear in the texts. Since all three texts deal with the same subject matter, they reveal by this very fact differences in grammar and in the vocabulary.

From the point of view of phonetics, B is somewhat more archaic, Ǧ more progressive, than M. In B ancient *t has been shifted only to / č / [ts]. Ancient *q and *k are realized differently in the three villages. In B they developed into a strongly post-velar / ḳ/ and a slightly palatalized / k/. In M they correspond to a slightly post-velar / ḳ/ and a strongly palatalized / k/ which sometimes approaches [kj]. Ǧ has shifted *q to / k/ and *k to / č/, whereby the latter

*Field work was carried out thanks to a dissertation scholarship of the DAAD (German Academic Exchange Service), for whose support I would like to express here my gratitude. Likewise I would like to thank Professor Otto Jastrow for scholarly supervision of my dissertation project.

coincided with / č / < *t. In loanwords from Arabic, / ǧ / is taken over in M and Ǧ as the / ž / of Damascene pronunciation, whereas B like the surrounding villages has / ǧ / [dž].

M	B	G	Ancient	Arabic[1]
č	ć	č	t	t
ḳ	ḳ[2]	k	q	q
k/[kj]	k	č	k	k
ž	ǧ	ž	-	ǧ

An exception is the relative particle / ti/ (M, Ǧ), which in B is always / ći/ (II, 39). However, in M as well as in Ǧ, / ti/ has also the variant / či/.

Ǧ has a / b/ instead of a / p/ in M and B in / bayṯa/ (III, 24). Cf. M / payṯa/ (I, 25), B / payṯā/ (II, 9).

Concerning the vowels, it is remarkable that in B and Ǧ the final -e of the suffixes of the 3rd person singular alternates with -i, whereas in M it remains stable. Examples:

B: mišwille (II, 17)   "they make for him"
       mišwilli (II, 2)   "they make for him"

       šaḳlille (II, 22)   "they take him along"
       šaḳlilli (II, 24)   "they take him along"

Ǧ: mnakkaṭille (III, 25)   "they give presents to him"
       mnakkaṭilli (III, 26)   "they give presents to him"

B and Ǧ in some cases have / u/ where M has / i/. In the texts one can find:
B: uḳdum (II, 37)   "before"
M: iḳdum (I, 20)   "before"

B: busənyōṯa[3] (II, 14)   "girls"
M: bisənyōṯa (I, 30)   "girls"

However, / i/ and / u/, even in pretonal syllables, are not the allophones of a single phoneme as is shown by the following minimal pair:
B/ M: ḥkumyōṯa   "governments"
        ḥkimyōṯa   "women doctors"
Ǧ: ḥčumyōṯa/ ḥčimyōṯa

In the field of nouns it is remarkable that in Ǧ a second form of the masculine plural in / -ōya/ is used, which no longer exists in B and M. Examples:
ḥḍuṯō (III, 18) alongside ḥḍuṯōya (III, 21) "bridegrooms"

---

[1] In loanwords.
[2] For technical reasons this sound will henceforth be rendered / ḳ /.
[3] The shwa is an auxiliary vowel with no phonemic status in all three dialects.

busunōya (III, 5) "boys"

In Ǧ geminate consonants in word-final position can be shortened, in which case the preceding vowel will be lengthened. If the preceding vowel is an /e/, this is usually shifted to /ī/. Additional geminate consonants occur in Ǧ as a result of the loss of the 3rd person masculine plural object suffix (-un > -0).

Examples:

Ǧ	M	
xūl (III, 2)	xullun (I, 19)	all of them
aspīl (III, 24)	aspill (I, 35)	they take along
maytīl (III, 9)	maytyill (I, 21)	they bring
awwal mīt (III, 3)	awwal mett	first (adv.)
zlīl (III, 26)	zlillun (I, 33)	they go
xīt (III, 28)	xett (I, 31)	also

In B and Ǧ the feminine enumeration plural is not formed by adding the suffix /-(y)an/, as it would be in M, but simply by deleting the feminine singular ending /-ṭa/ /-ča/ (B: /-ṭa/ /-ča/):

B: ṭarč bisnī (II, 1)   "two girls."

In M this form would be /ṭarč bisnīyan/. In the text we have

exma ṭannūryan (I, 6)   "some clothes."

In B and Ǧ verbs of the IInd form can be formed with an /-a-/ preceding the last radical. This vowel does not affect the stress pattern.

Examples:

M: mičkattma (I, 9)   "she hands over"
    mfarrgin (I, 11)   "they look on"
    mahaddrill ba'dinn (I, 38)   "they ready themselves"
B: mnákkaṭin (II, 54)   "they give presents"
    mzayyanill lanna ḥṣōna (II, 22) "they adorn this horse"
Ǧ: mnakkaṭille (III, 25)   "they give presents to him"
    msažžallille b-warkṭa   "they write it for him on a
    (III, 27)   sheet of paper"
    mfarrgin (III, 2)   "they look on."

The texts yield the following example of the IIIrd form of the verb:

M	B
mbarixilla (I, 46)	mbarxilla (II, 18).

The vowel /i/ preceding the last radical in the M form is due to the special formation of the IIIrd form in M. All forms of the perfect, with the exception of the third person singular and plural, as well as all forms with plural suffixes in the imperfect and all forms with feminine and plural suffixes in the participle, are formed with a long /-ī-/ in the second syllable. This /-ī-/ is shortened to /-i-/ whenever, through the addition of object suffixes, it is shifted into pretonal position. In B and Ǧ such forms are unknown, as the following paradigm of sōfar "to travel" will show:

Perfect:		M	B	Ǧ
Sg.	3 m	sōfar	sōfar	sōfar
	f	safīraṭ	sōfraṭ	sōfraṭ
	2 m	safîrič	sōfrić	sōfrič
	f	safîriš	sōfriš	sōfriš
	1 c	safîriṭ	sōfriṭ	sōfriṭ
Pl.	3 c	sōfar	sōfar	sōfar
	2 m	safiričxun	safrićxun	safričəx
	2 f	safiričxen	safrićxun	safričxen
	1 c	safirinnaḥ	safrinnaḥ	safrinnaḥ
Imperative:		M	B	Ǧ
Sg.	c	safār	sōfar	safōr
Pl.	m	safirōn	sōfrun	safrōn
	f	safirēn	sōfrun	safrēn
Imperfect:		M	B	Ǧ
Sg.	3 m	ysōfar	ysōfar	ysōfar
	f	čsōfar	ćsōfar	čsōfar
	2 m	čsōfar	ćsōfar	čsōfar
	f	čsōfar	šsōfar	šsōfar
	1 c	nsōfar	nsōfar	nsōfar
Pl.	3 m	ysafîrun	ysōfrun	ysōfrun
	f	ysafîran	ysōfrun	ysōfran
	2 m	čsafîrim	ćsōfrun	čsōfrun
	f	čsafîran	ćsōfrun	čsōfran
	1 c	nsōfar	nsōfar	nsōfar
Participle:		M	B	Ǧ
Sg.	3 m	msōfar	msōfar	msōfar
	f	msafîra	msōfra	msōfra
	2 m	čimsōfar	ćimsōfar	čimsōfar
	f	čimsafîra	šimsōfra	šimsōfra
	1 m	nimsōfar	nimsōfar	nimsōfar
	f	nimsafîra	nimsōfra	nimsōfra
Pl.	3 m	msafîrin	msōfrin	msōfrin
	f	msafîran	msōfrin	msōfran
	2 m	čimsafîrin	ćimsōfrin	čimsōfrin
	f	čimsafîran	ćimsōfrin	čimsōfran
	1 m	nimsafîrin	nimsōfrin	nimsōfrin
	f	nimsafîran	nimsōfrin	nimsōfran/in

In M and B the verbs tertiae infirmae display a /y/ as third radical in all feminine and plural forms of the first participle (in Ǧ this /y/ appears only in the feminine forms), thus:

M: mayṭyin ḥalyūṭa (I, 32)   "they bring sweets"

Ǧ: mayṯin semla (III, 10)   "they bring a ladder"
The second participle in M and Ǧ displays the vowel sequence /a-e/ (/a-i/ in pretonal position). In B one finds the sequence /i-e/ (/i-i/ in pretonal position), except for verbs in which the consonantal environment (ḥ/r) preserves the sequence /a-i/. In the texts we find the following example:
M: šawwiyilla (I, 45)   "they had made for her"
B: šiwwiyilla (II, 41)   "they had made for her"
The verbal paradigm with object suffixes which expresses definiteness by means of a second, infixed /-l-/ differs very markedly in Ǧ from the forms prevailing in M and B. Example:
Ǧ: mayṯlūle ḥḏučča (III, 26)   "they bring him the bride"
B: šakəllille 'arūsća (II, 38)   "they fetch the bride for him"
Notable, in particular, is the similarity of many forms (in the perfect, e.g., 3p f, 2p m, 1p c) and the almost total abandonment of gender distinction (except for the second person singular in the participle). Compare the following paradigms of the perfect and the participle with object suffixes of the third person masc. sg. on the basis of the verb "to write":

Perfect:		M	B	Ǧ
Sg.	3 m	xaṯəplēle	xaṯəplēli	xaṯəplēle
	f	xaṯəplalle	xaṯəplalli	xaṯpičlēle
	2 m	xaṯəplične	xaṯəplićli	xaṯpičlēle
	f	xaṯəplišlu	xaṯəplišli	xaṯpišlīlu
	1 c	xaṯəplille	xaṯəplilli	xaṯpičlēle
Pl.	3 m	xaṯəplulle	xaṯəplulli	xaṯəplūle
	f	xaṯəplalle	xaṯəplulli	xaṯəplūle
	2 m	xaṯpičlulle	xaṯpićlulli	xaṯpičlūle
	f	xaṯpičlalle	xaṯpićlulli	xaṯpičlūle
	1 c	xaṯəplaḥlēle	xaṯəplaḥlēli	xaṯəpnaḥlūle

Participle:		M	B	Ǧ
Sg.	3 m	xaṯəplēle	xaṯəplēli	xaṯəplēle
	f	xaṯəplōle	xaṯəplōli	xaṯəplēle
	2 m	čxaṯəplēle	ćxaṯəplēli	čxaṯəplēle
	f	čxaṯəplōle	šxaṯəplōli	šxaṯəplīlu
	1 m	nxaṯəplēle	nxaṯəplēli	nxaṯəplēle
	f	nxaṯəplōle	nxaṯəplōli	nxaṯəplēle
Pl.	3 m	xaṯəplille	xaṯəplilli	xaṯəplūle
	f	xaṯəplalle	xaṯəplilli	xaṯəplūle
	2 m	čxaṯəplille	ćxaṯəplilli	čxaṯəplūle
	f	čxaṯəplalle	ćxaṯəplilli	čxaṯəplūle
	1 m	nxaṯəplille	nxaṯəplilli	nxaṯəplūle
	f	nxaṯəplalle	nxaṯəplilli	nxaṯəplūle

The verb /amar/ "to say" in the imperfect has a different inflectional basis in B from that in the other two villages, whenever the verb carries an indirect object suffix:

M: nšinnaḥ nmallax (I, 35)   "I forgot to tell you"
B: inšiṯ namrēx (II, 33)   "I forgot to tell you"

For the sake of completeness the imperfect paradigm with the object suffix for the 2p m sg, as it appears in M and B, is here given for comparison:

			M	B
Sg	3	m	ymallax	yamrēx
		f	čmallax	čamrēx
	1	c	nmallax	namrēx
Pl	3	m	yumrullax	yamrullax
		f	yumrallax	yamrullax
	1	c	nmallax	namrēx

The frequent verbs "to sit," "to go (away)," and "to come" (M: /ḳʻōle/, /zalle/, /ṯōle/) have been variously combined with an /l/-suffix in the three villages. To the participle /ḳaʻēle/ (II, 46) in B (same in M) corresponds /kōʻ/ (III, 22) in G. The verb /ṯōle/, by replacing its third radical /y/ in most cases by /l/, was thus assimilated to the verb /zalle/ in B. For the participle we have the following examples in our texts:

B: s   2   f   zlōla (II, 11)   ṯlōla (II, 19)
    pl   3   m   zlillun (II, 3)   ṯlillun (II, 60)
as opposed to
M: sg   2   f   zlōla   ṯyōla (I, 25)
    pl   3   m   zlillun (I, 33)   ṯyillun (I, 1)

Ǧ does mostly without the forms with a suffixed /l/ in these three verbs. As an example the paradigm of /aṯa/ "to come" is given together with the forms of M and B for comparison's sake:

Perfect			M	B	Ǧ
Sg.	3	m	ṯōle	ṯōli	aṯa
		f	ṯalla	ṯalla	aṯaṯ
	2	m	ṯičlax	ṯičlax	aṯič
		f	ṯišliš	ṯišliš	aṯiš
	1	c	ṯill	ṯill	aṯiṯ
Pl.	3	m	ṯōlun	ṯōlun	aṯun
		f	ṯōlen	ṯōlun	aṯan
	2	m	ṯičxun	ṯliċxun	ṯičəx
		f	ṯičxen	ṯliċxun	ṯičxen
	1	c	ṯinnaḥ	ṯinaḥlaḥ	ṯinnaḥ
				ṯininnaḥ/ṯilinnaḥ	

Imperative		M	B	Ǧ
Sg.	m	ṭāx	ṭōx	ṭō
	f	ṭāš	ṭēš	ṭōy
Pl.	m	ṭalxun/ṭōn	ṭalxun	ṭōn
	f	ṭalxen/ṭō	ṭalxun	ṭēn

Imperfect		M	B	Ǧ
Sg.	3 m	yṭēle	yṭēle	yīṭ
	f	čṭēla	ṭṭēla	čīṭ
	2 m	čṭēx	ṭṭēx	čīṭ
	f	čṭīš	šṭīš	šīṭ
	1 c	nṭīl	nṭīl	nīṭ
Pl.	3 m	yiṭyullun yiṭyillun (I/41)	yiṭlullun	yīṭun
	f	yiṭyallen	yiṭlullen	yīṭan
	2 m	čiṭyullxun čiṭyillxun	ćiṭlullxun	čīṭun
	f	čiṭyallxen	ćiṭlullxun	čīṭan
	1 c	nṭēḥ (I/4)	nṭēḥ	nīṭ

Participle		M	B	Ǧ
Sg.	3 m	ōṭ/ṭēle (I/10)	ōṭ/ṭēle (II/37)	ōṭ/ṭēle (III/6)
	f	ōṭya/ṭyōla (I/29)	ōṭya/ṭlōla (II/19)	ōṭya/ṭyōla
	2 m	čōṭ/čṭēx	ćōṭ/ṭṭēx	čōṭ
	f	čōṭya/čiṭyōš	šōṭya/šiṭlōš	šōṭya
	1 m	nōṭ/nṭīl	nōṭ/nṭīl	nōṭ
	f	nōṭya/niṭyōl	nōṭya/niṭlōl	nōṭya
Pl.	3 m	ōṭyin/ṭyillun (I/1)	ōṭyin/ṭlillun (II/60)	ōṭin/ṭīl (III/6)
	f	ōṭyan/ṭyallen	ōṭyin/ṭlillun	ōṭyan/ṭyallen
	2 m	čōṭyin/ čiṭyillxun	ćōṭyin/ ćiṭlillxun	čōṭin
	f	čōṭyan/čiṭyallxen	ćōṭyin/ćiṭlillxun	čōṭyan
	1 m	nōṭyin/niṭyillaḥ	nōṭyin/niṭlillaḥ	nōṭin
	f	nōṭyan/ niṭyallaḥ	nōṭyin/ niṭlillaḥ	nōṭyan

Finally, attention is drawn to some differences in vocabulary as exemplified in our texts:

M	B	Ǧ	
lina	lina	lihan	whither
ḥdūṯa	ʿarīsa	ḥdūṯa	bridegroom
ḥdučča	ʿarūsća	ḥdučča	bride

maščūṭa	ʿorsa	maščūṭa	wedding
mayṭyin	mēšṭin	mayṭin	they bring
yīb	yīb	ib	(conditional particle)
blōta	ḳrīṭa	blōta	village

Text no. I — Maʿlula

The text is by the 24 year old Ṣālḥa Mḥammad Ḥusni Diyāb. She grew up in M, being the daughter of the imam of the mosque there. For a few years she has been married to the son of the Muslim mayor of M.

As many, especially younger, speakers do, she uses the pseudo-verb / batte/ also preceding verbs in the plural, where according to the rules the forms would be m / battayhun/ and f / battayhen/. Collective nouns that are formally f sg are often treated by her as plurals:

> hann əgmōʿča (I, 1)   these people
> lōʾ-ʾommṭa (I, 8)   these people

As in Ǧ the Muslims in M sometimes use the word /ʿarūfča/ in the sense of "week." The Christians use only /šoppṭa/.

1. ṭyillun hann əg̣mōʿča ti batte yxuṭbun. ṭalpill əḥḍučča m-tiḏōya. 2. tiḏōya iza ilun mšawarnō mšawirillun w-əmšawirill bisnīṭa. 8. iza aḳəblaṭ bisnīṭa rattillun žwōba mrillun: "waḷḷa, aḳəblaṭ bisnīṭa." 4. "emmat baḥ nṭēḥ nixṭub?" 5. yōma flanō ṭyillun, nōḥčin ʿa ṣōg̣ta zōbnin ṣīg̣ta. zabnilla žezʾa m-waʿyōṭa yōmil xeṭəpṭa. 6. yaʿni čup xull waʿyōṭa zabəllilla. zabnilla exma ṭannūryan, exma wʿōy xann yaʿni Aʿaynūnatan ʿan nās. A⁴ 7. ē, mayṭyillun w-ṭyillun liʿlayy yōmil xeṭəpṭa. 8. maʿzmill lōʾ-ʾommṭa. ṭyillun yxuṭbun. 9. mxasslilla hōṣ ṣīg̣ta. ṭabʿan mičḳattma eḥda rappa b-ʿomra, mxasslōla lə-ḥḍučča ṣ-ṣīg̣ta. 10. ḥḍūṭa ču ṭēle ʾimmayy, bess tiḏōye w-ahlōyṭe. 11. ē, mišwin mḍayafča w-fartill lann waʿyōṭa ḳommil lōʾ-ʾommṭa, mfarrg̣in ʿlayy mō ayṭ. 12. mbarixillun hōʾ-ʾommṭa bōṭar hōḏ ḏīfṭa. 13. ḳōymin atar, uxxul mōn zelle ʿa payṭe bōṭar ḥafəlṭa.

14. ṭēn yōma ṭyillun bē ḥḍūṭa mbarixill bē ḥḍučča. 15. ṭēleṭ yōma ṭyillun bē ḥḍučča mbarixill bē ḥḍūṭa. 16. w-ṭyillun bē ḥḍūṭa zyōrča ḥetta yḥattitull ẋeṭəbla xṭōba. 17. ē, mḥattitill xeṭəbla xṭōba. xaṭpille g̣appiš šayxa. 18. šarʿan g̣appaynaḥ anaḥ yaʿni gappis sarḳōy xaṭpille g̣appiš šayxa iḳdum. baʿdēn nōḥčin ʿa maḥkamṭa. 19. xaṭpill xṭōba rasmay, msažžlilla bə-ḥkūmča, xaṭpilla Aməṭʿaddem w-məṭʾaxxerA w-žezʾa m-waʿyōṭil payṭa aw xullun ti battayy hū w-sōlḳin mḥattitill maščūṭa.

20. ē, yōmil maščūṭa, yōmil batte yḥattitull maščūṭa, batte ynuḥčun iḳdum m-maščūṭa yžahhzun. 21. mkammlill əžhōza, waʿyōṭa ti batte yayṭillulla w-g̣arḍōya w-mayṭyill g̣orfṭiḏ ḍmōxa. 22. payṭa ti batte yfurəslulla farsille. w-mḥattitill maščūṭa. 23. maʿzmin w-ṭyillun másalan yōmil ḥenna. 24. iḳdum m-

---

4A ...... A = Arabic.

ḥenna b-yōma, yīb yaddīʿa ḥdučča, mišwa ḥafəlṭa lə-rfiḳyōṭa, mišwa ḥafəlṭa lə-rfiḳyōṭa. 25. ṭēn yōma ṭyōla hōḥ ḥallōḳča ʿa payṭa mišwlōla saʿra, mišwlōl ərfiḳyōṭa saʿren w-ṣamtilla yaʿni w-minṣamtin hinn w-hī. 26. yīb layyišill lōḥ ḥenna w-naḳḳišilla p-šamʿa w-warta zayyinilla. 27. ṭyillun maʿzmill rappō yizlullun yṭuʿnun ṣaḥnōyil ḥenna. ti mbaḳḳar yʿann ṭōʿen ṣaḥnil ḥenna w-ʿōbar. 28. ē, uxxul-aḥḥad mbaḳḳar ẓalġūṭča mẓalġeṭla, mbaḳḳar ʿunnīṭa mʿannēla, mbaḳḳar mawwōla mišwēle -ʿa hwōyil min yōdeʿ aḥḥad maḥək. 29. w-baʿdēn, bōṭar menna, ṭyōla xann eḥda rappa b-ʿomra ḳaʿyōla ḳommle ḥdučča. 30. mayṭyilla šamʿa aw ḥūṭa, ḳatərlilla b-ʿīda w-mḥannyilla. mnaḳḳišlōla ḥenna w-mḥannyōla w-hann bisənyōṭa mẓaləġṭalla wə-mʿannyalla. 31. baʿdēn minṣaffan p-tawra ti batte yḥannan xett. mḥannyan w-mẓaləġṭillun. 32. bōṭar ḥenna mišwin naḳrašča, mayṭyin ḥalyūṭa w-mdayīfin šāy. mdayīfin xett yaʿni mlabbas, šukalata, ti batte ydayifunne. 33. bōṭar menna tōḳḳin w-rōḳdin, šōhrin xann l-ʿemmil ʿaṣofra, ḳōymin zlillun. 34. ṭēn yōma ṭyillun bē ḥdūṭa mbarixilla p-ḥenna. 35. bōṭar menna ṭyi ... ʿafwan, nšinnaḥ nmallax dukkil innu aspill žhōza yōmil ḥenna. aspill marfḳōṭa wə-l-waʿyōṭa ti žahhizillun w-zlillun bē ḥdūṭa. 36. ṭēn yōma ṭyillun mbarixillun xett p-ḥenna w-tōḳḳin w-rōḳdin ḳalles, yīb ḥdučča xassīya ṭarəhṭa ḥuwwōr w-ṣmīta wə-šbičča xett ṣmīta ḳomma w-hann bisənyōṭa xullen ṣmītan. w-ʿamtōḳḳin w-rōḳdin. 37. xett bē ḥdūṭa tōḳḳin w-rōḳdin. mžamilillun ḳalles — šaʿṭa, ṭarač wə-zlillun. 38. ē, zlillun, mḥaddrill baʿdinn l-muʿṭīṭlə ḥdučča. 39. ē, yīb bē ḥdučča xett šawwīyin xōla, baššīlin, maḥəšmin bē ḥdūṭa, maḥəšmin dayfōyil bē ḥdučča xett. bōṭar min maḥəšmidd dayfayy w-maḥəšmin batte yuspull əḥdučča. 40. ē, aspill əḥdučča w-sōlḳin. šōhrin l-ḥatti ʿṣofra.

41. l-ʿaṣər, iḳdum ma yiṭyillun yuspull əḥdučča, mišwin ḥallaḳūṭa lə-ḥdūṭa, ḥalḳille. ḥalḳille wə-mʿannyille hū w-ʿamḥōleḳ. 42. mayṭyille ḥallōḳa ʿa payṭa ḥōleḳ. ḥalḳille wə-mʿannyille, lēle w-lə-rfiḳōye xett wə-šbīne. 43. ṭyillun aspill əḥdučča wə-zlillun šōhrin l-ḥatti ʿṣofra. 44. misḳillin xann iṭər, ṭlōṭa yūm l-ḥatti šobʿa yūm. tōḳḳin w-rōḳdin w ... yaʿni minbaṣtin ahlōyṭa baʿda baʿda. 45. bōṭar ʿarūfča mišwilla mbaraxča. ṭyillun tidōya w-ahlōyṭa, ġarība yīb naḳḳīṭla yōmil maščūṭa, šawwiyilla yaʿni šawbišilla. 46. amma ti ... ḳarribōya wə-stiḳōyit tidōya w-ʿahlōyṭa ṭyillun mbarixilla.

47. w-bess w-is-salām.

1. The people come who want to ask [for the hand of the bride] in marriage. They request the bride from her relatives. 2. Her relatives, in case they have counsellors, take counsel with them and with the girl. 3. When the girl has consented, they give them an answer saying: By God, the girl has consented. — 4. When shall we come to finalize the betrothal? — 5. On the [agreed] day they come and go down [to Damascus] to the jeweller and buy jewels. They buy her part of her things on the day of the betrothal. 6. I.e., they do not buy her all her things [at once]. They buy her a few clothes, a few kitchen utensils, i.e. that there is something for the people to see. 7. Well, they bring them [i.e.,

these things] and come to them on the day of the betrothal. 8. They invite the people. They come to celebrate the betrothal. 9. They deck her out with that jewelry. Of course an older woman hands [it] over to her, she decks the bride out with the jewelry. 10. The bridegroom does not come with them, only his relatives and family members. 11. Well, they offer something to them [food and drink] and they spread out the things in front of the people. They look over what he has brought. 12. The people congratulate her after the hospitality. 13. Then they get up and everyone goes home after the party.

14. The next day, the family of the bridegroom comes to congratulate the family of the bride. 15. On the third day, the family of the bride comes to congratulate the family of the bridegroom. 16. And then the family of the bridegroom comes for a visit to draw up the marriage contract. 17. Yes, they draw up the marriage contract. They write it in the presence of the Sheikh [imam of the mosque]. 18. It is the law with us, i.e., with the Muslims, to write it first in the presence of the Sheikh. Then they go down [to Damascus] to the registry. [There] they write up the official marriage contract. They register [the bride] with the government and they write for her the amounts to be paid before the marriage and after the divorce and her part of the furnishings of the house and whatever they want [into the contract] and they come up [from Damascus to M] to schedule the wedding.

20. Yes, on the day of the wedding, on the day on which they want to schedule the wedding, first they will go down [to Damascus] to do [all the] errands. 21. They complete her outfit, the clothes they want to bring her and her [other] things, and they bring the bedroom [furniture]. 22. The house they want to furnish for her they furnish for her. And they schedule the wedding. 23. They send out invitations, and they come for example on the Day of the Henna. 24. One day before the Henna celebration, [the date of] which must be known to the bride, she organizes a party for her friends. 25. The next day this hairdresser comes to her house. She does her hair and that of her friends, and they display her, that is to say, they [the friends] and she [the bride] are displayed. 26. They must have kneaded [beforehand] the henna and adorned it with candles and flowers; they have beautified it. 27. They invite the old people that they go and carry the plates with the henna. Whoever can sing carries a plate of henna and enters. 28. Yes, everybody who can trill trills for her, whoever knows a song sings it to her, whoever knows a poem recites it — each one will talk according to his ability. 29. After that an older woman comes and sits down next to the bride. 30. They bring her wax or a thread and bind it to her hand and dye it [i.e., her hand; with wax or thread they design a pattern on her hand] with henna. She embellishes it for her with henna and sings for her, and those girls trill and sing for her. 31. Then all those who also want to be dyed with henna line up. They are dyed with henna and they trill for them. 32. Thereafter they bring snacks and sweets and offer tea. They also offer candies and chocolate; whatever they wish they offer. 33. Thereafter

they beat the drum and dance, they spend the night this way until morning, then get up and leave.

34. The next day, the bridegroom's relatives come to congratulate her for the henna. 35. Then come ... excuse me, I have forgotten to tell you that they take the dower along on the Day of the Henna. They take the cushions and the things they have prepared for them and then the relatives of the bridegroom leave with them. 36. The next morning they also come and congratulate [her] for the henna and beat the drum and dance a little, while the bride is supposed to wear a white veil, and she is displayed and the marriage witness is also displayed before her and all these girls [bridesmaids] are displayed. And they beat the drum and dance. 37. The relatives of the bridegroom, too, play the drum and dance. They stay a little for politeness' sake, one or two hours, and leave. 38. Yes, they leave and get ready for fetching the bride. 39. The bride's family is supposed to have prepared a meal, to have cooked. The relatives of the bridegroom eat supper as do the guests of the bride's family. After they and the guests have eaten their supper, they will take the bride along. 40. Yes, they take the bride along and go up [into the house]. They celebrate the whole night until morning.

41. In the afternoon before they come to take the bride along, they undertake the haircut and the shaving of the bridegroom. They give him a haircut and shave him and sing for him, while he is being shaved. 42. They fetch him a hairdresser to his home who grooms him. They shave him and sing for him and his friends and his witness, too [get a shave]. 43. They come, take the bride with them, go and celebrate the whole night until morning. 44. They do that for two, three days — up to seven days they play the drum and dance and ... well, the relatives have a good time with each other. 45. After one week, they pay her a visit to congratulate her. Her relatives and family members come, [likewise one or the other] stranger, if he had given her presents on the wedding day, that is those who presented her [with things or money]. 46. The relatives and the friends of her family come and congratulate her.

47. That's all.

Text no. II — Bax‘a

The text is by the twenty-five year old Faṭṭūm ‘abd-ir-Raḥīm, daughter of the imam of Bax‘a, who grew up in Bax‘a and is still unmarried. She works in the house and in the fields.

She talks very fast and she was always somewhat nervous in front of the microphone for which reason some sentences get off to a wrong start and others are broken off. I have marked such cases by ... .

1. awwal yōma nma‘zmin anaḥ busənyōṭa. minǧam‘in, ya‘ni zelle ṭarć bisnī ma‘zminil ‘arūsća minšōnil ḥammōma, w-iṯṯar šapp ma‘zminil ‘arīsa, ya‘ni ‘arīsa w-‘arūsća. ‘arīsa bass ću ḥammōmi wakća bass ‘arūsća. 2. ma‘zmin š-šahərṭa, ću m-mōma bass šahərṭa. mišwin ḥafəlṭit tabbūle atar ći mawǧut mišwilli w-hanna. mišwin ḥafəlṭa l-‘arūsća.

3. ṭēni yōma 'ṣofra zlillun ma'zmin mark'in minšṓll ḥenna. ya'ni waḳə'ṭil ḥenna. 4. mawḳfa 'arūsća mić'áṭṭala m-'ukəbL̯alūla xann misḳilla waḳḳīfa l-ša'ṭa eḥḏa'asər, ṭarć'asər. 5. ḥenna eḥḏa, ṭarəć ya'ni exma mā bṓ'in hann šahurṓ misḳillin. 6. zlillun miṣṭill ḥenna. 'arīsa šaḳell ḥenna m-ǧappil'arūsća. 7. mḥannanill 'arīsa šappṓ w-'arūsća mḥannanilla busənyṓṭa. 8. mḥasslin atar, mḥannanilla w-mḥasslin, mišwin xett waḳə'ṭil ḥenna—xōla ya'ni. mišwin m-xušš šiklṓ. 9. ćbṓ' nxušəplēx mā?—lā? mišwin kuppṓ mḳallyin, mišwin ḳulḳṓṣ, mišwin baytinǧṓn, mišwin hann—ma ešme—fawōkih, mišwin ḥilwiyāt, mišwin ǧilē, mišwin ṣofra atar ya'ni m-ći mawǧut ya'ni m-payṭa. 10. w-ma ešme, w-hṓḏ ommṭa atar hann busənyṓṭa bass; ću misḳel ǧayr busənyṓṭa. ćūṯ ćisḳel, nakkīḥin ćūṯ bayntinn, bass busənyṓṭa, l-'arūsća ya'ni. 11. maḥašmin w-ći misḳilla ǧappa ḏōmxa misḳilla w-ći ću bṓ'a zlōla 'a payṭa. 12. ḳṓymin ə'ṣofra ša'ṭa e'sar, eḥḏa'asər ḏaḥwṭa, xett mark'in tōyrin ṭarć bisnī minšṓn ya'zmunnil busənyṓṭa yfukklulla ḥenna l-'arūsća. 13. mḥannallilla ḏwōṭa la'inn, ṭarć eṯlaṭ spa'. awwalća wībin xull kaffṓ. imṓḏ la', ya'ni abəṭlaṭ, iṯḳan bass ṭarć, eṯlaṭ spa'. 14. ma'zmin busənyṓṭa l-ǧappil ... ya'ni rfiḳyṓṭil 'arūsća zlillun fakklilla ḥenna w-mišwilla xett ḥafəlṭa. 15. m'annyin ya'ni w-rōḳḏin w-mišwilla ḥafəlṭa w-xulL̯aḥḥaḏ m'ṓwet 'a payṭe. 16. zlillun mark'in xann zlōla 'arūsća mić'aṭṭala. 'arīsa xett, yīb šappo xett xann. 17. 'zīmin w-xett mišwin waḳə'ṭil ḥenna w-mḥannanille ext ma ǧappaynaḥ ya'ni bil-lēlya w-ṭēni yōma ma'zmille xett. mišwille ḥafəlṭa w-fakklille ḥenna.

18. xett ... ē, mark'in ... 'arūsća zlōla mić'áṭṭala. ṭēni yōma hṓḏ yṓmil ḥenna. zlillun ommṭa mbarxilla p-ḥenna. 19. zlōla mić'áṭṭala, ṭlōla xann əl-'aṣər. hṓḏ ommṭa zlōla le'la. 20. l-'aṣər ykūn 'arīsa l-ḥammṓmi waḳća. ṭēni yōma šaḳlill 'arīsa mḥammamille. 21. i'zem másalan ǧappil ebril ḥṓle, ǧappil ebriḏ ḏṓḏe, 'a hwṓyil ma i'zem. šaḳlille mḥammamille. 22. mišwille ḥafəlṭa w-šaḳlille xett—hṓš awwalća wībin xann, imṓḏ la arke' ḥayla hanna—miṣṭille ḥṣōna, mzayyanill lanna ḥṣōna w-marəxpilli w-šaḳlille 'a trṓ. 23. 'a trṓ hanik ya'ni? p-ṭarfli ḳrīṭa ǧappaynaḥ. ya'ni trṓ mi'nṓyṭa inni ḏokkṭa faḏḏīya, b-barrīya ya'ni, p-ṭarfli ḳrīṭa ešma trṓ.

24. šaḳlilli mišwilli xett ḥafəlṭa hel. misḳillin tṓ ... zlillun xalīṭa šappṓ w-busənyṓṭa w-zalmṓṭa w-xulli sawa roḥəl lōḏ ... roḥəl 'arīsa. 25. misḳilla 'arūsća l-ḥōla, batta aḥḥaḏ yawḳef ǧappa. 26. 'ṓṭta hṓxa ya'ni iḏa 'arūsća sḳillaṭ, naǧpilla šappṓ. 27. mišwilla b-gayr ḏokkṭa minšṓn ya'ni inni nafeḳlun. iḏ'ić ya'ny̑ inni naǧpunna nafeḳlun e'la. 28. ē, hōxa misḳilla eḥḏa ǧappa, misḳilla nṭīra ǧappa w-ǧappil 'arīsa aḥḥaḏ. 29. 'arīsa šaḳlille 'a trṓ. mišwin atar tabəḳṭa 'a trṓ w-ḥafəlṭa w-misḳillin xann l-'okəb battax ćīmar, l-uḳḏum mn-ə'rōba p-ḳalles, l-'oḳbil 'aṣər. 30. ḥafəlṭa ya'ni mišwin tabəḳṭa w-reḳḏa w-šunyṓṭa l-ḥalēn w-zalmṓṭa l-ḥalēn. 31. šunyṓṭa 'al̯ētra w-zalmṓṭa 'al̯ētra; w-xett iḏa bṓ'in šunyṓṭa kṓ'min 'emmil zalmṓṭa p-tabəḳṭa wə-p-hanna.

32. m'ṓwtin. busənyṓṭa mafərḳill 'arūsća w-šappṓ zlillun lə'_'arīsa, 'emmil 'arīsa. 33. hṓxa ṭṓḳen waḳćil aḥəšmūṭa. xett ṓṭ aḥəšmūṭa hā! xull yṓma ṓṭ

aḥəšmūṯa—inšiṯ namrēx. xett mišwin aḥəšmūṯa. 34. busənyōṯa maḥəšmin ġappil 'arūsća w-šunyōṯa ya'ni w-xalīṯ xullun ṭiflō xann, hanna ġappil 'arīsa w-šappō w-zalmōṯa xulli. 35. xett 'arīsa mišw aḥəšmūṯa w-'arūsća mišwa ḥəšmūṯa; xett bil-lēlya atar, uḵḏum ma yšuḵlull 'arūsća l-'arīsa p-ḵalles, mišṯill 'arīsa l-'arūsća. 36. mwakkalill 'arūsća. šaḵlill wkōlća menna, mappyilla wkōlća w-hanna w-zlillun. 37. ṯēle 'arīsa rōḵeḏ hū w-hī waḵća ya'n.uḵḏum mett ṭarč šō'. ⁵ ē, w-mnaḵḵeṯla ya'ni hōḏ wkōlća. zelli. 38. zelli atar. 'oḵbil meṯṯ ṭarč šō' šaḵəllille 'arūsća. ša'ṯa ehḏa'asər, ṭarć'asər 'a ša'ṯa ćūṯ waḵća mḥattat ya'ni. šaḵəllile 'arūsća. 39. ōṯ ommṯa ya'ni marəġbin yišwun ... ġappil 'arīsa waḵćil šaḵəllille 'arūsća atar ... waḵćiš šaḵlill 'arūsća xett mēšṯin ḥṣōna ći arəxpull 'arīsa e'le l-'a trō, mišṯille hū. 40. mzayyanilli w-xett mark'in marəxpill 'arūsća e'le w-zaffṯa rohil 'arūsća, šunyōṯa w-zalmōṯa, ext ma zaffṯil 'arīsa waḵćiz zalle 'a trō, šunyōṯa w-zalmōṯa, w-'arūsća xann. 41. šaḵlilli. bikūn 'arūsća hōxa šiwwiyilla xomərṯa—ḥmīra ya'ni. ka'mlilla b-īḏa w-mapplilla—mišwilla p-ḥaṣṣa ōṯ ommṯa misəryōṯa, ommṯa mišwilla warta—'a hwōyil ma bō'in. 42. lazzḵōla 'a ṯar'iḏ ḏōrća uḵḏum ma ći'bar. ya'ni 'ōṯṯa ġappaynaḥ xann. 43. 'ōbra 'arūsća. ōṯ ommṯa ya'ni mišwin ḥafəlṯa l-'arīsa wə-l-'arūsća, mraḵḵaḏillun. 44. bikūn 'arīsa ćūb hā! 'ōber 'arīsa ... 'arūsća 'ōbra ćūb 'arīsa b-gorfṯa. b-gorfṯa ya'ni ći lēla ćūb. b-gorfṯiḏ ḏmōxa bikūn ćūb. 45. šaḵlilli ya'ni rfiḵōyi, iṯṯar šapp ṭamrilli. 46. ṯlōla 'arūsća ḵa'yōla mett rob'iš ša'ṯa, e'sar tḵīḵ hanna—mišṯill 'arīsa, 'ōber hū e'la atar. 'ōber ḵa'ēle hū w-hī. 47. mišwillun ḥafəlṯa, mraḵḵaḏillun. ōṯ ommṯa lā, zlillun m'ōwtin tugray 'a payṯēn. 48. imōḏ xulli 'ammišwin. mišwin ḥafəlṯa xann z'ōra mett ša'ṯa w-mṭaššarillun w-zlillun.

49. ṯēni yōma atar ṯōḵen ṣuphōyṯa, ešma ṣuphōyṯa. kōymin 'arisō mn-ə'ṣofra. 50. 'arūsća mxassya xann. ćū mxassya ext 'arūsća mićkállala ya'ni, mxassya hanna lupsa. 51. ōṯ busənyōṯa mxassyin ya'ni 'a rayšēn išōra la'innu xalīṯ. ćū ġappaynaḥ ya'ni hanna. 52. mxassya ṭawwel mġayyra bēll lōḏ ommṯa w-ḵa'yōla hī w-'arīsa. 53. ṯlillun ommṯa mbarxillun. l-'arīsa w-l-'arūsća. 54. bikūn ōṯ aḥḥaḏ ḵa' msaġġel. ya'ni haćć náḵḵaṭić xann. ḥrēna ḥrēna, flanō flanō, bikūn xulli msaġġalilli. ana ma náḵḵaṭiṯ, hanna ... mnáḵḵaṭin atar. 55. w-mišwin ḥafəlṯa atar. mabəṯya ḥafəlṯa, ṣuphōyṯa ešma, ešma ṣuphōyṯa. mn-ə'ṣofra mišwin ḥafəlṯa l-'oḵəbl.alūla. 56. alūla ṯōḵen šawba. xull.ommṯa zelle—ya'ni waḵćil aḵərṯūṯa—xull ommṯa, xull.ahḥaḏ zelle 'a ḏokkṯe, 'a payṯe.

57. 'oḵəbl.aḵərṯūṯa, xann əl-'aṣər xett mabəṯya xann š-ša'ṯa ehḏa, ṭarć ōṯ ommṯa, ōṯ ommṯa ṭarć'asər—ya'ni ćūṯ waḵća mḥattat. 58. xett ōṯ aḥəšmūṯa hā! xett mišwin aḥəšmūṯa, maḥəšmin ġappil 'arīsa yōmiṣ ṣuphōyṯa. 59. ḥōsel 'orsa. ōṯ ommṯa 'oḵbil 'orsa atar mišwin ḥafəlṯa ṯēni yōma, ōṯ ommṯa xalaṣ—

iḥsel hanna 'orsa. 60. misḳilla hōḏ ommṭa ṭlillun mbarxillun. 'ōṭṭa ya'ni exət ḏayfō.

61. hanna 'orsa. 'uḳbōlća lə-bnōx.

1. The first day we invite girls. They come together, i.e., two girls go to invite the bride for the bath, and two young men invite the bridegroom, thus the bridegroom and the bride. But it is not yet time for the bath of the bridegroom, only [for] the bride. 2. They invite for the evening, not during the day, only [for] the evening. They prepare a *tabbūle* party [*tabbūle* being a kind of salad made from parsley], well, whatever is available they prepare and all that. They organize a party for the bride. 3. The next morning they invite again, for the henna, i.e., for the proceeding of [dyeing with] henna. 4. The bride hangs around with nothing to do from the afternoon until eleven, twelve o'clock [at night]. 5. The dyeing with henna [takes place] at one, two o'clock [at night]. The guests stay as long as they wish. 6. They go and fetch the henna. The bridegroom fetches the henna from the bride. 7. The young men dye the bridegroom with henna and the girls dye the bride with henna. 8. When they have finished — have dyed with henna and finished, they prepare the banquet for the henna party. They make all kinds [of food]. 9. Shall I enumerate to you what [they make]? — no? — They make fried dumplings made of crushed wheat, they make potatoes and eggplants; they make - what do you call it? — fruit, sweets, jelly; they make a banquet, that is, from all that is available in the house. 10. And, well, these people, the girls, only the girls stay. You cannot stay; married people are not present, only the friends of the bride. 11. They eat supper and whoever wants to stay sleeps at her place and who does not goes home. 12. They get up in the morning around ten, eleven o'clock, and again two girls make the round to invite the girls to remove the henna from the bride [which is put like a bandage around her fingers for the night]. 13. For they dye her hands, two or three fingers. Formerly they used to dye the whole hand. Not nowadays, i.e., it is no longer so, only two, three fingers [will be dyed]. 14. They invite girls for ... i.e., the friends of the bride come and remove her henna and organize also a party for her. 15. They sing thus and dance and make a party for her and everybody returns home [after that]. 16. They leave and the bride goes to rest. [With] the bridegroom it is likewise, concerning the young men it is also like that. 17. They are invited and also have a henna party and they dye him with henna as it is with us [i.e., the girls], that is to say, in the night and on the following day they invite him, too. They prepare a party for him and remove the henna.

18. Also ... yes, again ... the bride goes to rest. The following day is the real Henna Day [because on this day the fingers are red after having been dyed during the night]. People come and congratulate her for the henna. 19. She goes to rest and comes [back] in the afternoon. The people go to her. 20. In the afternoon it is time for the bath of the bridegroom. On the second day they invite the bridegroom and bathe him. 21. He is invited, e.g., by his cousin on

his mother's side or his cousin on his father' side; depending on who has invited him [to him he goes]. They fetch him and bathe him. 22. They prepare for him a party and bring for him — now [I am talking] about former times, then they did it like that, today not much of it remains — they bring him a horse. They embellish this horse, put him on it and take him to the threshing-floors. 23. To the threshing-floors, that is where? At the side of the village [here] with us, i.e., the threshing-floors are an empty spot, outside [of the village] that is, at the edge of the village, which is called "the threshing-floors."

24. They take him along and prepare for him also a party there. They stay, dan[ce] ... they go in a mixed group, boys and girls and men all of them together behind this [fem.] ... behind the bridegroom. 25. The bride remains alone. She needs someone to stay with her. 26. It is the custom here that the bride will be stolen by the young men, if she remains [alone]. 27. They [then] bring her to another place, so that [something] comes out of it for them. You know, when they steal her, something will come out of it for them [i.e., they will receive a ransom for her]. 28. Yes, therefore some [girl] stays with her. She stays with her so that she will be guarded, and someone stays with the bridegroom, too. 29. The bridegroom they take to the threshing-floors. They dance a round dance on the threshing-floors and have a celebration and stay thus until after, let's say [lit.: you will say] until shortly before the evening, until the late afternoon. 30. Celebration means that they perform a round dance and dance, and the women keep to themselves and the men keep to themselves. 31. The women are on one threshing-floor and the men are on [another] threshing-floor; however, if the women wish, they can hold the men [by their hands] in the round dance and all that.

32. They return. The girls accompany the bride and the young men go to the bridegroom, with the bridegroom. 33. Now it is time for the supper. There is also supper [the exclamation 'ḥā!' is meant to direct the attention of the listener to something important, in this case the supper]. On each of these days there is a supper — I forgot to tell you! They prepare supper, too. 34. [Only] the girls eat their supper with the bride; the [married] women and everybody else mix, the children, etc., this [is] at the bridegroom's, the youths and men, everybody. 35. The bridegroom likewise prepares a supper, and the bride prepares a supper. Likewise, in the night, shortly before they take the bride to the bridegroom, they take the bridegroom to the bride.

36. They authorize the bride. They take the authorization from her, they give her the authorization and all that and leave. 37. The bridegroom comes and dances with her for a while, that is, about two hours before. Yes, he gives her presents, i.e., that is the authorization. He leaves. 38. He leaves now. After about two hours they come to fetch the bride. Around eleven, twelve o'clock; the time is not fixed to the hour. They bring him his bride. 39. There are people who like to ... on the bridegroom's side, when they fetch his bride for him ... when they fetch his bride for him, they also take that horse on which

they let the bridegroom ride to the threshing-floors, they bring it. 40. They embellish it and let the bride ride on it and the wedding procession is behind the bride, women and men, like the wedding procession of the bridegroom when he went to the threshing-floors, men and women, and with the bride it is likewise. 41. They fetch him [i.e., the bridegroom; they fetch him when she enters into his house]. At this point in time they are supposed to have prepared bread dough for the bride, i.e., sour dough. They take her hand and give it to her. There are people who put some money on top of it or flowers, as they wish. 42. She sticks it on the door of the house, before she enters. Thus it is the custom with us. 43. The bride enters. There are people who arrange a party for the bridegroom and the bride. They let them dance. 44. Note that it may be that the bridegroom is not there. The bridegroom enters ... the bride enters and the bridegroom is not in the room, that is, he is not in her room. It may be that he is not in the bedroom. 45. His friends have taken him along; two young men keep him hidden. 46. The bride comes and sits around for a quarter of an hour, ten minutes, something like that — they bring the bridegroom. He enters and stays together with her. 47. They have a party for them and let them dance. There are people who do not do that, in that case they return immediately to their homes. 48. Nowadays everybody does it [thus]. They have a little party, about one hour, and leave them alone and go away.

49. The following day there is a breakfast called /ṣupḥōyṭa/. Bride and bridegroom get up in the morning. 50. The bride wears normal clothes. She does not don her wedding dress, she wears totally normal clothes. 51. Some girls wear a scarf on their heads, for it is mixed [men and women]. This [going without a scarf] does not exist among us. 52. She changes clothes and wears a long dress among all the people and is sitting there with the bridegroom. 53. People come and congratulate them, the bridegroom and the bride. 54. Possibly someone sits there and writes everything down, i.e., [how much money] you have given, the next one, and the next, and such-and-such and such-and-such, everything they write down. What I have given, this one ... they thus make gifts [of money to the newlywed]. 55. And they have a party, as indicated. The party starts, it is called /ṣupḥōyṭa/, breakfast. Starting in the morning until the afternoon they have a party. 56. Around noon it gets hot. All people leave, as it is time for lunch, anyway — all people, everyone goes home.

57. After lunch, in the afternoon, [the party] starts again until one or two o'clock [a.m.] with some people, with some people only until twelve o'clock, i.e., the time is not limited. 58. There is also supper. They also prepare supper and sup at the bridegroom's on the day on which the breakfast also [takes place]. 59. [With this] the wedding ends. There are people who have a party even after the wedding, on the following day, with other people it is the end, the wedding has come to an end. 60. However, people continue to come and

congratulate them. They are received in that case as guests as it is customary with us.

61. That is the wedding. All the best for your children!

Text no. III — Ğubb'adīn

The speaker is the forty-three year old peasant Ražab al-Akḥal who is called Abu Mḥammad in the village. Apart from his work as a farmer he also makes and repairs agricultural tools made of wood, such as plows.

1. awwalča, 'a zamōn kadīm, maščūṯa b-ġuppa'ōḏ wa xḥōla. 2. wa mižčam'an hān blatō ti čuləḥčullaynaḥ xūl w-ṯīl mfarrġin e'lah — 'a maščūṯa. 3. awwal mīt mišwin či'līlča. m'állalin 'asra yūm, ḥammešča'sar yūm. tōpčin, rōkḏin w-mišwin čimṯilyōṯa. 4. bōṯar mennah tōr mišwin 'urrabōyin. wa mšammīl 'urrabōyin. kōm zaləmṯa mišwille rō'ya. 5. ōseb busunōya, 'isər ṯlēṯ psūn. ōspin žarṣō. zelle 'a šenna bōn ra'ēl. 6. ṯīl 'urrabōyin naġpīl lann ġḏō. kōm ṯēle hū, mišəččay l-ḥōčma. 7. mišwin maḥčamṯa w-ḥōčma. mišəččay l-maḥčamṯa innu nahəplūlay ġḏōy. 8. zlōla tawəlṯa—'asčarōyin—m'awtīl m-'urrabōyin. 9. w-mayṯīl lann ġḏō, w-mayṯīl ra'īsi 'urrabōyin 'a maḥčamṯa. mahəčmilli bə-šnōka. 10. kōymin, mayṯin semla w-marnḥille w-mtantlill lanna ra'īsi 'urrabōyin bēh. 11. kōm ra'īsi 'urrabōyin mušw muḥōmi tifā', xwō muḥōmi tifā' me'le. 12. kōm sōlek 'a lanna semla hanna muḥōmi tifā' w-m'ān iṯṯir ṯlōṯa bayṯ w-mameləl: A" 'alēhun yā 'arab!"A. 13. kōymin 'urrabōyin hōžmin 'a tawəlṯa w-mxallṣill lanna zaləmṯa minnāy.

14. kōymin bōṯar minnāy mišwin tafakžōyin. mintōrin bə-blōta. mšammīl tafakžōyin. mtáwwaḥin bə-blōta.

15. bōṯar mennah kōymin mayṯīl əḥdūṯa. mxassille p-ṯar'i žēm'a, ib aybin šob'a, ṯmōnya sawa — 'asra ḥdūṯ. 16. mxassīl b-žēm'a w-msawwīl w-mayṯin ġamlō, uxxul aḥḥa ġamla. 17. mzayyanill lanna ġamla p-šaršfō, bə-ḥramō w-p-šawryōṯa w mišwill əḥdūṯa w-mxassille w-mišwille rīšča b-'ukōle w-marxpille 'a lanna ġamla w-mtawwarilli bə-blōta xullah. 18. w-aspilli 'a škifōyi ḥdutō, mšammīl škifōyi ḥdutō. 19. w-bōṯar miz zayrill əškifōyi ḥdutō m'ōwtin mtawwarill blōta. 20. m'ōwtin lihan? l-sahəlta ti 'ammišwīl ḥafəlta bāh. 21. ṣaffīl lann əḥdutōya ṣeffa w-kō'in tōpčin w-rōkḏin w-mišwin abu ne'ṣi. 22. hanna abu ne'ṣi maġrlūle ffōye p-ḥuwwar w-mxassilli kamṣō xān w-mišwilli rīšča b-muḥḥe mn-ann riḥōṯa w-kō' mnakket b-ō ḥafəlta. 23. mameləl: "xara 'arab, xara 'arab" w-ḏōḥeč 'lāy w-mnakket mišwēl nahfōṯa w-čō'min b-ō tabəčta w-maḍillin tōpčin l-ḥatta 'rōba.

24. 'arōba aspīl — mah hešme — aspīl əḥdutōya uxxul-aḥḥa 'a bayṯe w-mišwin ḥafəlta. rōkḏin, tōpčin w-mišwin əḥšamūta. 25. mahəšmin hōḏ ommṯa xulla mahəšma ġappil hanna ḥdūṯa w-kōymin tōr mnakkaṯille — lə-ḥdūṯa. 26. zlīl mayṯlūle ḥducča w-mnakkaṯilli. hanna mnakketle ḥiməš warək, hanna em'a warək, hanna 'isər w-ḥammeš warək. 27. lammill lann nkūṯa w-msažžallille b-warkṯa. 28. xīt yōmi ṯōken hanna ti nakkīṯle ḥdūṯa m'ōwet mnakkaṯlēle ti nakkīṯlēle. Akird w-wafa ya'ni.A 29. maḍilla hō saləfta 'asra, ḥammešča'sar yūm w-minčahya.

1. Formerly, in the olden days, the wedding feast in Ǧubb'adīn was beautiful. 2. The [inhabitants of the] villages around us all gathered together and came to watch the wedding feast. 3. First they have the celebration. They celebrate for ten, fifteen days. They dance round dances and other dances and make performances. 4. Thereafter they play the Bedouin. They called it the "Bedouin." They made one man the shepherd. 5. He takes boys along with him, twenty, thirty boys. They take bells with them. He goes with them up on the rock and herds them [because the boys have to play the kids]. 6. The Bedouins come and steal those kids. Then he [the shepherd] sets out and lodges a complaint with the judge. 7. They play court and judge. He complains at the court: They have stolen my kids. 8. Then the government sets out — [in the form of] soldiers — and they retrieve them from the Bedouins. 9. And they bring those kids back and bring the bedouin chief to court. They sentence him to [death by] hanging. 10. They go and fetch a ladder and put it up and let the bedouin chief down from it. 11. Then the bedouin chief makes someone his advocate, an advocate for himself. 12. He then ascends this ladder, this advocate, and he sings two, three verses and cries out: Upon them, you Arabs! 13. At that the bedouins attack the government and free this man.

14. Thereafter they [the village people] set out and form patrols. They go around the village. They call them patrols. They go around the village [to invite the people to the wedding feast].

15. After that they set out and fetch the bridegroom. They dress him up at the door of the mosque; it should be seven or eight together — [maybe] ten bridegrooms. 16. They dress them up at the mosque and make them ready and bring camels, one for each. 17. They embellish this camel with blankets and large and small pieces of cloth, and they get the bridegroom ready and dress him and stick a feather into his head-band and put him on this camel and parade him through the whole village. 18. And they take him to the Rocks of the Bridegrooms. They call them "Rocks of the Bride and the Bridegroom." 19. And after they have visited the Rocks of the Bridegrooms, they again lead the village around [i.e., the inhabitants]. 20. Whereto do they return? To the place where they will have the celebration. 21. The bridegrooms all line up in one row and start dancing and they make one [among their midst] the Abu Ne'ṣi. 22. They paint this Abu Ne'ṣi's face white and they dress him in such [ridiculous] shirts and put such a long feather on his head, and then he makes jests during the feast. 23. He says to them "Shit Arabs, Shit Arabs" and laughs about them and makes jokes for them, and they join hands in this round dance and continue to dance until the evening.

24. In the evening they bring — what do you call it? — they bring each bridegroom to his home and have a party. They dance and prepare supper. 25. They eat supper. The people all eat supper at this bridegroom's and then they give presents to him — the bridegroom. 26. They go and fetch the bride for him and give presents to him. This one gives him fifty lira, that one one

hundred lira, this one twenty-five lira. 27. They collect the [money] gifts and note them down on a piece of paper. 28. If the one who has given him a present becomes a bridegroom himself one day, he [the present bridegroom] will again give him what that [man] has given him. [It is] thus a loan and repayment. 29. The whole affair lasts for ten, fifteen days and then it is over.

THE BOOK OF RUTH IN NEO-ARAMAIC

Gideon Goldenberg and Mordekhay Zaken

The oral traditions of a Jewish literal Bible translation, *šara'* [< Arab. *šarḥ*], in Neo-Aramaic have already attracted the attention of scholars. Large parts of such versions were written down, in the fifties, by Kurdistani rabbis on the initiative of J. J. Rivlin; tape-recordings of oral *šara'*-traditions have been made at the Hebrew University Language Traditions Project on the initiative of H. J. Polotsky and S. Morag. A thorough study of the orally transmitted Neo-Aramaic Bible translations has been undertaken by Y. Sabar, whose edition of *The Book of Genesis in Neo-Aramaic in the Dialect of the Jewish Community of Zakho* appeared in Jerusalem in 1983 (as vol. IX of '*Eda ve-Lashon*, Publications of the Hebrew University Language Traditions Project). Sabar's 35-page introduction instructively summarizes the main characteristics of the translation.

As there is much individual and ad hoc variation in the traditional reading of the Bible in the colloquial, it is necessary to study as many examples as possible of those traditions in order to discover their sources and understand the various developments. The text here presented is the Neo-Aramaic version of Ruth as read by Ze'ev (Gurgo) Ariel, a native of Zakho. The Book of Ruth, which is read in the synagogue on Shavu'ot, the Jewish feast of Pentecost, used to be read to the congregation first in Neo-Aramaic by the cantor in the synagogue, on the Sabbath before Shavu'ot also in the *mišmara*, study and prayer gathering in commemoration of the dead in the house of mourning or in the synagogue. Ze'ev Ariel was born in Zakho, Iraqi Kurdistan, in 1914, and like all Jewish boys there learnt the Bible in Hebrew and then in the traditional oral translation in the Colloquial. His teacher was Rabbi Moshe 'Alwan. Ariel used to read the Book of Ruth in Neo-Aramaic to the public in Zakho and, since his arrival in Israel in 1935, to the elderly Kurdistani Jews in the village of Elro'i where he lived, then in Jerusalem.

It will be noticed that the recorded version abounds with suggested alternative translations of various terms and phrases; it is a combination of a sound tradition with not a few improvisations. In many cases Ariel adds explanations as needed in his opinion by the audience to understand the text; such digressions are mostly given in the following text in parentheses. The recitation of the Neo-Aramaic has a typical melody, with pausal lengthenings (unmarked in the text).

The text is given in a rather broad transcription, but not systematized. In Ariel's pronunciation vowel-length is neutralized (and therefore unmarked) in word-final position, also often in non-final unstressed open syllables. His glottal stop is rather unstable and usually weak, e.g. "land"—['ar'a / 'ara], "in the land"—[bar'a / b'ara / bara], "to the land"—[lar'a / l'ar'a], "door"—[tar'a / tara], "who comes" (f.)—[dasya / d'asya], "no"—[la' / la / lā]; his o is closer than usual, and intervocalic w is often weak. A special feature of Ariel's speech is the clearly audible bilabial on-glide before n-: in his pronunciation nīxūsa (i 9) will be heard as [mnīxūsa], napqātən (ii 22) as [mnapqātən], nāpəl (iii 18) as [mnāpəl]. Compare to that the sporadic off-glide audible after g where ggazdila "they reap it" (in the long explanatory addition after ii 14) clearly sounds [gugrazdīla].

The general characteristics of the translational style as described in Sabar's introduction are also true for Ḥaxam Gurgo's version of Ruth, like the inclusion of Hebrew words (i 2.11.13, ii 5, iv 1.7.9.11), the omission of the conjunction u "and" (i 22, iv 1.11, and passim), the literal translation of את by 'āl (iv 10.11.13.16.18-22), the ungrammatical construction of Predicate + indep. pers. pron. instead of Pred. + copula (iv 9.10), or the use of 'ōd for אשר regardless of gender and number (i 7, iii 4, iv 11.15).

In several instances the Neo-Aramaic translation, rather than being literal, follows some Midrashic or exegetic tradition, as, e.g., iii 13 where Ṭov is said to be the proper name of Naomi's nearer kinsman, iii 15-17 where sēs'sə'ōrīm is understood as "six measures of barley." In some other cases (e.g. ii 14, ii 19, iv 11) the translation is mistaken.

The text was recorded by M. Z., who also prepared the first draft of the transcription;* it was then checked up, revised and edited with the assistance of G. G.

Chapter I

1 hwēle bəd yōmāsəd šərā'ət šarā'e pəšle kəpna bəd 'ar'a (grāni wēla). zəlle gōra mən Betleḥem Yehuda ləskāna bəd daštəd Mō'āv 'āwa ubaxte ukutru yalunke dīde.

2 šəmməd gōra 'Elimelex šəmməd baxte Na'omi ušəmmət kutru bnōne dīde Maḥlon u-Xəlyon 'efrātim mən Betleḥem Yehuda, sēlu ldaštəd Mō'āv wēlu tāma (skənnu tāma).

3 mətle 'Elimelex gōr Na'omi, pəšla 'āya ukutru bnōne dīda.

4 gurru ta gyānōhun baxtāsa Mō'āvāye, šəmmət xa 'Orpa səmməd day trē Rut; tūlu tāma mux 'əṣra šənne.

*M. Z.'s research was supported in part by the Memorial Foundation for Jewish Culture.

5 mətlu ham kuturtōhun Maḥlon u-Xəlyon, pəšla 'ē baxta mən kutru yalunke dīda umən gōra.

6 qəmla 'āya ukalāsa dīda d'ərra mən daštəd Mō'āv did šme'la bəd daštəd Mō'āv did txərre 'əstaz 'ōlam qōm dīde līhāwa ṭalōhun laxma.

7 mpəqla mən day dūka 'ōd wēla tāma kutru kalāsa dīda 'əmma. zəllu bəd 'urxa wēlu bīzāla ləd'āra lar'əd Yehuda.

8 mərra Na'omi ta kutru kalāsa dīda: sāwun d'ōrun baxta 'əl bēs yəmma; 'āwəz 'əstaz 'ōlam 'əmmōxun hawūsa kud dax 'uzlōxun 'əmməd mīse u'əmmi.

9 yāwəl 'əstaz 'ōlam ṭalōxun xāzētun nīxūsa baxta bēs gōra. nšəqla 'əllōhun mōrəmlu qālōhun bxēlu.

10 mərru ṭāla did 'əmmax bda'raxni [l]qōm dīdax (la gēzax 'əl bēsa).

11 mərra Na'omi: d'ōrun bnāsa dīdi, tamā bāsētun 'əmmi, xōla hēš 'ətli brōne bəd mē'ewāsi pēši ṭalōxun 'əl gūre?

12 d'ōrun bnāsa dīdi usāwun did pəšli sōtənta mən hwāya lgōra; 'īkan 'amrāna 'ətli təqwa (sparta), ham 'əzlal hōyāna lgōra (hakan 'əzlal žəg gōrāna gōra) uham mhōyāna brōne.

13 xōla 'əllōhun msaprētun hīl rāwe, xōla 'əllōhun pēšētun mə'uggānōt 'əlləd la hwāya 'əl gōra?! la bnāsa dīdi did marərtala 'əlli rāba mənnōxun did mpəqla 'əbbi 'īz 'əstaz 'ōlam.

14 mōrəmlu qālu bxēlu hēš, nšəqla 'Orpa 'əl xmāsa, Rut 'əlṭəxla 'əbba (mərra: 'āna la gēzan).

15 mərra: hōna d'ərra 'izamsax 'əl qōm dīda ulma'būde dīda, d'ōr basər 'izamsax.

16 mərra Rut: la ṭapyat 'əbbi rāba ləšwāqa dīdax ləd'āra mən basrax. dūkəd 'āhat 'āzātən 'āna bāzāna, dūkəd damxātən bdamxāna, qōm dīdax qōm dīdi, 'ilāha dīdax 'ilāha dīdi.

17 dūkəd mēsātən 'āna bmēsāna, tāma 'asyāna qwāra. hatxa 'āwəz 'əstaz 'ōlam 'əlli hatxa māzəd did mōsa mafrəš bēni ubēnax.

18 xzēla did pəšla bəhīvi la gba 'āza mən kəsla, bṭəlla lmaḥkōye 'əmma.

19 zəllu kuturtōhun hīl 'īsāya dōhun sēlu l-Betleḥem. dammət sēlu l-Betleḥem [m]tūšəšla kulla bāžēr 'əllōhun, mərru: mo 'ēha-la Na'omi?

20 mərra ṭalōhun: la ṣarxətuli Na'omi, ṣrōxun 'əlli marrā, marətta, did mōmərre šadday 'əlli rāba.

21 'āna mlīsa zəlli mən kəslōxun, spəqta qam mad'ərri 'əstaz 'ōlam. tamā ṣarxətuli Na'omi? 'əstaz 'ōlam mǧōyəble 'əbbi, šadday muxrūle 'əlli.

22 d'ərra Na'omi [u]Rut Mō'āvēsa kalsa 'əmma, 'an did d'ərru mən daštəd Mō'āv, 'āni sēlu Betleḥem bəd 'awwələd ġẓādəd sa'āre.

Chapter II

1 ta Na'omi 'əswa xa nāš gyāna lgōra, xa nāša gabbār xēla (wēle) mən 'ōǧāġ 'Elimelex šəmme Bo'az.

2 mərra Rut Mō'āvēsa ta Na'omi xmāsa: bāzāna 'atta go dašta blaqtāna xapča bəšuble, bāzāna basər dūkəd xazyāna ḥəsən bəd 'ēne. mərra ṭāla: sē brāti.

3 zəlla usēla mg̊ōme'la go dašta basər ġaẓāde. tfəqla tfaqta dīda go zaviyəd dašta did Bo'az, 'ōd mən 'ōg̊āg̊ 'Elimelex.

4 hōna Bo'az sēle mən Betleḥem, mərre ta ġaẓāde: 'əstaz 'ōlam 'əmmōxun. mərru ṭāle: mbārəxlox 'əstaz 'ōlam.

5 mərre Bo'az ta ġolāma dīde 'ōd wēle ḥmīla 'əl ġaẓāde (mux mənahel 'avōda): máni-la 'ē yalta 'ēha ('ōd kxāzənna xa yalta ġarib 'axxa)?

6 mg̊ōyəble 'ō yāla dīle ḥmīla lġaẓāde mərre: 'ē yalta Mō'āvēsa-la 'āya, 'ay did d'ərra 'əmməd Na'omi mən daštəd Mō'āv.

7 mərra ṭāli: bāzāna bəmg̊am'āna 'atta bəd malōqe, blaqṭāna basər ġaẓāde; sēla ḥməlla mən bənōke hīl 'atta, 'ōha ləytāwa dīda go bēsa čūča (gēr go bēsa tūla bas 'axxa hēš lēwa tūta).

8 mərre Bo'az ta Rut: hala šmō' brāti, la 'āzātən ləmg̊amō'e bəd dašta xa xēta, ham mən 'axxa la 'ōrātən, 'axxa laṭxātən 'əmməd ġolamwāsa dīdi.

9 'ēnax bəd dašta 'ōh[a] did ġaẓdi mēnəx 'əbbōhun 'āzātən basrōhun; 'āna mōṣēli 'əl ġolamwāsa dīdi 'əlləd la nḥāqa 'əllax (čuxxa la maḥke 'əmmax). ṣahyātən, bāzātən 'əl 'amāne bšatyātən mən did garši ġolamwāsa (tāma 'īs māya, 'īs kulle məndi).

10 [m]pəlla 'əl paswāsa kəpla l'ar'a (qāme) mərra ṭāle: tamā xzēli ḥəsən bəd 'ēnox ləfrāqa dīdi? 'āna xa baxta nuxrēsa wan (muḥkēlox 'əmmi 'ō maḥkōye hatxa qam 'āzəzətti).

11 mg̊ōyəble Bo'az mərre ṭāla: maḥkōye sēle maḥkōye ṭāli kulle mād 'uzlax 'əmməd xmāsax basər myās gōrax, trəklax bābax yəmmax 'ar'əd mawlūde dīdax zəllax basər qōm 'ōd la ki'atte təmmal bōma-xēt.

12 maġrəm 'əstaz ōlam pa'lūsa dīdax hōya kərre dīdax tamām mən kəs 'əstaz ōlam 'ilāhəd Yisrā'ēl 'ōd sēlax ləmṭalōle xē damāne dīde.

13 mərra: xazyāna ḥəsən bəd 'ēnox 'əstāzi did qam mdalxəšətti rāba did muḥkēlox 'əl ləbbəd g̊ēriyye dīdox, 'āna la kəsyan mux xa g̊ēriyye dīdox.

14 mərre ṭāla Bo'az wa'dəd 'īxāla: qrū 'axxa 'axlātən mən laxma, ṭamšātən pərtxa dīdax bəd xāla, yatwātən mən dəpən ġaẓāde, qlē ta gyānax ši qalatqat! qlēla xəlla swe'la umūzədla.

(bəd daw wa'da kəxlīwa 'īxāla gšātēwa, tamā? bsəbxāṭər la ṣahēwa. kṭamšīwale pərtxa dōhun go xāla, kəxlīwa. bəd daw wa'da laswa la mašqā'ōt la məndi, bəxlāl, laswa mən danya masā'əl. laxma umāya wēlu, 'eqa xāla gōzīwa ta gyānu, ḥōmeṣ, kṭamšīwale sabxāṭər hāwēlu hənna, te'avon, makušīwa 'īxāla. uqalatqat maylu? la kī'əttu 'āhət. xəṭṭe guġaẓdīla hēž ra'əzta- la xapča...gmēsēla gdēqīla gmēsē ži dōqa, kī'əṭṭe dōqa? gdāre gāwe unūra gōzi xēse qālēla; 'eqa kəxlīwa, gəmrīwala qalatqat, rāba basəmta-la. 'e naqla 'uzla ta gyāna Rut, xəlla žig gəmrāwala: bšōqan ta xmāsi žig blablanne ṭāla šud 'ap 'āya 'axla, mən daw qalatqat.)

15 qəmla ləmg̊amō'e, mōṣēle Bo'az ta ġolamwāsa dīde mərrēlu: ham bēn malōqe šud laqṭa, la manxəpətula.

16 ham mšalšōle ži mšalšəlētun ṭāla mən dastāsa ušōqētun šud laqṭa ulā nōzētun 'əbba.

17 'əlqəṭla go dašta hīl 'āṣərta, qam dēqālu mād mǧōmeʻla wēlu mux xa 'ulba saʻāre.
18 ṭ'ənna usēla 'əl bāžēr, xzēla xmāsa mā did mǧōmeʻla, mpəqla hulla ṭāla mən daw 'īxāla mād mōzədwāla mən swā'a dīda.
19 mərra ṭāla xmāsa: 'ēka tfəqlax, 'ēka mǧōmeʻlax 'ədyo, 'ēka 'uzlax 'anya masā'əl? hāwe frāqa dīdax mburxa! muḥkēla ta xmāsa mā did 'uzla 'əmme; mərra: šəmməd daw gōra 'ōd 'uzli 'əmme 'ədyo—Boʻaz īle šəmme.
20 mərra Naʻomi ta kalsa: mburxa-le 'āwa 'əstaz 'ōlam 'ōd la šuqle hawūsa dīde 'əmmət ṣāx u'əmməd mīse. mərra ṭāla Naʻomi: bala kī'ātən, 'āwa qarīwa dēni-le, 'aw gōra, mən maxəlṣāna dēni-le 'āwa.
21 mərra Rut Mō'āvēsa: ham did mərre ṭāli žig: 'əmməd ġolamwāsa dīdi laṭxātən hīl xalṣi kulle ġẓāda mād 'ətli (ču dūka xēt la 'āzat gēr).
22 mərra Naʻomi ta Rut kalsa: bāš īla brāti did napqātən 'əmməd ġolamwāsa dīde did la tafqi 'əbbax nāše nuxrāye bəd xa dašta xa xēta (kēfa sēle rāba).
23 'əlṭəxla bəd ġolamwāsəd Boʻaz ləmǧamō'e hīl xlāṣ ġẓādət saʻāre uġẓādət xəṭṭe. tūla 'əmmət xmāsa.

Chapter III

1 mərra ṭāla Naʻomi xmāsa: brāti, halā bṭa'yāna ṭālax xa nīxūsa 'ōd šapra 'əllax (yaʻni gəba magūrāla. hēš yalta-la! brāta-la!).
2 'atta halā Boʻaz nāš gyāna dēni-le, mən 'ōǧāġ dēni, 'ōd did wēlax 'əmməd ġolamwāsa dīde, hōna 'āwa bəmdāre 'əl bədər saʻāre 'əzlal (bədər kī'ət mayla? gmēse lamašal xa 'əmma gūniyye, trē 'əmma gūniyye, 'ē naqla 'əmməd hənna...'əmmət tūna kāye. laswa kombayn, laswa hənna, gmēsēwa xa hənna did sīwa, wēla 'uzta, dārēwala xē danya hatxa, 'əl pōxa, tūna gēzəlwa lxa 'al ġabara, usaʻāre pēšīwa 'əl xa 'al. 'ēha gəmrīwa bəmdāre, mdarōye).
3 bxēpātən, bdahnātən, blōšat ǧulle dīdax 'əl gyānax, kōšātən go bədra; la pāyəš 'aškara ta ču gōra hīl xlāṣa dīde 'əl 'īxāla u-ləštāya.
4 hāwe bəd dmāxa dīde yā'ātən 'əl day dūka 'ōd dāməx tāma, 'asyātən galyātən xē 'aqlāse udamxātən, 'ē naqla 'āwa maḥke ṭālax mā did 'ōzātən.
5 mərra ṭāla: mād 'amratti 'āna bōzāna.
6 kušla 'əl bədra (bəd lēle) 'uzla kud dax mād qam muṣyāla xmāsa.
7 xəlle Boʻaz uštēle, špərre ləbbe, sēle lədmāxa bəd dūmāyək did bədra, sēla Rut bəd hēdi glēla xē 'aqlāse udməxla.
8 wēle go palgəz-lēl 'ō gōra pət'om r'əlle, čfəlle, kxāze xa baxta wēla dməxta xē 'aqlāse ('āwa xšūle šēda-la, 'āwa la kī'e Rut īla, lēle-le).
9 mərre: mani-wat 'āhat? (hnəlle, zde'le), mərra: 'āna Rut ǧēriyye dīdox, parsētən damāne dīdox 'əl ǧēriyye dīdox, did maxəlṣāna wētən 'āhət.
10 mərre: mbōraxta 'āhat qam 'əstaz 'ōlam ya brāti, mušpərrax hawūsa dīdax 'ē xarēsa mən dē qamēsa 'əlləd la zəllax basər ǧwanqe, 'īkan faqīr 'īkan 'āšīr / 'īkan xīzan 'īkan dōlamand.
11 'atta brāti la zad'ātən, kulle mād 'amrātən ṭāli 'āna gōzən ṭālax, did kī'e

kulle tar'əd qōm dīdi did 'āhat 'ēšet-ḥayil wātən / did baxta ṣaddāqa wātən 'āhat.

12 'atta did ṭrōsa did maxəlṣāna wēna 'āna, bas 'īs maxəlṣāna bəš qarīwa mənni / 'atta 'omnam did 'āna wən maxəlṣāna, bas 'īs xa maxəlṣāna xēta bəš qarīwa mənni.

13 dmōx 'əzlal, hāwe bəd bənōke 'īkan maxləṣlax ṭōv (šəmme Ṭōv īle) maxləṣ, 'īkan lā 'āǧəble lmaxlōṣe dīdax maxəlṣənnax 'āna, ḥay qayyam 'əstaz 'ōlam; dmōx hīl bənōke.

14 dməxla xē 'aqlāse hīl bənōke, qəmla bəd qabəl fārəq gōra 'əl xōre ('ah, hēš hənna lēwa, čuxxa la kxāze zġas), mərre: la pāyəš 'aškara did nāše xāzēla did sēla baxta lbədra (ba'dēn maḥke 'əlle).

15 mərre: mēsēla məṭpaḥat (čarčafke, ṭabaqta) 'ōd 'əllax, dōq 'əbba. duqla 'əbba, tqəlle ṭāla 'əšta fətre sa'āre, maṭ'ənnu 'əlla, sēla lbāžēr.

16 sēla kəs xmāsa, mərra: mani-wat brāti? (m'ēka 'anya šu'āle mēsēlax?). muḥkēla ṭāla kulle mā did 'uzle ṭāla 'ō gōra.

17 gəmra: 'āwa hulleli 'anya mərre ṭāli.../ 'əšta fətre sa'āre 'anya hulle ṭāli gēmər: la 'āzātən spəqta kəs xmāsax (gēr 'ēba-le).

18 mərra: də-tū brāti hīl did pāyəš 'aškara 'ō xabra xāzax māṭō nāpəl 'ō məndi, did la gnāyəx 'ō gōra hīl lā xāləṣle šūla dīde 'ədyo.

Chapter IV

1 Bo'az ysəqle go tar'a tūle tāma, hōna gō'el ('aw did wēle bəš qarīwa mənne) 'urre, 'ō did muḥkēle Bo'az. mərrēle: flānkas, xlōf ysa tū 'axxa! xləfle utūle.

2 šqəlle 'əṣra gūre mən zaqēnīm (mən sawōne) did bāžēr mərre (ṭalōhun: rābōtay ysālōxun) tūn 'axxa, tūlu.

3 mərre ta dō maxəlṣāna (la mərrēle duġri 'əl Rut, mərre ta maxəlṣāna): xa zaviyəd dašta 'əswa ta 'axōnēni 'Elimelex, Na'omi gəba mzabnāla, 'ay did d'ərra mən daštəd Mō'āv ('ay zaviyəd dašta).

4 'āna mərri: kašfēna go nāsox bamrənnox: zōn ta gyānox barqul danya dīlu tīwe barqul zaqēnīm (sawōne) qōm dīdi (mux sahze kāwe), 'īkan maxəlṣētən maxləṣ, 'īkan la 'āǧəblox maxəlṣētən maḥki ṭāli byā'ēna, did lēs mənǧid mənnox ləmaxlōṣe u'āna wən basrox. mərre: la', 'āna maxəlṣən ('āna bzōnənna 'ay zaviyəd dašta).

5 mərre Bo'az gēmər: damməd zwāna dīdox 'ay dašta mən 'īz Na'omi [u]mən Rut Mō'āvēsa bax mīsa žig bzōnətta, lāzəm maqīmēta šəmməd mīsa 'əl məlk dīde.

6 mərre gō'el (maxəlṣāna): la, la mṣēna 'āna lmaxlōṣe ta gyāni, lēbi mahəlkēna 'əl məlk dīdi, maxləṣ 'āhət ta gyānox 'āl xulāṣi dīdi, did 'āna la mṣēna lmaxlōṣe.

7 'ēha wēla 'āde bəd Yisrā'ēl 'əl mzabōne u'əl mxalōpe, 'əl maqōme kulle məndi, šləple gōra pēlavte qam yāwəlla ta xōre, 'ēha wēla 'āde bəd Yisrā'ēl / 'əswa 'āde qamāye bəd Yisrā'ēl, 'aw did zāwən u...'əl gaola tamora, 'əl maqōme kulle xabra, qam šāləpla gōra 'āl pēlavte qam yāwəlla ta xōre, 'ēha wēla 'āde bəd Yisrā'ēl.

8 mərre gṓ'ēl ta Bo'az: zṓn ta gyānox 'āhət ('āna mrāšut dīdi gyāwənna kulla ṭālox), 'ay damma Bo'az šləple pēlavte.

9 mərre Bo'az ta zaqēnīm (ta sawṓne) [u]ta kulla ǧamā'a mād dīlu tīwe: sahze 'axtṓxun 'ədyo did zunni mād 'əswa ta 'Elimelex mā did 'əswa ta Xəlyon u-Maḥlon mən 'īz Na'omi.

10 ham 'āl Rut Mṓ'āvēsa bax Maḥlon zunni ta gyāni 'əl baxta 'əl maqṓme šəmməd mīsa 'əl məlk dīde, did lā qāṭe' šəmməd mīsa mən kəs 'axawāse umən tar'əd qṓm dīde. sahze 'axtṓxun 'ədyo.

11 mərru kulla qōm, kulla ǧamā'a bəd tar'a [u]sawṓne: sahze! (kullu pe 'eḥad), yāwəl 'əstaz 'ōlam 'āl dē baxta dasya 'əl bēsox mux Rāḥel mux Lē'a 'ōd bnēlu kuturtṓhun 'āl Bēt-Yisrā'ēl, 'uzlu xēla bəd 'Efrat ṣrəxlu šəmma bəd Betlaḥem.

12 hāwe bēsox mux bēs Pereṣ 'ōd yzəlla Tamar ta Yehuda, mən daw barzar'a 'ōd yāwəl 'əstaz 'ōlam ṭālox mən dē yalta 'ēha.

13 šqəlle Bo'az 'āl Rut pəšla ṭāle 'əl baxta sēle kəsla hulle 'əstaz 'ōlam ṭāla smāxa yzəlla brōna.

14 mərru baxtāsa ta Na'omi: mburxa 'əstaz 'ōlam 'ōd lā mubṭəlle maxəlṣāna 'ədyo, 'āse ṣrāxa šəmme bəd Yisrā'ēl.

15 hāwe ṭālax 'əl mad'ōrəd gyānax ləmdabōre sēvūsa dīdax, did kalsax 'ōd qam maḥibatta qam mhōyāle 'ōd wēla ṭālax 'āya bāš mən šṓ'a bnōne.

16 šqəlla Na'omi 'āl yāla qam daryāle go xpāqa pəšla ṭāle 'əl dahīne.

17 ṣrəxlu ṭāle šəwāwe šəmma līmāra: hwēle brōna ta Na'omi, ṣrəxlu šəmme 'Ōved, 'āwa bābəd Yīšay bābəd Dāvid.

18 'anya mawlūdəd Pāreṣ: Pereṣ muhwēle 'āl Ḥəṣron,

19 Ḥəṣron muhwēle 'āl Rām, Rām muhwēle 'āl 'Amminadav,

20 'Amminadav muhwēle 'āl Naḥšon, Naḥšon muhwēle 'āl Salma,

21 Salmon muhwēle 'āl Bo'az, Bo'az muhwēle 'āl 'Ōved,

22 'Ōved muhwēle 'āl Yīšay, Yīšay muhwēle 'āl Dāvid.

VI. Philological and Literary Studies

La Complainte sur la Peste de Pioz

Bruno Poizat

En l'an 2049 des Grecs, soit encore 1738 du Christ, le choléra ravagea le pays de Mossoul, et s'acharna en particulier sur le village de Pioz; ces épidémies étaient alors fréquentes, et nous aurions tout oublié de celle-ci si le prêtre (qàšà') du village, Sàwmo, n'avait composé quelques temps après un long poème à la mémoire de ses victimes.

La fonction de cette oeuvre était tout à la fois de tirer une leçon morale de cet épouvantable fléau, considéré comme une punition divine, et d'évoquer le souvenir des disparus; par l'intérêt historique de la description d'une communauté villageoise touchée par l'épreuve, et aussi par l'émotion que l'auteur a su nous faire partager, elle échappe aux poncifs de la tradition de littérature pieuse dont elle est issue; elle nous fait parcourir les ruelles du village, nous en laisse deviner les principaux personnages, elle décrit les souffrances des mourants, elle évoque la disparition d'un ami ou d'un être cher.

Mais ce qui, pour nous, en fait l'intérêt principal, c'est la langue dans laquelle elle a été écrite, car ce prêtre lettré, connu par ailleurs pour des compositions en syriaque, le langage savant des clercs, choisit de s'adresser à ses villageois dans leur dialecte araméen quotidien, le surèt. En effet, si, à partir du 19ème siècle fleurit une abondante poésie en araméen vernaculaire, fortement soumise aux influences des missions latines et américaines, puis à celle de la littérature européenne, les compositions anciennes en cette langue sont assez rares, et n'ont que très peu attiré l'attention du monde savant.

Pioz est situé à 45 km au nord de Mossoul, à peu près à 5 km à l'ouest d'Aïn Sifni, sur le front de collines qui borde au nord la plaine de Mossoul; il se compose de deux villages, celui du bas et celui du haut, que nous trouverons dans la complainte. Il était peuplé de chrétiens chaldéens et nestoriens jusqu'à la dernière guerre, ainsi que de kurdes yazidis; il est aujourd'hui exclusivement yazidi. On trouvera dans FIEY 1965, p. 473-474, quelques renseignements sur l'histoire ancienne du village ainsi que sur qàšà' Sàwmo, qui serait mort en 1742.

Dans cet article, je dresse un bref tableau des auteurs anciens en surèt; je décris les manuscrits contenant le texte de notre complainte; j'en analyse le contenu, ainsi que les procédés de versification; je fais quelques remarques

161

d'ordre linguistique, en particulier sur les formes verbales qu'on y trouve; enfin je publie 59 de ses strophes, sur un total de 248.

J'utilise le système suivant de transcription, signe pour signe, de l'alphabet syriaque tel qu'il est utilisé pour noter le surèt:

1. *consonnes*, dans l'ordre de l'alphabet:
' b g d h w z x T y k l m n s & p S q r š t

2. *voyelles*: zqàpà': à; ptàxà': a; zlàmà' qešyà': è; zlàmà' pšiTà': e; rwàxà': o; rḅàSà': u; xḅàSà': i

3. *autres signes*: rukàḵà': ˍ; magˆlyànà': ˆ; mtalqànà': /; syàm¨è': ¨; point pour emphatiques arabes: ◦

Pour être plus lisibles, ces signes, sauf rukàḵà', sont écrits après la lettre qu'ils affectent.

A - Collections de poèmes anciens en surèt

Plusieurs recueils de poésies sont conservés dans des bibliothèques accessibles aux chercheurs; voici ceux dont j'ai connaissance:

a - Collection SACHAU. Une importante collection de manuscrits en surèt, accompagnés d'une traduction arabe, rassemblée par Eduard Sachau au cours de deux voyages en Mésopotamie à la fin du siècle dernier, et conservée à la Staatsbibliothek de Berlin.

Elle a fait l'objet d'un catalogue détaillé (SACHAU 1899), et de deux publications (SACHAU 1896 et LIDZBARSKI 1896); dans la première, publication d'une traduction en surèt du "Chérubin et du Larron" de Narsaï, attribuée à David Kora (mort en 1889); le P. Jacques Rhétoré, qui a bien connu David, attribue cette pièce à un "Cacha Maroguen de Farachin," date inconnue; la deuxième publie deux poèmes plus anciens (123-3 et 123-6); signalons également la publication dans SOCIN 1882 de 121-6, un poème de t'omà' sinjàri, mort en 1860.

Trois volumes, dont la copie a été achevée en 1882 et 1883, contiennent des poésies d'époques diverses, 121-122, 123-124, 134.

b - Collection KATOLA. Deux volumes manuscrits copiés par Joseph Katola, évêque chaldéen de Tell Kaif, en 1889, acquis par Budge en 1891, et conservés au British Museum.

c - Collection MINGANA. Quatre compositions en surèt dans cette collection conservée à Birmingham, 567-F, 19-E, 51-C, 51-D; voir MINGANA 1933.

d - Collection RHÉTORÉ. Deux cahiers de poésies, conservés à la bibliothèque des PP. Dominicains de Mossoul, recopiés par le P. Jacques Rhétoré (né à la Charité-sur-Loire en 1841, mort à Mossoul en 1921); ce missionnaire est lui-même auteur de nombreuses compositions en surèt, qu'il signait yà&qo nuxràyà', "Jacques l'Etranger"; voir GALLAND 1921, HADDAD 1980, POIZAT 1982, CHEVALIER 1985.

e - Collections HABBI. Sous ce titre commode, je regroupe trois volumes utilisés par le P. Joseph Habbi dans son article (HABBI 1978): 1 - un manuscrit achevé en 1931 au couvent de N.D. des Semences, à Alqosh, aujourd'hui conservé à Bagdad; 2 - un manuscrit daté de 1938, conservé au Patriarchat Chaldéen de Mossoul; 3 - un manuscrit de 1933, dans une reproduction imprimée en facsimilé à Santiago, Californie, en 1977.

f - Editions imprimées. Les PP. Dominicains imprimèrent à Mossoul en 1896 (nouvelle édition 1954) un "Recueil de Chants Religieux en langue chaldéenne vulgaire"; il contient 64 cantiques assez courts, attribués à David Kora, mais qui sont en réalité du P. Rhétoré, qui était absent de Mossoul lors de cette édition, ainsi que d'autres poésies du 19ème siècle, et enfin la Complainte sur la Peste de qàšà' Sàwmo. Enfin, à la liste des publications que j'ai déjà signalées, il faut ajouter celle de 25 strophes de cette même complainte à la fin de RHETORE 1912.

Quand on regroupe ce qu'on trouve dans ces collections, on obtient la liste suivant d'auteurs antérieurs au 19ème siècle:

1 - mar xnanišo& dbet rustàqà'.

xnanišo& est le nom générique des évêques du district ("rustàqà'") de bet šamesdin, en Azerbaijan, entre Ushnu et la frontière turque; voir FIEY 1965, p. 785.

- sur la peste, signé et daté 1591, RHÉTORÉ.
- sur la pénitence, signé, sans date dans le texte; RHÉTORÉ, SACHAU 123-6 (éditée par LIDZBARSKI, p. 386-392), HABBI 1, 2; Habbi donne 1723 comme date de composition: l'auteur serait alors un successeur du précédent sur le siège de bet šamesdin.

2 - mar yuxànan, évêque de màwànà', en tergàwar (tout proche de šamesdin).

- sur la création, composé en 1662; SACHAU 121-8 & 123-8, KATOLA, RHÉTORÉ, HABBI 1, 2.

3 - qàšà' hormiz, d'Alqosh.

- sur la pénitence, SACHAU 123-4 (attribué à qàšà' yawsep jemdani, de Tell Kaif), MINGANA 51-D, HABBI 1, 3 (donne 1608 comme date de composition).

4 - qàšà' isràyel, d'Alqosh, fils du précédent.

Voir FIEY 1965, p. 394; le Prêtre Israel aurait eu quelques soixante-dix ans en 1611.

- sur la perfection de l'oeuvre divine, signé et daté 1611, SACHAU 123-5, RHÉTORÉ, HABBI 1, 2, 3.
- sur le péché, SACHAU 123-7, HABBI 1, 2 (avec 1611 comme date de composition).
- sur les bné' šmuni, signé et daté 1611, SACHAU 123-11 (mais avec 1632 comme date de composition), RHÉTORÉ, KATOLA.
- hymne à la Vierge, MINGANA 19-E.

Par ailleurs, Habbi attribue à cet auteur une complainte sur une épidémie qui aurait eu lieu à Alqosh en 1611; *mais* Rhétoré, après avoir cru que cette pièce appartenait à ce Prêtre Israel, ajoute la note suivante: "La pièce ne montre aucune date, mais on sait que la peste d'Alcoche eut lieu en 1828."

L'auteur s'est inspiré de la pièce de Cacha Somo sur la peste de Pioz et la copie assez souvent. On l'appelle Cacha Israel le Jeune pour le distinguer de Cacha Israel l'Ancien qui écrit en 1611 du Christ."

Il y eut toute une dynastie de qàšà' israyel à Alqosh, se succédant de père en fils, si bien qu'il n'est pas sûr que tous ces poèmes soient du même; Joseph Habbi signale que l'un d'eux composa en 1766 une traduction de l'évangile en surèt.

5 - qàšà' yawsep bar jamaleddin, de Tell Kaif.

Voir FIEY 1965 p. 359-360; la présence d'un prêtre Joseph est attestée à Tell Kaif en 1654 et 1664.

    - sur le plan divin, signé et daté 1662, SACHAU 123-10, KATOLA, HABBI 1, 2, 3.

    - sur la vérité révélée, SACHAU 123-1, KATOLA, HABBI 1, 3 (daté 1663).

    - l'enfance du Christ, d'après Warda, SACHAU 123-4.

    - sur les paraboles de l'Evangile, composé en 1666, SACHAU 123-3 (publié par LIDZBARSKI), MINGANA 51-C (attribué à qàšà' hormiz), HABBI 1, 3.

    - sur les paroles du Christ, SACHAU 123-2 (daté 1590), HABBI 1, 3 (daté 1668).

6 - qàšà' haydèni dgesà'

    - hymne à la Vierge, 1723, HABBI 1,2,3.

7. - sàmàšà' t'omà', fils de qàšà' &aḇdišo&.

    - hymne à la Vierge, 1744, MINGANA 567-F.

8 - qàšà' Sàwmo, de pioz.

    - sur la peste de Pioz, peu après 1738, SACHAU 121-13, KATOLA, RHÉTORÉ.

Parmi les auteurs postérieurs qu'on trouve dans ces collections, trois sont sans repères chronologiques: qàšà' marogen de farašin, qàšà' brahim de txumà', 'arsanis dmalek gˆamgˆànà'; pour les autres on obtient la liste suivante:

qàšà' hudèni, de txumà' (1825)

qàšà' israyel le jeune, d'Alqosh (1828)

qàšà' damianos, du Couvent (1832, 1855, 1856), qàšà' 'ablahad du Couvent, qàšà' &aḇdišo& du Couvent (ce couvent est celui de Rabban Hormiz, à Alqosh, restauré en 1808)

t'omà' tektek sinjàri (mort en 1860, voir FIEY 1965, p. 371)

qàšà' dawud de Barzané (mort à Kanifalan vers 1871, voir FIEY 1965, p. 169-171 et 374)

šàmàšà' yonan, de txumà' (1870)

qàšà' denxà', de Baz (1884)

dawud korà' (l'aveugle) de Ba Nuhadra (mort à Mossoul en 1889)

išàyà' de Tchamba (1908, 1910)

la poétesse henna an-nabiyah, de Tell Kaif (1911)

šàmàšà' kˆonà', de Teleskof (1913)

ya&qo nuxràyà' (le P. Jacques Rhétoré, né en 1841, mort en 1921).

B - Les manuscrits de la complainte

Pour notre poème sur la peste de Pioz, nous disposons donc de trois manuscrits, SACHAU, KATOLA et RHÉTORÉ, que je note respectivement S, K, R, de l'imprimé des dominicains, et des 25 strophes de la grammaire du P. Rhétoré que je note respectivement I et G.

Le manuscrit Sachau S

C'est celui que je prends comme base de l'édition; il est complet, à part un télescopage entre les strophes 9 et 10; je ne le corrige que lorsqu'il y a erreur de rime, ou bien dans le compte des pieds, ou si le sens est tout à fait défectueux.

C'est un volume relié en 8, avec 15 lignes par page d'une belle écriture chaldéenne; il a été achevé à Tell Kaif, en 1883, par le diacre Francis Mèrè; comme dans tous les manuscrits de poésie anciens, les strophes sont écrites bout à bout, sans aller à la ligne: un double point sépare les vers, et un quadruple les strophes.

Le système d'orthographe est celui qui était traditionellement utilisé pour noter le surèṯ avant que, sous l'influence des missions protestantes et catholiques, on y introduisit des prétentions savantes et étymologiques. Il est le plus phonétique possible, avec toutefois une dérogation constante, qui est cet ' ('alap) qui termine obligatoirement chaque substantif, suivant l'habitude araméenne ancienne; cet ' note aussi le pronom masculin singulier de la troisième personne affixé à la particule *l*-; les formes verbales sont en général écrites en un seul mot, ce qui correspond à la langue parlée, qui en fait une seule unité d'accent. Le trait annullateur est peu fréquent. Le & est très souvent remplacé par ', et le ḇ par w ou o; le x est une rareté: il est presque systématiquement remplacé par ḵ, qui est d'ailleurs bien plus lisible, et permet une jolie calligraphie en finale.

Ce manuscrit est accompagné d'une traduction en arabe, faite à Mossoul, en 1882, par le diacre Armya Chamir d'Ankawa, dans une écriture difficilement lisible, avec une ponctuation négligée; on y rencontre souvent des mots surèṯ ou kurde; c'est une traduction rapide, mot-à-mot, qui, lorsque le texte original est obscur, le transcrit fidèlement par une égale obscurité.

Le manuscrit Katola K

Ce manuscrit est très semblable au précédent; il a été écrit dans un village voisin et à la même époque; il lui manque les strophes 181-190 et 225; lorsqu'il y a divergence entre les différentes sources, K et S son en général d'accord par rapport aux autres, à l'exception de la strophe 42.

K a une écriture encore plus phonétique que celle de S, marquée de particularités dialectales de la plaine de Mossoul; u pour i ou e: lušànà' pour lišànà' (24c, 25a), nuqbà' pour neqḇà' (84b); T pour t, Tar'à' pour tar&à' (200a), qu'on trouve aussi dans S (170a), Telaṭ pour telat (179a, K, S), etc. Plus remarquable est l'emploi, à la première personne du pluriel, du pronom affixe sujet, normalement affixé au participe, à la place du pronom affixe objet, affixé à la préposition l: là' preš luḵ (48a), là' 'wed luḵ (64c, 65a), "nous

n'avons pas séparé," "nous n'avons pas fait," et non pas "tu n'as pas séparé,"
"tu n'as pas fait"; ces formes sont reprises exceptionellement par K là' preš lek̲,
là' 'wed lek̲, et même par I là' &bed luk̲.

Le manuscrit Rhétoré R

Ce manuscrit, qui semble appartenir à une tradition différente, a été recopié
sur un manuscrit de Gawar (aujourd'hui Yüksekova, en Turquie, près de la
frontière iranienne); il est possible que le P. Rhétoré ne l'ait pas transcrit tel
quel, car l'écriture est assez conforme aux règles du "soureth régulier" qu'il
expose dans sa grammaire: les mots sont le plus proche possible de leur forme
syriaque, d'où usage fréquent du trait annullateur; x et & sont maintenus, le
pronom de troisième personne est h et non ': griš lèh pour grešlè' dans K et S;
de même h/ wà' h/ wà' pour wàwà' dans K et S, etc.; il est également possible
que cette orthographe corresponde tout simplement à celle préconisée par la
mission de l'American Board d'Urmi: le P. Rhétoré s'est plaint plus d'une fois
du peu de cas qu'on faisait dans la plaine de Mossoul de l'orthographe des
livres en surèt̲ imprimés en Perse.

Le texte de la grammaire du P. Rhétoré G

Le P. Rhétoré a publié, en appendice de RHÉTORÉ 1912, un choix
particulièrement heureux de textes en surèt̲,   ḑont 25 strophes de la
complainte: 119, 124-134, 138-143, 147, 209-211, 213, 215, 247; c'est là que je
l'ai rencontrée pour la première fois. Cette version reprend R, en en
normalisant entièrement l'orthographe suivant le système préconisé par la
grammaire; elle est accompagnée d'une traduction en français.

L'édition imprimée I

Le P. Rhétoré avait peu d'estime pour cette édition: "L'impression se fit
sans m'informer et on se servit de textes écrits par des scribes ignorants
auxquels joignirent leur lumières des correcteurs sans méthode...les Fables et
les Cantiques furent imprimés sous le nom de David l'Aveugle qui m'avait
aidé dans mes compositions, et on donna à cela pour raison que grâce au nom
de David ces livres seraient mieux accueillis par les indigènes."

Le texte de notre complainte y est en effet fort maltraité: rimes
défectueuses, mauvais décompte de pieds; elle donne beaucoup de versions
aberrantes, à la limite du non-sens, avec une tendance systématique à
exagérer le nombre des morts; elle suit plus R que K et S; il lui manque six
strophes, 120, 125, 243-246.

Son mérite aura été cependant de maintenir vivant le souvenir de l'oeuvre
de qàšà' Sàwmo, et j'ai des amis qui se souviennent l'avoir chantée, dans leur
jeunesse, au petit séminaire, ou bien l'avoir lue lors de veillées familiales.

C - Analyse du poème

La Complainte sur la Peste de Pioz se compose de 248 strophes,
comprenant chacune trois vers de sept pieds; c'est une disposition peu
fréquente dans les oeuvres que nous avons considérées, dont les strophes ont
en général quatre vers.

Le décompte des pieds n'est pas toujours extrêmement rigoureux, et pour en trouver sept il faut parfois avaler les particules comme w ou d, ou bien au contraire les prononcer. La langue fournit au poète divers procédés pour accorder ce nombre de pieds; par example, il a la faculté de faire ou de ne pas faire l'accord du participe passif au féminin singulier ou au pluriel; il peut employer une form légère lay, ou contraire une forme lourde layhi, pour le pronom affixe de troisième personne du pluriel; il peut aussi user des prépositions lwàt- ou làl- au lieu d'un simple l-; plus curieusement, il semble ne pas attribuer à l'insertion de wà (h/wà' dans R) dans le parfait la valeur d'un passé que lui donne toutes les grammaires; par example, en 177b, pleTlè', wl'el iseq wàlè', "il est sorti et il est monté vers le haut," et non pas "il était monté"; il faut considérer cette forme comme un équivalent de iseqlè', sauf qu'elle donne un pied de plus. On a de même de nombreuses alternances qTelè', qTelwàlè'.

Le trois vers de chaque strophe riment, et il est clair que l'auteur a recherché la rime la plus riche possible, chose qui lui est facilitée par l'uniformité des flections verbales et nominales en surèt.

Un procédé de versification constant dans la première partie, qui est également utilisé pour les passages narratifs de la deuxième (décrivant le passage de la peste dans le village), consiste à répéter le dernier vers d'une strophe dans le premier de la strophe suivante, en en modifiant l'ordre des mots, en remplaçant un terme par un synonyme, ou bien en variant un accord, de manière à changer la rime. Cette figure de style est fréquente dans ce genre de composition, mais elle est ici assez lourde, puisque, comme il n'y a que trois vers par strophe, presque tout est dit deux fois. Elle permet au linguiste d'observer d'intéressantes permutations; on y constate une extrême mobilité, une très grande liberté dans l'agencement des mots, en particulier dans les formes verbales, bien plus grande que ce qu'on trouve dans un texte d'aujourd'hui; cela semble indiquer que le système verbal du surèt, dans la plaine de Mossoul, était moins figé du temps de qàsà' Sàwmo que maintenant, mais il faut aussi faire la part de la licence poétique, qui peut produire des formes artificielles.

La monotonie de ce procédé est interrompue par un deuxième, dans l'introduction de la deuxième partie, dans les énumérations de cette même partie, et dans la conclusion, qui consiste à introduire une série de strophes en parallèle, de même structure, et sur la même rime.

Passons maintenant au contenu du poème; comme le dit, dans une note, le P. Rhétoré "Le travail de Cacha Somo comprend 246 strophes [en fait 248], dont les 118 premières forment des préliminaires où sont exposés les causes morales du fléau, les péchés du peuple. C'est un thème que les poètes soureth aiment à exploiter, mais qui est ici très encombrant."

1-15 Introduction, invocation à la Trinité

Ensuite vient l'énumération des péchés, dans un ordre quelque peu sinueux:

15-20 Irrespect de la foi

20-33 Oppression des pauvres, arrogance, avarice
34-42 Indignité des prêtres et des diacres
43-51 Insouciance, jalousie, etc.
52-56 Irrespect de l'eucharistie
57-73 Querelles, mépris des pauvres et des prisonniers, avarice
74-90 Péchés sexuels
91-96 Les tourments de l'enfer
97-106 Débauches, beuveries, manquement au jeûne
107-114 Irrespect des chefs, calomnie, avarice, manque de charité
115-124 Annonce du fléau, avec sa date en 119 (2049 de l'ère des Séleucides, soit 1738 de notre ère)
125-130 La peste part de Aqra (100 km au nord-est de Mossoul, 50 km à l'est de Pioz), tue 40.000 personnes à Mossoul, et s'installe à Pioz le 20 avril.
131-137 Trois maisons touchées par la peste, qui, pour une raison inconnue, sont mises en avant au lieu de figurer avec les autres: celles de šàbo, 'aprem, 'abdàlà'.
138-151 Les gens s'enfuient du village, l'épidémie s'intensifie.

Ensuite la peste parcourt le village, maison par maison, en suivant un itinéraire un peu confus:

152-155 Elle détruit les maisons de 'esxaq, 'abu son frère, mušé'; elle tue 80 personnes
156-159 Dans le quartier d'en bas, elle frappe ḳošàbu et hormez
160-184 Elle s'acharne sur le village, et détruit les maisons de Sàwmu (= Slilà'), ḳawšu, qogˆà', 'adam, &aḅdiš et šem'on, boṭà', màmu, yàwsep, hormez, sa&yà', garibu, bašo, xanà', celle du chef du village (gˆem&à', šonè' sa femme ?), gˆamu, Sàwmu, ḳàtu, ḳàwšàbu
185-210 Elle va vers le haut, s'installe chez &aḅdiš, chez les bi qàšà' (les prêtres), yàldà', bedè'; elle revient vers le bas chez yàwnan, dàwedu, gˆerbo, kanun, le diacre yàwnu, meSrè' (une femme chef de famille !), 'elià', "le Persan," le diacre matè'; elle remonte du coté de la montagne chez xanu &abdàlà', yàldà' le montagnard, šem'on d'Alqosh, xaydu, 'àwro, hormez, mezà'
211-225 Les souffrances des mourants: 350 morts (strophe 213); mort des enfants, des adolescents, des jeunes femmes
226-241 Les effets de la maladie: troubles de la vue, ivresse, soif, larmes, fièvre; sépultures sommaires
242-248 Conclusion: souhaits d'une vie meilleure pour les défunts, et pour les auditeurs.

D - Les formes verbales dans la complainte

Le moment est venu de faire quelques remarques sur la langue de notre poème; il est en effet intéressant de tenter quelques comparaisons entre l'usage présent et un texte vieux de plus de 200 ans, écrit dans le dialecte de la plaine de Mossoul, qui est celui de la majorité des araméophones, mais qui est aussi celui qui a été le moins étudié.

Pour ne pas trop prendre de place, je ne parlerai que du système verbal, qui est d'ailleurs la partie du langage la plus expressive, et la plus délicate à décrire, du surèt; qàšà' Sàwmo a habilement joué de ses possibilités combinatoires; il permute des formes presque semblables, ou bien différentes, mais de même sens, ou bien il varie les accords, inverse l'ordre des composants, pour briser un vers, pour en constituer un autre, de même assonance, mais de rythme différent; ou bien encore il met en parallèle une série de strophes avec des terminaisons verbales toutes semblables, ce qui donne, grace à ce procédé répétitif, de l'ampleur à son sujet.

On sait que le néo-araméen a abandonné l'ancienne conjugaison sémitique, à l'exception de l'impératif, qui apparait deux fois dans la complainte: 88c (au négatif! voir MACLEAN 1895, p. 147) là' hwàw ḵayàr̈è', "ne soyez pas chercheurs," 215a ḵzaw, "voyez."

Il l'a remplacée par une nouvelle, formée de participes actifs ou passifs auxquels sont agglutinés des pronoms affixes; cette "nouvelle conjugaison" n'est d'ailleurs pas si neuve pour l'araméen; elle est bien attestée en syriaque. Les participes ont les flections de l'ancien état absolu de l'araméen (gdimà', ou forme abrégée) qui, en surèt, ne s'applique plus aux substantifs: dans cette langue ce sont de pures formes verbales. Pour cela, je suivrai l'excellente terminologie de Rhétoré, et j'appellerai cette conjugaison "conjugaison paradigmatique."

C'est que cette conjugaison est en concurrence avec une autre conjugaison encore plus récente, qui est formée avec le verbe h/wàyà', être (conjugué paradigmatiquement!), et de véritables substantifs, portant les flections de l'ancien état emphatique, c'est-à-dire les flections nominales normales en surèt, et qui peuvent être l'adjectif verbal, le nom verbal, ou même le nom d'agent! Elle est qualifiée de "non-paradigmatique" car la construction en est si mobile et si explicite qu'on hésite à la tabuler comme une conjugaison figée. Si d'ailleurs on le fait, on a du mal à voir où il faut s'arrêter, et en combinant toutes les possibilités on finit par obtenir des formes composées et surcomposées de valeur toute théorique.

Dans certains dialectes d'Iran et du Hakkari, cette conjugaison non-paradigmatique est devenue la façon la plus naturelle de s'exprimer, si bien qu'elle finit par se figer en des formes véritablement verbales, qui sont décrites comme telles dans les monographies de GARBELL 1965 et JACOBI 1973; il convient toutefois de noter chez ces auteurs une tendance à rapprocher des formes de sens voisins ou identiques, mais de bases différentes (par exemple des parfaits). Cette façon de faire serait tout-à-fait inadaptée au verbe de notre complainte, où ces formes, moins fréquentes, sont plutôt des périphrases, dont tous les composants sont bien isolés; d'ailleurs MACLEAN 1895 signale la persistance de la conjugaison paradigmatique comme une particularité dialectale de la plaine de Mossoul, qui ne pouvait qu'être plus accentuée à l'époque ancienne.

Au cours de la longue histoire, l'araméen nous a permis d'observer toute une évolution de la conjugaison sémitique; il semble que nous soyons témoins, à l'époque contemporaine, d'un nouveau phénomène de substitution; pour le décrire, il est impérieux de classer les formes verbales par leur constituants et non par leur sens; et il est vain de distinguer des nuances de sens ou d'emploi entre formes concurrentes: bien que ce soit contraire à un principe d'économie, il faut admettre, au moins dans une phase transitoire, l'emploi de formes de bases très distinctes mais équivalentes quant au sens.

Pour permettre au lecteur de s'y retrouver, je vais dresser un tableau des participes et des noms verbaux intervenant dans la conjugaison, pour les quatre formes dérivées du verbe; en général la forme I est neutre, intransitive, la forme II est active, la forme III est causative; quant à la forme IV, elle est réservée aux racines quadrilittères, qui sont souvent des doublets de racines de trois lettres. Ce tableau est totalement artificiel, d'abord parce que le verbe paradigme gràšà', tirer, n'est pas dans notre texte, et qu'il n'a pas de formes II et III attestées; son doublet gargošé' est dans MACLEAN 1901 et ORAHAM 1943.

Forme I	masc. sing.	fem. sing.	pluriel
participe actif	gàreš	gàršà'	gàrši
participe passif	greš	grišà'	griši
adjectif verbal	grišà'	greštà'	grišè'
nom verbal	gràšà'		
nom d'agent	garàšà'		

Forme II			
participe actif	mgareš	mgaršà'	mgarši
participe passif	mgureš	mguršà'	mgurši
adjectif verbal	mguršà'	mgureštà'	mguršè'
nom verbal	mgarošè'		
nom d'agent	mgaršànà'		

Forme III			
participe actif	magreš	mageršà'	magerši
participe passif	mugreš	mugeršà'	mugerši
adjectif verbal	mugrešà'	mugreštà'	mugrešè'
nom verbal	magrošè'		
nom d'agent	mageršànà'		

Forme IV			
participe actif	gargeš	gargešà'	gargeši
participe passif	gurgeš	gurgešà'	gurgeši
adjectif verbal	gurgešà'	gurgeštà'	gurgešè'
nom verbal	gargošè'		
nom d'agent	gargešànà'		

La conjugaison paradigmatique
Avant toutes choses, il faut donner la liste des pronoms:

	isolé	affixe sujet	affixe objet
1° pers. m. s.	'ànà'	-en	li
1° pers. f. s.	'ànà'	-an	li
2° pers. m. s.	'at	-et	luḵ
2° pers. f. s.	'at	-at	laḵ
3° pers. m. s.	'àhu	-φ	lè'
3° pers. f. s.	'àhi	-à'	là'
1° pers. p.	'aḵni	-eḵ	lan, leḵ, luḵ
2° pers. p.	'aḵtu	-itu	lawḵu
3° pers. p.	'anhi, 'ànay	-i	lay, layhi

Les premières et deuxièmes personnes du singulier ne figurent pas dans notre texte, et sont données à titre indicatif; il en est de même de la forme 'àhi, qui est donnée dans MACLEAN 1901 comme le pronom isolé de 3ème pers. f. s. à Alqosh, et qui correspond bien à 'àhu.

Les pronoms affixe sujet sont affixés à un participe actif ou passif; à la troisième personne, ils ne sont rien d'autre que les flections de l'état absolu de ce participe; aux autres personnes, il s'agit de cette flection combinée avec une forme tronquée des pronoms isolés.

Les affixes objets sont donnés en combinaison avec la particule l-, comme ils interviennent dans la conjugaison; affixés à un substantif, ils deviennent pronom possessifs (dans certain dialectes, les troisièmes personnes singulier sont alors différentes; ce n'est pas le cas dans notre texte; toutefois les possessifs seront systématiquement écrits -èh, -àh, même dans S ou K).

La forme pleine de la conjugaison paradigmatique est composée de deux groupes: participe + sujet 1 + objet; on peut insérer wà (h/ wà' chez R, car cette particule appartiendrait à la racine h/ wàyà', être) entre les deux groupes, ce qui, en principe, donne un passé; enfin, et dans le cas du participe actif seulement, on peut donner à la forme une valeur modale en la faisant précéder de l'une des particules k-, bed, kem.

La conjugaison du participe passif est une tournure originellement passive, où l'agent de l'action décrite est le pronom objet introduit par la particule l-; cela est particulièrement net quand on la rencontre sous la forme pleine, par exemple dans MAROGULOV 1935 p. 45 & 59, ou SIMONO 1974 p. 38-43, où le pronom affixe sujet désigne le patient de l'action. Cette forme pleine n'est possible qu'avec un verbe transitif: avec un verbe intransitif, elle est réduite à une forme minimale participe + 1 + pronom objet; mais aussi, la plupart du temps, seule apparait cette forme minimale, et, dans notre texte, il n'y a pas de pronoms sujets de 1ème ou 2ème personnes affixés au participe passif.

Le sujet du participe, c'est-à-dire le patient de l'action, peut être exprimé par un nom, qui est placé avant ou après le verbe: 8c haymànuṭà' mḵulpàlan 9a mḵulpàlan haymànuṭà', "altérée par nous la foi=nous avons altéré la foi";

suivant la logique de la forme pleine, le participe devrait s'accorder avec son sujet, mais, dans bien des dialectes, cet accorde ne se fait plus et le participe reste au masculin singulier; dans celui de la Complainte, cet accord est devenu facultatif, et on constate qu'il se fait à peu près une fois sur deux; il est difficile de dégager des raisons qui font qu'il y ait accord ou pas accord, et en particulier la place du sujet ne semble pas avoir d'influence; parfois on peut voir dans cet accord la valeur d'un rappel du sujet: 148c wbàt˙è' dkabir˙è' ksep̲l̲è' 149a k̲sep̲l̲è' bàt˙è' wk̲riwilè', "les maisons de nombreuses gens elle a écrasé(es)," "elle a écrasé les maisons et les a ruinées"; mais en général il semble aléatoire, ou guidé par des raisons de versification.

Dans cette forme minimale, le sens passif se perd quelque peu, et d'ailleurs l'opposition entre actif et passif n'est pas toujours très nette; par exemple, notre texte emploie en 192c sTemlè', et son dérivé II en 175c musTemlé' avec le sens de "il a démoli"; mais en 120c, sTem lay signifie "elles se sont effondrées." Toutefois notre Complainte n'en est pas encore au point de produire des formes participe passif + 1 + pronom objet + 1 + pronom objet, dénoncée comme fautive par SIMONO 1974 (voir aussi ses remarques sur l'accord du participe), ou même participe passif + 1 + pronom sujet + 1 + pronom objet, comme dans le dialecte décrit par JACOBI 1973, où participe passif + 1 fonctionne comme un participe actif.

Si l'agent de l'action, celui qui est représenté par le pronom objet, est un nom, la façon normale de s'exprimer est de mettre ce nom en tête, en maintenant le pronom comme rappel: 123a dešman pleTlè', "l'ennemi il est sorti"; 123c màwtànà' bàtan dbeqlè', "la peste nos maisons elle a pris" (et non "prises"!); mais en 6b, 74b-c, 76c, notre complainte remplace ce pronom par le nom, et obtient une construction nom-sujet + participe passif + 1 + nom-objet, qui est logique, mais qui n'est signalée dans aucune grammaire.

Le sens premier de cette forme est celui d'un parfait: elle désigne une action qui s'est accomplie; par un glissement naturel, elle a acquis une connotation de passé, et a aussi la valeur d'un prétérite, d'un temps de narration, et c'est avec cette valeur qu'elle est omniprésente dans notre Complainte. Comme je l'ai déja dit, l'insertion de wà ne lui donne pas la valeur d'un plus-que-parfait; dans notre texte elle ne fait que spécifier cette valeur de passé, et les formes avec ou sans wà sont équivalentes.

La conjugaison du participe actif est moins usée que celle du participe passif; sa forme minimale est participe actif + pronom sujet; si le sujet est exprimé par un nom, il y a toujours accord; l'objet est exprimé par 1 + pronom ou 1 + nom, mais, dans le cas d'un nom, le 1 peut être omis. Le sens est celui d'un imparfait, d'une action non-achevée, et l'insertion de wà a toujours valeur d'un passé.

En l'absence d'indicateur modal, cette forme a la valeur d'un subjonctif, d'un optatif ou d'un jussif: 248c lmalkutèh màwseqlawk̲u, "dans son royaume qu'il vous fasse monter"; avec l'indicateur k-, qui est parfois omis, surtout au négatif, on obtient un indicatif, qui prend souvent une valeur de "présent général": 10b hàdak̲ kmàwdè' kresTyànà', "ainsi confesse le chrétien"; avec b-ou bed on obtient un futur, un éventuel: 94a bmaprešàlay xaTàÿ'è', "elle fera fondre les pécheurs"; enfin la particule kem a l'effet curieux de transformer cette construction en un parfait, en un équivalent du participe passif avec permutation du sujet et de l'objet: 116c kem šà̲beq lan (équivalent de šb̲iqex lè') "il nous a laissés"; cette tournure est bien attestée dans les grammaires, où on indique qu'elle est surtout employée dans la plaine de Mossoul.

La conjugaison non-paradigmatique

On trouve dans la Complainte une forme de sens progressif (l'action est en cours d'accomplissement) ayant pour base le nom verbal: verbe h/ wàyà + b + nom verbal; 104 wek̲wà' beSyàmà', "nous étions en train de jeûner"; dans certains dialectes, cette forme est l'expression normale de l'imparfait, mais elle est loin de constituer une forme verbale figée dans celui de notre texte; on ne peut s'empêcher de la rapprocher de 101a zmeran bštàyà', "nous avons chanté en buvant," 138a kmelè' bqTàlà, "il a parachevé sa tuerie," 138b pešlè' ber'àlà', "il s'est mis à trembler," que personne ne songerait à tabuler dans la conjugaison des verbes štàyà', qTàlà', r&àlà'; de plus, notre Complainte omet souvent le verbe auxiliaire, le nom verbal nu suffisant à exprimer la concomittance: 25b be&šànà', "et de croître," 59a dlà' k̲zàyà', "qui ne voyait pas," 233b beg ˆràyà', "et de couler."

Quant à l'adjectif verbal, il se comporte partout comme un véritable adjectif; à la rigueur on pourrait voir une forme verbale dans 12a wewà' nk̲ità' "il était descendu"; il est parfois juxtaposé à un nom, sans verbe auxiliaire; il sert à former le passif, avec le verbe h/wàyà' ou le verbe pyàšà' comme auxiliaire 96c pešlè' nešyà', "il a été oublié," 103a là' wèwà' qbeltà', "elle n'était pas acceptée" (et non pas: elle n'avait pas accepté).

On pourrait mettre dans la conjugaison non-paradigmatique une autre tournure employée par notre poète, qui forme un imparfait avec le nom d'agent (qui est plus un "faiseur" qu'un "faisant") et le verbe auxiliaire: 41c waywà' mar̈ekšànè' "ils étaient entraineurs," 43a mbaqràr̈'è' là' hàwaywà', "questionneurs ils n'étaient pas," 88c là' hwàw k̲ayàr̈'e`' "ne soyez pas chercheurs." Peut-on considérer qu'il s'agit de l'ébauche d'une nouvelle conjugaison que, finalement, la langue n'a pas retenu? Le système verbal du surèt̲ finit par ressembler à un jeu de construction qui se développe à l'infini, et il faut bien que l'usage fasse des choix!

En conclusion, notre poème connait fort peu de ces formes non-paradigmatiques qui sont si envahissantes dans les dialectes du nord, et il semble avoir conservé à la conjugaison paradigmatique toute sa mobilité primitive; est-ce un signe d'archaïsme? On trouvera cette conclusion quelque peu téméraire, puisqu'elle repose sur l'étude d'un texte court, et de nature très particulière; pour avoir des bases plus solides, il n'y a que deux directions à suivre: éditer plus de textes anciens, étudier d'avantage les dialectes iraqiens.

Texte (Voir l'appendice, p. 199)

durekṯà' &el màwṯànà' dgaw pioz
dilà' dqàšà' Sàwmo

Complainte sur la peste de
Pioz de qàšà' Sàwmo

1 šuḇxà' lšemà' dgaḇàlan
mà' Taḇtà' hḇelèh Tàlan
msabab &àwlan w&amàlan

Louange au nom de notre créateur
Quelle récompense il nous a donnée
Pour nos fautes et nos oeuvres

2 msabab &àwlan uḵT˙iàtan
p°andan wp°e&lan wḵaS˙làtan
rugẕèh mšuderè' lwàtan

A cause de nos fautes et de nos péchés
Nos méfaits, nos actes et nos vices
Il a envoyé sur nous sa colère

3 lwàtan rugzèh mšuderè'
šaḇTèh &àwlan mquderè'
wbàlèh menan muḵderè'

Sur nous il a envoyé sa colère
Il a mesuré son baton à nos fautes
Et détourné de nous sa sollicitude

4 muḵderè' menan pàtèh
demḵulp°ilan 'ur ˙ḵàtèh
wlà' 'raylan tanàyàtèh

Il a détourné de nous son visage
Nous qui nous sommes écartés de ses voies
Et n'avons pas reçu ses paroles

—

8 kresTyànuṯà' ḵsip°à' lan
ma&modiṯà' tlip°à' lan
haymanuṯà' mḵulpàlan

Le christianisme, nous l'avons aboli
Le baptême, nous l'avons souillé
La foi, nous l'avons altérée

9 mḵulpàlan haymanuṯà'
deqn˙omè' detliṯàyuṯà'
bḵà' kyànà' d'alàhuṯà'

Nous avons altéré la foi
Aux personnes de la Trinité
En une seule substance divine

10 tliṯàyuṯà' bxàd/ kyànà'
hàdaḵ kmàwdè' kresTyànà'
tànyàṯà' w&àqel wgyànà'

Trinité en une seule substance
Ainsi confesse le chrétien
Dans sa parole, sa pensée et son âme

11 brà' melṯà' '/nàšà' lḇešlèh
b'/nàšutèh tray là' pešlé'
&almà' bdemèh mqudešlè'

Le Fils-Verbe s'est vêtu en homme
En s'humanisant il n'est pas devenu deux
Il a sanctifié le monde par son sang

12 mqudšàlè' bdemèh briṯà'
Tà' hàdaḵ wèwà' nḵiṯà'
dmanTep°wàlan meḵTiṯà'

Il a sanctifié la création par son sang
C'est pour cela qu'il est descendu
Pour qu'il nous lave du péché

13 meḵTiṯà' dmanTep°wàlan
puq˙dànè' nSuḇ lè' Tàlan
dmaqešTeḵwà' p°&àlan

Du péché pour qu'il nous lave
Il a établi pour nous des commandements
Afin que nous rectifions nos actes

—

86 bpuqdànà' 'itwà' ḵṯiḇà'
dkud de'weḏlay šulà' ḵriwà'
'anhi wneqḇà' raḡ miwà'

Dans les commandements il y avait d'écrit
Que tous ceux qui ont fait chose honteuse
Eux et la femme on devait lapider

87 raḡ miwàlay zanày˙è'
b'ànay šar˙&è' qamày˙è'
d&amà' debnay˙isràyel

Ils lapidaient les fornicateurs
Dans ces premières lois
Du peuple des fils d'Israel

88 rḡ àmà' 'eṯwà' lgayàr˙è'
wmàran mèrè' bbašàrèh
bbaḵtà' là' hwàw ḵayàr˙è'

Lapidation était le sort des adultères
Et Notre Seigneur a dit dans son évangile
"Ne recherchez pas la femme!"

89 'imà' dḵerè' wmšuhyàlè'
xàS°er blebèh giràlè'
wgihànà' 'iriṯàlè'

Dès qu'on l'a cherchée et convoitée
On est prêt dans son coeur à commettre l'adultère
Et on a mérité l'enfer

90 ham merwàlè' Tà' mušè'
kud dTàye& lebèh l'en˙šè'
rugzi 'elèh bed qàšè'

Il avait aussi dit à Moïse
Quiconque dont le coeur penche vers les femmes
Ma colère sur lui sera dure

91 rugzi 'elèh bed qàwè' Ma colère sur lui sera forte
ķu gam̄'è' wģ'ehw̄'è' bthàwè' Sous chagrins et tourments il sera
wbķartà' bnurà' bed mTàwè' A la fin dans le feu il grillera

116 Tà' hàdak pešlan mlom̄'è' Ainsi étions-nous fautifs
dwèlan lšar&èh Toàlomè' Nous qui étions rebelles à sa loi
kem šàḫeqlan yatum̄'è' Il nous a abandonnés orphelins
117 yatum̄'è' kemšàḫeqlan Orphelins il nous a abandonnés
wmàrà' là' kemnàpeqlan Le Seigneur ne nous a pas délivrés
wbmàwṭànà' kem sàxeqlan Dans la peste il nous a broyé
118 Kem sàxeqlan bmàwṭànà' Il nous a broyé dans la peste
ķà' quyà' wķà' xemṭànà Une forte et une ardente
ķzaḫnà' dmušé' Tuḫànà' Comme au temps du bienheureux Moïse
119 bšàtà' d"mT lmenyànà' L'année 2049 selon le compte
d'àleķsandros qarnànà' D'Alexandre le Cornu
npelè' 'àḏi màwṭànà' A eu lieu cette peste
120 bay šà'tà' dmalk̄'è' Tolemlay Cette année où les rois ont opprimé
wdarqul deķdàd̄'è' qemlay Et se sont dressés l'un contre l'autre
bmàwṭànà' bàṭ̄an sTemlay Dans la peste nos maisons se sont écroulées
121 b'ày šà'tà' rèšà' dķu̇'lè' Cette année commencement de l'enfantement
dmar̄dwàṭà' lzaḫnan dsulè' Des chatiments que notre temps a subits
màwṭànà' bàtan ķrulè' La peste a ruiné nos maisons
122 b'ay šà'tà' d&àwlan zedlè' Cette année où notre faute s'est accrue
Tur̄'è' wdaš̄tàṭà' tleķlè' Monts et plaines elle a ravagés
nàwṭànà' bàtan gweķlè' La peste a dévasté nos maisons

125 šuràyèh m&aqrà' hwèlè Son commencement a été à Aqra
wmek nurà' b'aṭrà' Tpèlè' Comme le feu elle a gagné le pays
dlà' r̄axmè' qTèlè' wspèlè' Sans pitié elle a tué et enflammé

128 kud dweqlè' bmàwSel wšpeķlè' Quand elle a pris Mossoul elle a débordé
'arbi 'alpàȳ'è' kseķlè' Quarante mille elle a décapité
wsàmèh gàw pioz bèķlè' Puis elle a craché son venin sur Pioz
129 beķlè' sàmèh ķtaninà' Elle a craché son venin comme un dragon
bmanzal dpioz &ašinà' Sur le riche pays de Pioz
'weḏlè' 'iqiḏà' wxqinà' Elle l'a rendu brûlé et consumé
130 'esri bnisan mšurèlè' Le 20 avril elle a commencé
wqeTmà' bmàṭà' mdurèlè' Elle a répandu de la cendre sur le village
bmàxàlè' ķtayṭà' šrèlè' Elle s'est établie au quartier d'en-bas

152 kud d'erè' hwèlè' bàlèh Quand elle est revenue elle s'est dirigée
lbayṭà' d'esxaq 'erwàlè' Vers la maison d'Isaac, elle (y) est entrée
'àhu w'ȳ'àlèh qTelwàlè' Lui et ses fils elle a tués
153 kud mbayṭà' d'esxaq pleTlè' Quand elle est sortie de chez Isaac
meķ berqà' mķèlè' wšbeTlè' Comme la foudre elle est tombée et a frappé
&abu w'aķonèh mpurpeTlè' Elle a massacré Abu et son frère
154 tàmà' b'alolà' seqlè' Alors elle a remonté la rue
bsapoilà' dmušè' tpoeqlè' Elle est tombée sur le pauvre Moïse
baytèh melyà' msupeqlè' Sa maison pleine elle a vidée

155 qTelè' tmàn¨è' nap°š¨àţà'   Elle a tué quatre-vingt personnes
    bini gur¨è' wbaḵ¨tàţà'   Parmi elles des hommes et des femmes
    kulay ğwanq¨è' wḵàm¨àţà'   Tous jeunes gens et jeunes filles

156 mbater dmumxèlè' baytèh   Après avoir frappé sa maison
    mtàmà' lteḵ ḵderè' pàtèh   Alors vers le bas elle a tourné sa face
    lḵàwšàbu wbaḵtèh wb¨nàtèh   Vers Khoshabu, sa femme et ses filles

157 'àwà ham baytèh dxèlè'   Cette maison aussi elle a broyée
    wmn tàmà' pleTlè' wtèlè'   Et de là elle est sortie et est venue
    lhormez dalàlà' mḵèlè'   Frapper Hormiz le Colporteur

158 'àhu wham ḵaltèh qTelè'   Lui et sa bru elle a tués
    wlebronèh zarip° bkelè'   Elle a convoité son fils Zarif
    sep° lè' bèh ḵdè'bà' wšqelè'   Avide comme un loup elle l'a emporté

159 mbater dmàxalè' šbeTlè'   Après avoir frappé le quartier
    ḵliSàlè' wmenah pleTlè'   L'avoir achevé et en être sortie
    tàmà' màţà' mxuweTlè'   Alors elle s'est acharnée sur le village

160 tàmà' 'eryàlè' màţà'   Alors elle s'est emparée du village
    wmeḵ ğala'd dsaypèh ḵàţà'   Comme un bourreau au sabre neuf
    kseḵlè' ğwan¨qè' wḵàm¨àţà'   Elle a décapité jeunes gens et jeunes filles

161 ğwan¨qè' wkàm¨àţà' kseḵlè'   Jeunes gens et jeunes filles elle a décapités
    là' bTelè' wqaT neḵlè'   Elle n'a cessé ni pris de repos
    wxemtèh bbay Sàwmu bèḵlè'   Elle a craché son venin chez Somo

162 qTelè' baḵtèh w'aḵonèh   Elle a tué sa femme et son frère
    tetay bnàt¨èh wham bronèh   Ses deux filles et aussi son fils
    šqilà' mek xeţnà' dbegnonèh   Beau comme un marié dans la chambre de noce

163 wkud mbi Slilà' d'erè'   Quand elle est revenue de chez Slila
    lbayţà' dešḅàbèh 'werè'   Elle est entrée chez son voisin
    wḵàSà' dbi ḵàwšu twerè'   Elle a brisé l'échine de Khošu

164 'àhu wham bronèh qTelè'   Lui et son fils elle a tués
    w'àw bayţayhi mbulbelè'   Elle a bouleversé leur maison
    w'arbà' mbi qog ˆà' šqelè'   Quatre de chez Qodja (Blaireau!) elle a pris

165 šqelè' qog ˆà' wtray bnon ¨èh   Elle a pris Qodja et ses deux fils
    'yàl¨è' meTyè' wğwanq¨onè'   Grands enfants et jeunes adolescents
    wham qTelè' baḵt d'àḵonèh   Elle a aussi tué la femme de son frère

166 mtàmà' mbi qogˆà' pleTlè'   Alors elle est sortie de chez Qodja
    wbTapàyà' dsulà' seqlè'   Elle est montée au dépôt de fumier
    wbayţà' dmàm 'àḍàm sxeqlè'   Elle a broyé la maison de Mam Adam

167 sxeqlè' baytèh wḵruwàlè'   Elle a broyé sa maison et l'a ruinée
    w'àhu wkaltèh qTelwàlè'   Lui et sa bru elle a tués
    wrašu bronèh wham 'y¨àlèh   Et son fils Rachu et ses enfants

168 wkud mbi màm 'àdam d'erè'   Quand elle est revenue de chez Mam Adam
    b'aloltà' d'umrà' 'werè'   Dans la rue de l'église elle est passée
    gàw bàt¨è' qeTmà' bderè'   Dans les maisons elle a répandu de la cendre

                                    —

213 ḵqaSàbà' bmàţà' npelè'   Comme un boucher elle est tombée sur le village
    wbyàwmà' wblaylè' là' bTelè'   Ni jour, ni nuit elle n'a cessé
    Tlàţà' 'em¨è' wḵàmši qTelè'   Trois cent cinquante elle a tués

214 kud yàwmà' demSabxiwà'   Tous les jours au matin
    šta'sar šḅa'sar mayţiwà'   Seize, dix-sept mouraient
    wḵàkmà' dlà' qḅàrà' payšiwà'   Certains restaient sans sépulture

215 ḵzàw yà' galeg sur"àyè'   Voyez, ô Chrétiens
    mà' brèlè' bpioz"nàyè'   Ce qui est arrivé aux gens de Pioz
    b'àni zaḇn"è' ḵar"àyè'   En ces derniers temps

—

226 dèk dmàḵewà' 'elayhi   Quand elle les frappait
    mašpelwàlay mḵàylayhi   Elle amoindrissait leurs forces
    wmbalbelwàlay 'ayn"ayhi   Et brouillait leur vue
227 'aynay"hi mbalebliwà'   Leurs yeux se brouillaient
    dxàmrà' kaskun Tam'iwà'   Comme s'ils goûtaient un vin fort
    kud ràwaywà' wnapliwà'   Quand ils étaient ivres ils tombaient
228 napliwà' mèḵ r"awàyè'   Ils tombaient comme des ivrognes
    wpayšiwà' sar"hawàyè'   Ils devenaient agités
    hibay qaT 'iwà' mḵàyè'   Ils n'avaient plus l'espoir de vivre

—

232 mayṭiwà' b'àḍ kurhànà'   Ils mouraient dans cette maladie
    wšayTiwà' bad yuqdànà'   Ils se consumaient dans cette fièvre
    wlaṭ wàlay mapiḵànà'   Il n'y avait rien pour les rafraichir
233 Talbiwà' màyà' màyà'   Ils demandaient de l'eau, de l'eau
    wdem"è' m'aynayh"i beg`ràyà'   Les larmes coulaient de leurs yeux
    là' mxezmay wlà' mnuḵràyà'   (Avec eux) ni parent ni étranger
234 kapniwà' wlayṭ maḵlànà'   Ils avaient faim, et personne pour leur
                                       donner à manger
    wSàhàywà' wlayṭ maštyànà'   Ils avaient soif, et personne pour leur
                                       donner à boire
    wšḇiq"è' bḵeškà' w&amTànà'   Abandonnés dans la sombre ténèbre

—

242 kun 'alàhà' mànèḵ lay   Que Dieu les fasse reposer
    wbay malkutèh mapSeḵ lay   Qu'il les rende heureux dans son royaume
    wbnuhrà' dpàtèh mapqeḵ lay   Qu'il les fasse prospérer à la lumière de sa face
243 mxàsèylay ham qaràyè'   Qu'il pardonne aux gens instruits
    šamàšè' w'esk"ulàyè'   Diacres et écoliers
    whàway qàmèh kalàï"è'   Qu'ils se tiennent devant lui
244 kun ḵaweḵlay ham Tlày"è'   Qu'il joigne les petits enfants
    be'y"àlè' qTï"lè' d&eḇr"àyè'   Aux enfants tués des hébreux
    wyarṭi bmalkutèh ḵày"è'   Qu'ils héritent de la vie dans son royaume
245 wkun màseq lay ham ḵam"àṭà'   Qu'il fasse monter les jeunes filles
    'am b"nàṭà' xakï"màṭà'   Auprès des Vierges Sages
    w'emay hàway ḵur"àṭà'   Qu'avec elles elles soient amies

—

247 kun yàrṭi kulay nyàḵà'   Que tous héritent du repos
    wqànay ḵoš"yè' wpSaḵà'   Et possèdent bonheur et joie
    mbadal &udàbay d'àḵà'   En place de leurs tourments d'ici-bas
248 w'aḵtu mhaymn"è' dSetlàwḵu   Et vous, croyants, qui avez écouté
    mmar"dwàtà' naTeràwḵu   Des épreuves qu'il vous préserve
    lmalkutèh màwseqlawḵu   Qu'il vous fasse monter dans son royaume

Notes

9-10   Cette invocation à la Trinité est à sa place normale, en début du poème; peut-on
voir dans cette insistance sur l'unité de la nature du Christ l'influence de la propagande

romaine, qui aboutira à la reconnaissance par le patriarche chaldéen de l'autorité du pape, au début du 19ème siècle?

12b   Exemple de conjugaison de l'adjectif verbal; les wà insérés dans les formes verbales de 12c, 13a, 13c (et pas 13b!) sont dus à une concordance avec wèwà'.

87c   isràyel se prononce isràyè'.

88c   Citation évangélique purement imaginaire!

90a   Pour une fois, ce wà peut avoir une valeur d'antérieur.

117   màwṯànà' est un nom d'agent de même radical que màwṯà', mort; c'est un masculin; je l'ai traduit par le mot "peste," qui à l'inconvénient d'être féminin, ce qui est ennuyeux surtout dans les passages où le fléau est comparé à un guerrier.

118c   A quel évènement biblique fait-il allusion? A la dernière plaie d'Egypte?

119   Jusqu'au 19ème siècle, les chrétiens syriens comptaient dans l'ère des Séleucides, en avance de 311 ans sur la nôtre; 2049 = 1738; la date en lettre se lit comme un mot ordinaire; ici, on a " au lieu de b pour 2000. En Orient, Alexandre de Macédoine est qualifié de "cornu" (en arabe, ḏū l-qurūn ou ḏū l-qarnayn), les cornes étant le symbole ancien de la puissance — on voit traditionnellement en cela une allusion aux deux parties, européenne et asiatique, de son empire.

120   Qui sont ces rois? La promenade militaire de Nadir Shah en Haute Mesopotamie a eu lieu en 1743, cinq ans après la peste de Pioz.

152ab   Exemple de traduction arabe par Chamir: lammā raja'a tawajjaha / li-bayti Isḥāqa daxala; comparer avec 163b; on peut considérer que l'accord du participe a une valeur de rappel.

152c   Le wà est sûrement introduit par la rime; on remarquera que toutes les rimes de cette strophe sont de nature distincte.

163a   Sàwmu et Slilà' sont synonymes; ils signifient "jeûne."

167b   même phénomène qu'en 152c.

168a   màm veut dire "oncle" en kurde; un titre de respect affectueux.

226c-227a   ambiguïté du passif et de l'actif.

244b   les "Saints Innocents."

246b   Celles de la parabole!

248a   Bel exemple de parfait. La pièce se conclut sans qu'y figure ni la date de composition (visiblement très peu de temps après le fléau), ni la signature du poète; mais la tradition est unanime à l'attribuer à qàšà' Sàwmo.

Références

CHEVALIER 1985   Michel CHEVALIER: *Les montagnards chrétiens du Hakkâri et du Kurdistan septentrional.* Paris: Départment de Géographie de l'Université Paris-Sorbonne

FIEY 1965   Jean Maurice FIEY: *Assyrie Chrétienne.* Beirut: Dar-al-Mashriq

GALLAND 1921   G. GALLAND: "Notice nécrologique du P. Rhétoré," *Année Dominicaine,* p. 201-203

GARBELL 1965   Irene GARBELL: *The Jewish Neo-Aramaic Dialect of Persian Azerbaijan.* The Hague: Mouton

HABBI 1978   Yūsuf ḤABBI: "Udabā' al-sūrith al-awā'il," *Majallah majma' al-lughah al-suryāniyah,* 4, p. 97-120. Bagdad

HADDAD 1980   Potros HADDAD: "Ya'qub 'al-gharīb," *Qàlà' suryàyà'*, no. 23

JACOBI 1973   Heidi JACOBI: *Grammatik des Thumischen Neuaramäisch*. Wiesbaden: Steiner

LIDZBARSKI 1896   Mark LIDZBARSKI: *Die Neu-Aramäischen Handschriften der Königlichen Bibliothek zu Berlin*. Weimar: Felber 1895; Hildesheim: Olms, 1973

MACLEAN 1895   Arthur John MACLEAN: *Grammar of the Dialects of Vernacular Syriac*. Cambridge: University Press, 1895; Amsterdam: Philo Press, 1971

MACLEAN 1901   id.: *Dictionary of the Dialects of Vernacular Syriac*. Oxford: Clarendon Press, 1901; Amsterdam: Philo Press, 1972

MAROGULOV 1935   Konstantin Isaakovitch MAROGULOV: *Grammatiqij qə mədrəsi d gurb*. Moscou; traduit par Olga KAPELIUK: *Grammaire néo-syriaque pour écoles d'adultes*, suppl. *GLECS*, t. 5, Paris: Geuthner, 1976

MINGANA 1933   Alphonse MINGANA: *Catalogue of the Mingana Collection of Manuscripts*. Cambridge: Heffer

ORAHAM 1943   Alexander Joseph ORAHAM: *Oraham's Dictionary of the Stabilized and Enriched Assyrian Language and English*. Chicago

POIZAT 1981   Bruno POIZAT: "Une bibliographie commentée pour le néo-araméen," *C. R. du GLECS*, 18-23, p. 347-414

POIZAT 1985   id.: Littérature néo-syriaque, dans *l'Encyclopédie Larousse des Littératures*, t. 2. Paris: Larousse

RHÉTORÉ 1912   Jacques RHÉTORÉ: *Grammaire de la langue soureth, ou chaldéen vulgaire*. Moussoul: Imprimerie des PP. Dominicains

SARA 1974   Salomon I. SARA: *A Description of Modern Chaldean*. The Hague: Mouton

SACHAU 1896   Eduard SACHAU: "Uber die Poesie in der Volkssprache der Nestorianer," *Sb. der K. Pr. Akad. der Wiss.*, 1, p. 179-215

SACHAU 1899   id.: *Verzeichniss der Orientalischen Handschriften der Königlichen Bibliothek zu Berlin*. Berlin: Asher

SOCIN 1882   Albert SOCIN: *Die neuaramäischen Dialekte von Urmia bis Mosul*. Tübingen

SIMONO 1974   *Meltà' dlisànà' 'atoràyà' swàdàyà' wper'oh*. Tehran; traduit partiellement dans Bruno POIZAT, "Un traité sur le verbe néo-araméen," *C. R. du GLECS*, 18-23, p. 169-192

TSERETELI 1965   *Sovremennyj assirijskij jazyk*, Moskva; traduit par Donatella LOCCHI & Fabrizio A. PENNACCHIETTI, *Grammatica di Assiro Moderno*. Napoli: Istituto Orientale, 1970; et Peter NAGEL, *Grammatik der modernen assyrischen Sprache*. Leipzig: VEB Verlag, 1978

WRITTEN TUROYO

Wolfhart Heinrichs

Among the three branches of Neo-Aramaic (Western, Central, and Eastern) it is only the Eastern branch which—at least in some of its manifestations—can pride itself on a certain historical dimension in that it has several centuries of attested history. This is true for both Christian and Jewish varieties of the language. The vernacular of the plain of Mosul was turned into a written idiom at least since the beginning of the seventeenth century, the time of its earliest attestation, but probably already much earlier, as can be deduced from the fact that, according to reports, this language was no longer fully understood in the nineteenth century due to its archaic features (cf. Macuch 1976, 91). The written form of this language had apparently been created by priests of the so-called school of Alqosh for both Bible translations and religious poetry for the common people. The oldest attested Neo-Aramaic Midrashim of the Kurdistani Jews belong to the same period (Sabar 1976, xxix). In the 1830s another dialect, that of Urmia in Persian Azerbaijan, was made the basis of another written language through the efforts of the American missionaries (Justin Perkins and others) who had been sent by the American Board of Commissioners for Foreign Missions to serve the Nestorian community in those parts. This developed into the most successful of all written Neo-Aramaic languages, and it is still very much alive today, although threatened by emigration and dispersal of its users in the West.

As for the Central branch of Neo-Aramaic and, more particularly, Ṭūrōyo, the language of the Jacobites in the Ṭūr 'Abdīn mountains in southeast Turkey (and the diasporas that have emanated from that region), it has been the prevailing view among specialists dealing with the culture of the Ṭūr 'Abdīn that the vernacular had, until a few years ago, never been reduced to writing. To quote a recent authority, Helga Anschütz in her documentation on the Syrian Christians of the Ṭūr 'Abdīn (Anschütz 1984) says (my translation): "Only recently has the Ṭūrōyo language been put down in transcription through the efforts of Hellmut Ritter and Otto Jastrow; until then it had been transmitted only orally." This statement needs certain qualifications. The first pertains to scholarly writing systems for Ṭūrōyo that precede the period of what we might call the Ritter renaissance in Ṭūrōyo studies. The second qualification refers to the practical writing system that has been devised and used during these past few years, and the third one will point out earlier attempts at writing Ṭūrōyo for practical purposes. Let me take up these three points separately in the order mentioned.

In singling out the work of Ritter and Jastrow, Anschütz has, of course, neglected to mention the respectable volume of Ṭūrōyo texts (in transcription and accompanied by a translation into German) that was published in 1881 by Eugen Prym and Albert Socin (Prym-Socin 1881). Their transcription system was extremely phonetic and detailed, so much so that Adolf Siegel in his *Laut- und Formenlehre des Neuaramäischen Dialekts des Tûr Abdîn* (Siegel 1923) introduced a simplified version of their system without, however, attempting anything like a phonemic way of spelling, for which the times were not yet ripe. But even Hellmut Ritter who initiated the recent revival of Ṭūrōyo studies could not be persuaded to use a phonemic transcription in the edition of his text collection. Ritter was a philologist of the highest caliber, but not a linguist in the modern sense of the word, and it seems to me that he had the feeling that, after a lifetime of dealing with written texts, he now wanted to reproduce a living language right from the mouths of its speakers without imposing on it the abstractions of a phonemic analysis. It is, however, only the first part of his corpus of texts (stories 1-92) which is presented in an elaborate phonetic spelling; the rest is given in a simplified orthography (stories 93-116) in which he dispenses with a great number of diacritics. This was done for practical reasons (Ritter 1967, *39*) and with the express hope that this system would be adopted by the speakers of the language. Indeed, some of Ritter's native informants have used his transcription in their letters to him (see facsimile in Ritter 1967, 36-37). I have no information whether it is still in use. What all this amounts to is the striking fact that in the scholarly field we have so far been presented with two full-fledged phonetic systems and two simplified ones, but with only one phonemic analysis and a transcription system based on it. The latter was devised by Otto Jastrow for his phonology and morphology (including some texts) of the dialect of Midin (Jastrow 1967, ³1985). It should be mentioned in passing that Prym-Socin 1881 and Siegel 1923 represent the town dialect of Miḍyaḍ (Miḍyoyo), while Ritter's collection contains texts in this as well as in the village dialects of ʿIwardo (ʿIwarnoyo), Anḥil (Niḥloyo), Kfarze (Kfarzoyo), Midin (Midwoyo), and of the region called Rāīte (comprising seven villages).

As far as the second rectification of Anschütz's statement is concerned, she had probably not been aware at the time she wrote her book that an effort was under way to create an orthography and a literary language for Ṭūrōyo. This was happening in Sweden where a considerable number of Ṭūrōyo speakers had found asylum and where according to Swedish law their children had the right to be taught at school in their mother tongue. So, in 1983, Dr. Yusuf Ishaq and his collaborators published a primer for first-graders entitled *Toxu qorena* ("Come, let's read") which was followed in 1985 by a workbook *(ktowo d cwodo)*. Prof. Jastrow has been a consultant for developing the spelling, and the result has been a very readable near-phonemic system with a fair, though not excessive, amount of diacritics. The language form chosen for "literarization" is apparently not any one single dialect, but rather a "mixture" (Ausgleichssprache). A form like *qorena* in the title is neither from the Midyaḏ dialect *(qurena)* nor from a village dialect *(qorina)*.

The third point I wanted to raise with reference to the statement of Dr. Anschütz is the main topic of this paper. It is the fact that, practically speaking, Ṭūrōyo had already been written in the last century. I am not alluding here to the Ṭūrōyo manuscripts that were compiled at the instigation of the German orientalist Eduard Sachau, when he was traveling in northern Syria and Mesopotamia (including the Ṭūr ʿAbdīn) in the years 1879-80. But let me briefly dwell on them, because they do have some importance for our main topic. Sachau was interested in the Neo-Aramaic languages, and he was in the habit of asking native informants who were literate to copy or compose manuscripts for him in their own dialects (including the old literary language of Alqosh). This procedure of his did not ingratiate him with the linguists interested in these languages, since in spite of the full vocalization adorning these texts they would have much preferred a collection of phonetically transcribed texts (see, e.g., Rosenthal 1939, 260). As far as Ṭūrōyo is concerned, his texts were all written by one man, a teacher and deacon in the village of Qillith (38 km west of Midyaḏ) by the name of Esha'yo (Isaiah). Most of these texts were apparently translated from Arabic and the Arabic original is included in the manuscripts. In the years 1884 and 1888 the Royal Library in Berlin bought these manuscripts from Sachau, and one of the texts—the Story of Ḥīqār the Wise—was later published by Mark Lidzbarski in a collection of Neo-Aramaic specimens which he had selected from the Sachau codices (Lidzbarski 1896a, 1-77 [Arabic pagination]). This was accompanied by the Arabic version *en face* and a translation into German (Lidzbarski 1896b, 1-41); the vocabulary of the Ṭūrōyo text was entered into the glossary at the end of Vol. 2 (Lidzbarski 1896b, 381-580). The language of the text—on which Lidzbarski did not and could not comment, because the dialect situation was unknown at that time—is the town dialect of Midyaḏ (cf. forms like *ketwi* "I was," *merle'len* "he said to them"—I transliterate the forms in the text, ' = *'ōlaf)*. Another small text from one of the Sachau codices, a translation of Genesis 1, was published in 1893 by Gottheil.

Now, not too long ago I went through the catalogue of Syriac manuscripts at Harvard compiled by M. Goshen-Gottstein, in order to search for Neo-Aramaic materials. Fortunately, the author, in an appendix, has included also the holdings of Syriac manuscripts in the Union Theological Seminary in New York. One entry there, listed as MS Syr 22 "The Gospel of John in Modern Syriac," caught my eye, because the author had added the following footnote: "In contrast to most dialectal volumes in these collections, this one is in the dialect of Tur Abdin. It includes the whole of John starting with 6:25. The pages extant are 23-89. The volume came from the collection of Henry Preserved Smith and is labelled on the outside: unidentified dialect of Modern Syriac. This MS was once listed as MS No. 27" (Goshen-Gottstein 1979, 127). I had Xerox copies made and sent to me for closer inspection. Most importantly for my purposes, the manuscript, though incomplete at the beginning, proved to contain a valuable colophon at the end. It runs as follows (there are a few uncertainties due to words that I could not find in my sources, transliteration: ī = i+y, ū = u+w; hyphens put in to facilitate grammatical analysis):

šrīḥ 'al 'īdeh d-'Eša'yo' b-Medyad qrīto' rabto' d-kityo' b-Ṭūr 'Abdīn d-as-Sūryōye' Ya'qūboye' m-ū-lešono' d-ū-ktowo' ktīw l-ū-lešono' d-ū-Ṭūro' da'reg̃ l-ī-manfa'a' d-ī-melle' d-Ya'qūboye' 'atīqe' [with syāmē] m-ū-'aṣyo' l-ū-msarḥo' d-az-z'ūre' [with syāmē] na'īme' d-fohmīle' w-'ek-ṭolbīna' m-ann-aḥe' [with syāmē] mhayemne' d-moṭe' l-sīdayye' [with syāmē] w-maqbelīle' lag̃an 'ī-manfa'a' d-a'r-roywoto' w-'ektīw 'al 'īde' [with syāmē] d-ūw-A'smar b-ī-madrase' d-kība' mo" na'īmh [sic] b-ī-madrase' d-a'-brūṭ b-š. [= šāto] mšīḥyt' [= mšiḥayto] 1877.

It was translated (?) at the hand of Esha'yo in Miḍyaḍ, the large town, which is in the Tur Abdin of the Jacobite Syrians, from the language which the Book was written (in) into the colloquial language of the Tur for the benefit of the nation *(millet)* of the Ancient Jacobites, from the difficult to the...so that the little children understand it. And we ask from our faithful brethren that it come to them and that they accept it, for the benefit of....And it was written by the hand of Asmar (?) in the school in which there are a hundred children, in the school of the Protestants, in the Christian year 1877.

The first thing to attract my attention was, of course, the date, because—if written in 1877—the manuscript predated the time when Sachau was traveling in those parts (1879-80), and it seemed to prove that attempts at reducing the vernacular to writing had been made, even before the great orientalist came along. I checked Sachau's account of his travel in the Tur and I came upon the following passage which I quote here in translation:

In Ḳyllith there is a school founded and supported by the American Mission in Mardin; it seems to have a very beneficial effect. The teacher at this school was a young man, Shammās (Deacon) Esha'jâ, who at the request of the mission had translated into Ṭôrânî (= Ṭūrōyo), his mother tongue, the Gospel of John; he showed me his manuscript, read some of it to me and later sent me a copy of it. While the men mostly know Kurdish and Arabic alongside with Ṭôrânî, the women and children only speak Ṭôrânî, and, in order to give a book of edification into their hands, the missionaries had commissioned this translation (Sachau 1883, 420; cf. also 410 and 422-23).

When comparing this passage with the colophon of the manuscript, there seems to be little doubt that the two Esha'yos are identical and that our manuscript is exactly the translation mentioned by Sachau, though apparently not in the handwriting of Esha'yo.

The cultural context of early written Ṭūrōyo, then, is clear. The American missionaries who had contributed so much to the development of the Eastern Modern Syriac (later Assyrian) language and literature also seem to have had their share in an attempt to parallel this successful enterprise in the domain of Western Modern Syriac. However, this attempt was undertaken on a much smaller scale; as a matter of fact, it may have been on such a small scale that our text is the only tangible result. Certainly, no printing press for Ṭūrōyo was founded and, as far as we can judge, the whole attempt was abortive. It would be very desirable to locate additional texts and, failing that, to discover further testimony and information on translations in the existing travel literature as well as in the archival materials of the American Board of Commissioners for Foreign Missions, which are now deposited in Harvard's Houghton Library. John Joseph in his study entitled *Muslim-Christian Relations and Inter-Christian Rivalries in the Middle East* (Joseph 1983) has already made ample use of these materials (for our topic see Joseph 1983, 74-78), but he was, of course, not overly interested in the—historically not very important—question of early written Ṭūrōyo.

What is the importance of the text we have before us? I would like to raise three points which would be at the same time topics for further research.

1) On the cultural side, we should ask ourselves why the creation of written Ṭūrōyo was such a timid affair that it went more or less unnoticed until now. Apart from the complicated vicissitudes of missionary history in the area, we should remind ourselves that the literary activities of the Jacobites had moved away from Classical Syriac into Karshuni (Arabic) on a much larger scale than had happened with the Nestorians. In Anatolia the Jacobites also developed Turkish Karshuni—a fact that does not seem to be well known in scholarly circles. All this means that the Jacobite community was linguistically divided into a number of speech-groups with Classical Syriac as church language being their only linguistic common denominator. As opposed to this, the Nestorian (including formerly Nestorian) population was much more homogeneous since—to the best of my knowledge and excluding the South Indian Nestorians—they were all speakers of Eastern Neo-Syriac dialects. They were also stronger in absolute numbers, and it made thus considerably more sense to develop a new literary language for them rather than for the Jacobites.

2) On the linguistic side, one might think that an older attestation of a language could represent an earlier form of that language. A time span of

slightly more than a hundred years is probably not sufficient for major changes to take place. Nevertheless, it might be worthwhile to have a closer look at the vocabulary, especially the loanwords, contained in this text with this in mind.

3) It is always interesting to see how a native speaker of a language deals with its phonetic and phonemic data when trying for the first time to represent it in writing. In our case we have, of course, to keep in mind that the writer lived in the tradition of Classical Syriac which is a closely related language. It is interesting to see that, on many occasions, Esha'yo manages to free himself of the dictates of the prestigious church language. A number of orthographical peculiarities of his system are enumerated in the list below. In this respect it is also noteworthy that the Story of Ḥīqār the Wise, commissioned by Sachau from the same Esha'yo, differs in some details from the spelling of our text, possibly due to the advice of the orientalist (e.g., consistent use of Rukkāḵā and Quššāyā).

The above sheds an interesting light on a hitherto little-known episode in the cultural history of the Ṭūrōyo language and, since historical attestation for it is scarce, even this little piece of evidence should be welcome.

Appendix

List of some of the spelling conventions in MS Syr 99 of the Union Theological Seminary "The Gospel of John in Modern Syriac" (Ṭūrōyo)

1. Geminated consonants are spelled as double consonants. Examples:

də-ḥzalle "that they saw him," spelled *de'ḥzalle'*

mərralle "they said to him," spelled *mirralleh*

Thus also with the plural article:

'a'-'ə́ḡbóne "the miracles," spelled *'a''ūgbone'* (with *syāmē*)

Even in Arabic loanwords:

m'alləm "master," spelled *mū'allem*

b-i-barriyye "in the desert," spelled *bibarriyye'*

2. Initial 'ōlaf is often left out, when preceded by a particle. Examples:

d-ú-bāḥar "of the sea," spelled *dūbaḥar*

d-abre "of his son," spelled *dabreh*

d-ú-isan "of man," spelled *dūysa'n*

d-əxli "that they eat," spelled *dokli*

k-əḏina "we know," spelled *koḏina'*

'i-emo "the mother," spelled *'iyemo'* (note glide)

However:

'ú-ābo "the father," spelled *'ūwa'bo'*

3. Final -a and -o is spelled with an 'ōlaf (-a', -o'), final -e partly as -e' and partly as -eh.

Cf. above *d'eḥzalle'* vs. *mirralleh*.

Also: *'a'le* "on him," spelled *'a'le'*, vs. *mēne* "of it," spelled *meneh*.

4. Medial -ā- is partly spelled -a- and partly -a'-. Examples for -a-:
d-ú-bāḥar spelled *dūbaḥar*
'ab-bābaydan "our fathers," spelled *'abbabaydan* (with *syāmē*)
nāḥət "it has come down," spelled *naḥet*

Examples for -a'-:
də-g-miḏāyə' "which will be lost," spelled *degmida'ye'*
hāno-yo "it is this," spelled *ha'noyo*

5. Prosthetic shwa preceding a consonant cluster is spelled 'e-, the 'ōlaf sometimes being omitted after an initial particle (which in any case may receive the vowel). Examples:
u k-ṭəlbina "and we request," spelled *w-'ek-ṭolbina'*
də-ḥzalle (see under 1) spelled *de'ḥzalle'*
də-g-miḏāyə' (see under 4) spelled *degmida'ye'*

6. Etymological spellings
mərralle spelled *mirralleh* (also *mərlelin* spelled *mirle'len*)
hātu "you (pl.)," spelled *ha'ntū*
kətyo spelled *keytyo* (i.e., the ktib is *kityo* and the qre is *ketyo*)

List of quoted literature

ANSCHÜTZ 1984 - Helga Anschütz: *Die syrischen Christen vom Tur 'Abdin. Eine altchristliche Bevölkerungsgruppe zwischen Beharrung, Stagnation und Auflösung.* Würzburg: Augustinus-Verlag. (= Das östliche Christentum. Neue Folge, Band 34).

GOSHEN-GOTTSTEIN 1979 - Moshe H. Goshen-Gottstein: *Syriac Manuscripts in the Harvard College Library. A Catalogue.* Missoula MT: Scholars Press.

GOTTHEIL 1893 - R. J. H. Gottheil: "The Judaeo-Aramaean Dialect of Salamās" in *JAOS* 15, 306-310 (for the Ṭūrōyo text).

ISHAQ 1983 - Yusuf Ishaq et alii: *Toxu qorena.* Stockholm: Skolöverstyrelsen.

ISHAQ 1985 - Yusuf Ishaq et alii: *Toxu qorena. Ktowo d cwodo. A.* Stockholm: Statens Institut för Läromedelsinformation.

JASTROW 1985 - Otto Jastrow: *Laut- und Formenlehre des neuaramäischen Dialekts von Midin im Ṭūr 'Abdin.* 3., ergänzte Auflage. Wiesbaden: Harrassowitz. [appeared first in 1967]

JOSEPH 1983 - John Joseph: *Muslim-Christian Relations and Inter-Christian Rivalries in the Middle East. The Case of the Jacobites in an Age of Transition.* Albany: SUNY Press.

LIDZBARSKI 1896a and 1896b - Mark Lidzbarski: *Die neu-aramäischen Handschriften der Königlichen Bibliothek zu Berlin. In Auswahl herausgegeben, übersetz und erläutert.* Erster Band (Texte). Zweiter Band (Ubersetzungen und Glossar). Weimar: Felber. (= Ergänzungshefte zur Zeitschrift für Assyriologie. Semitistische Studien hrsg. von Carl Bezold. Heft 4/9).

MACUCH 1976 - Rudolf Macuch: *Geschichte der spät- und neusyrischen Literatur.* Berlin u. New York: de Gruyter.

PRYM-SOCIN 1881 - Eugen Prym und Albert Socin: *Der neu-aramaeische Dialekt des Ṭûr 'Abdîn.* Erster Teil: Die Texte. Zweiter Teil: Ubersetzung. Göttingen: Vandenhoeck und Ruprecht.

RITTER 1967, 1969, 1971 - Hellmut Ritter: *Ṭûrōyo. Die Volkssprache der syrischen Christen des Ṭûr 'Abdîn.* A: Texte. Band I-III. Wiesbaden: Steiner.

ROSENTHAL 1939 - Franz Rosenthal: *Die aramaistische Forschung seit Th. Nöldeke's Veröffentlichungen.* Leiden: Brill.

SABAR 1976 - Yona Sabar: *Pəsaṭ Wayəhi Bəsallah. A Neo-Aramaic Midrash on Beshallah (Exodus).* Introduction, Phonetic Transcription, Translation, Notes and Glossary. Wiesbaden: Harrassowitz.

SACHAU 1883 - Eduard Sachau: *Reise in Syrien und Mesopotamien.* Leipzig: Brockhaus.

SIEGEL 1923 - Adolf Siegel: *Laut- und Formenlehre des neuaramäischen Dialekts des Tûr Abdin.* Hannover: Lafaire. (= *Beiträge zur semitischen Philologie und Linguistik* hrsg. von G. Bergsträsser. Heft 2).

TUROYO - FROM SPOKEN TO WRITTEN LANGUAGE
Yusuf Ishaq

The Turoyo-speaking community—background

Turoyo, as it is known among the people both in their homeland and the diaspora, is a Neo-Aramaic language, spoken originally by Christians in an area called Tur Abdin. This area is located in a mountainous region in the southeastern part of Turkey, in the province of Mardin. Here, the Turoyo-speaking community is settled in the town of Midyat and in some thirty villages surrounding it. The predominant church among the Christians in the Tur Abdin area is the Syrian Orthodox. As a result of World War II and continual emigration, the Turoyo-speaking community has drastically dwindled in size, and in recent decades the number of emigrants has exceeded the number of the group remaining in the homeland. Thousands of Turoyo speakers moved to neighboring countries such as Syria (especially Qamishli near the borders south of Midyat and Aleppo) and Lebanon (mainly Beirut and Zahle) where they found life more convenient than in Tur Abdin. In the early fifties and sixties, a small group also resided in Istanbul in search of better professional opportunities and a good education for their children. Many others turned to the European countries, North and South America, and Australia.

The Turoyo-speaking community in Sweden

The Turoyo-speaking communities in Sweden are found in about sixty different localities, among them Södertälje, Stockholm, Gothenburg, Jönköping, Västerås and Hallstahammar.

The first organized group entered Sweden in 1967 by special recommendation of the World Council of Churches (WCC) and the UN High Commissioner for Refugees (HCR). The group was comprised of about two hundred refugees from Lebanon who originally came from Iraq, Syria and Turkey. During the following years, a non-organized family-uniting immigration continued.

In 1975, large-scale immigration from both Turkey and West Germany started. According to the National (Swedish) Labor Market Board (AMS), during the year 1976 Sweden received approximately six thousand Turkish Syrians. They formed the largest group of immigrants since the arrival of

189

Hungarian refugees after the revolt of 1956. The members of the Turoyo-speaking community are not considered as political refugees (A-refug.) but as humanitarian refugees (B-refug.).

In February 1976, the Swedish government granted asylum to two thousand Turkish Syrians. At the same time, a compulsory visa system for Turkish citizens was introduced.

In spite of the stiffening of the regulations, an additional fifteen hundred Turkish Syrian refugees found their way to Sweden by October 1976. And since Denmark had no compulsory visa system for Turks, the immigration to Sweden via Denmark was able to continue.

In mid-November 1976, the Swedish government gave a clear sign that an additional two thousand Turkish Syrians could stay in the country. At the same time it was decided that no more Turkish Syrians except direct relatives were to be received in Sweden. Nevertheless, the immigration continued illegally.

In 1978, the number of Syrian immigrants had risen to about seven thousand. In 1980, according to information furnished by municipalities and their own churches, their number exceeded twelve thousand. Today, some estimate that the total number of the community surpasses eighteen thousand.

Home language teaching policy in Sweden

Of all the European countries coming into contact with various groups of immigrants, only Sweden has made a unique adjustment in its educational policy towards the newcomers. The major change in education aimed at immigrants took place during the years 1972-1976.

In 1976, the Swedish Parliament (Riksdag) decided that children and young people from immigrant families were to be given better opportunities to preserve and develop their native language. Due to this policy, Sweden now has one of the most progressive systems of bilingual education in the world.

As a matter of fact, Swedish authorities are convinced that bilingualism is an important target and that immigrant children need to be bilingual so that, when they grow up, they will be able to decide for themselves to what extent they wish to identify with Swedish culture, on the one hand, or to preserve the language, traditions and customs of their own group, on the other. Bilingualism has no doubt become one of the chief aims of immigrant education.

The purpose of home language teaching

The curriculum for the compulsory school of 1980 defines the purpose and the goals of home language teaching as follows:

> The purpose of instruction in home language is for the pupils to develop their language so that it will provide them with a means of growing into

individuals with a strong sense of identity and a clear opinion of themselves, their group identity and their living situation.

According to the curriculum (LGR 80), home language instruction is meant to help the pupils retain contact with their families and their language group, because a child's language is closely bound up with his or her personality and living situation. If this link is broken, both linguistic and personal development are stunted. Therefore, one of the important aims of home language instruction is to strengthen the pupils' self-esteem so that they will be unafraid to express themselves and to stand up for their opinions.

They also have to be helped to cope with linguistic and cultural strain which membership in a minority can entail, to be able to identify with two or more cultures and languages and to turn this into a beneficial experience, and to attain understanding of the living conditions and patterns of life in the country of origin.

The importance of home language instruction

It has been established among Swedish educators that home language instruction is very important even for further studies. They think it is more difficult for immigrant children than for Swedish to develop their own language because they speak a certain language at home with their families and another one with their Swedish friends and classmates.

They are also convinced that it is not only during childhood that people learn their home language. Language learning is a lifelong process. A child's home language is, in fact, not complete when he starts school. Therefore, it is very important for immigrant children to be given help in practicing and developing their home language even after they have begun to learn Swedish.

It has also been observed that not until the child is sure of his or her home language can he or she begin learning another language properly. If the child has a proper knowledge of one language (the home language), it becomes easier for him to learn another one. But if the child does not know the first language and he is only helped to learn Swedish, the Swedish he acquires will no doubt be limited. Language, as it is regarded by the educators, is an essential part of individual development as well as of human culture. This is the reason it is so important for immigrant children to be given special help in practicing their mother tongue, not only in school but in pre-school as well. Immigrant pupils are in danger of losing contact with their parents and their relatives because they no longer share a common language with them. For this and other reasons, the educational authorities, municipalities and other institutions in Sweden encourage home language instruction.

Home language practice on the pre-school and elementary school levels

The home language practice in pre-school plays a key role in the language learning process. In pre-school, children are given an opportunity to be together with other children and adults who speak the same language. Home language practice is, as a matter of fact, an integral part of pre-school activities, and the major duty of the home language teacher is to give help and stimulus. At pre-school level, home language practice can be organized for six-year-old immigrant children. In some municipalities, home language practice is also available for even younger children. In many cases, children have an opportunity to attend a single-language nursery school where children and the majority of the staff speak the same language. But when the immigrant children attend nursery school together with Swedish children, a home language teacher comes to meet with them once or twice every week. Moreover, the immigrant children on the elementary level are given a study guidance in their home language. This means that the immigrant pupil can be given lessons in different subjects in his or her own language. He or she can also be helped to understand Swedish textbooks and the wording of questions and tasks.

Home language teaching in Sweden is organized freely. Each municipality decides for itself how to run home language lessons. Diverse situations play a big role in planning. The home language teaching process depends on how many children there are in each language group and on how many are enrolled for voluntary home language practice periods. Planning is, of course, also affected by the children's ages and by their previous knowledge of their home language. If there is a sufficient number of pupils in the same grade belonging to the same language group, the school might organize preparatory classes in which most lessons are given in the home language.

All children, however, at the elementary school level are enrolled in ordinary Swedish classes. A large number of immigrant children attend the ordinary class and then get auxiliary Swedish lessons and home language guidance if necessary. If there is a large number of children in one grade belonging to the same language, the school then may plan for composite classes. A composite class usually includes a certain number of Swedish pupils and a group of immigrants. Both Swedish and home language teachers plan and conduct the teaching together. Home language lessons and home language study guidance are handled by the home language teacher so that immigrant children in this case receive more instruction in their mother tongue than they would in an ordinary Swedish class. Furthermore, if there is a sufficient number of immigrant pupils in the same grade and belonging to the same group, the municipality or the school administration itself can organize several preparatory classes in which most lessons are given in the home language. The school can also put children from the same language group in one and the same school. In this case, not all children will get the chance to attend the school nearest home; instead they will have the opportunity of receiving more teaching in their mother tongue.

The present arrangement is based in general on the principle that home language instruction must be optional. The immigrant children are entitled to extra Swedish lessons as well as tutoring in other subjects if the need arises. If the children cannot speak Swedish at all, they may be enrolled in a preparatory class for a certain period of time until they are ready to keep up with their ordinary class. The option for home language instruction applies in principle to all compulsory levels of education (1-3, 4-6, 7-9), as well as to the pre-school and the upper secondary school level. In grades 7-9 the home language instruction replaces two periods of other subjects, either compulsory or elective.

In 1979 the Swedish National Board of Education reported that at the compulsory school level there were twenty home language classes which had pupils of Turoyo-speaking origin. The educational authorities at Södertälje (a city south of Stockholm in which some four to five thousand Turoyo speakers reside) gave the following information about the enrollment figures for the home language program: Finnish, 1600; Syriac, 450; Arabic, 40; and Turkish, 15. In 1986 and 1987, the number of Syriac pupils in the compulsory school *(grundskolan)* in Södertälje is 1156 with about 48 home language teachers.

The Turoyo project

1) *The orthography*

Following recommendations made by experts on behalf of the Turoyo-speaking children with regard to the lack of teaching materials in that language, the Swedish National Board of Education resolved in 1981 to help these children by introducing Turoyo language instruction in schools attended by Turoyo-speaking children. The author of this paper was chosen to head a committee consisting of four home language teachers, selected from different schools, that was set up to develop textbooks and reading materials for Turoyo instruction. The first prerequisite of my work was to develop an orthography for the Turoyo project. After a considerable period of time, my research led to the following result:

a) *The consonants*

Symbol	Phonetic definition and comments	Syriac	Arabic
B b	Voiced bilabial plosive. Ex: babo [bá:bo]—father.	ܒ	ب
C c	Voiced pharyngeal fricative. (No English equivalent) Ex: cabër ['á:br̩]—he entered.	ܥ	ع
C č	Voiceless palato-alveolar affricate— pronounced like Eng. ch, "church." Ex: čiroke [tʃi.róke]—story.	ܫ̰	چ
D d	Voiced dental plosive. Ex: dahwo [dǽhuo]—gold.	ܕ	د

Ḏ ḏ	Voiced interdental fricative—pronounced like th in Eng. "this." Ex: ḏayëb [ðá:ib]—melt.	ڎ	ذ
Ḍ ḍ	Voiced pharyngealized interdental fricative—it is like ḏ with the addition of velarization. Ex: ḍayfo [ḍáifo]—guest.	ڏ-ڎ	ظ /ض
F f	Voiceless labiodental fricative. Ex: fayë̃s [fá:iʃ]—he stayed, remained.	ڢ	ڤ
G g	Voiced dorso-velar plosive. Ex: gelo [gé:lo]—grass.	ܓ	ܔ
G ǧ	Voiced velar fricative—it is like x with the addition of voicing. Ex: ǧalabe [ɤǽlabe]—much, plenty.	ܞ	غ
H h	Voiceless glottal fricative. Ex: hawxa [hǽuˌxa]—so, thus.	ܗ	ه
Ḥ ḥ	Voiceless pharyngeal fricative—an emphatic h pronounced with a strong and sustained expulsion of the breath. Ex: ḥawro [ḥǽuˌro]—friend.	ܚ	ح
J j	Voiced palatal affricate. Ex: jule [dʒú:le]—clothes.	ܓ	ج
K k	Voiceless velar plosive. Ex: kalbo [kǽlbo]—dog.	ܟ-ܞ	ك
L l	Voiced dental lateral. Ex: loqëṭ [łó:qit]—to pick up with the beak.	ܠ	ل
M m	Voiced bilabial nasal. Ex: malko [mǽlko]—king.	ܡ	م
N n	Voiced apico-dental nasal— Ex: niŝe [ni:ʃe]—women.	ܢ	ن
P p	Voiceless bilabial plosive. Ex: paṯyo [p'ǽθio]—broad, wide.	ܦ	پ
Q q	Voiceless uvular plosive—produced by making contact between the back of the tongue and the uvula. Ex: qolo [qó:lo]—voice.	ܩ	ق
R r	Voiced alveolar tremulant. Ex: rabo [rá:bo]—big, large, adult, great.	ܪ	ر
S s	Voiceless dental fricative. Ex: sowo [só:o]—an old man.	ܣ	س
Ṣ ṣ	Voiceless pharyngealized dental fricative—an emphatic s pronounced with the teeth slightly apart, pressing the tip of the	ܨ	ص

tongue against the lower teeth and raising
the tongue to press also against the upper
teeth and palate.
Ex: ṣacro [ṣáʿro]—hair.

S š Voiceless palato-alveolar fricative.
š is pronounced like the sh in Eng. "rush."
Ex: šëmšo [ʃəmʃo]—sun.

T t Voiceless dental plosive.
Ex: tarco [t'ǽrʿo]—door.

Ṭ ṭ Voiceless pharyngealized dental plosive.
(No English equivalent)
Ex: ṭuro [ʈúːro]—mountain.

T̲ t̲ Voiceless interdental fricative—
pronounced like th in English "thin."
Ex: t̲awbo [θǽubo]—piece of cloth, roll
cloth.

W w Labialized velar semivowel—pronounced like
w in English "way."
Ex: warzo [uǽrzo]—melon field.

X x Voiceless velar fricative—pronounced like
ch in Scottish "loch" or German "ach."
Ex: xabro [xǽbro]—word, news.

Y y Palatal semivowel—like English y in "yell."
Ex: yawmo [iǽumo]—day.

Z z Voiced dental fricative—pronounced like the z
in English "zeal."
Ex: zayto [záːito]—oil.

Z ż Voiced palato-alveolar fricative—pronounced
like the s in English "pleasure."
Ex: żabaš [ʒǽbæʃ]—watermelon.

b. *The vowels*

Symbol	Phonetic definition and comments	Syriac	Arabic

I i Voiced close front unrounded vowel.
Ex: biro [biːro]—well.

E e Voiced half-closed front unrounded vowel.
Ex: lebo [leːbo]—heart.

E ë Voiced half-closed central unrounded vowel.
Ex: kërfo [kʿúrfo]—snake.

A a Voiced open central unrounded vowel.
Ex: babo [báːbo]—father.

O o Voiced half-closed back rounded vowel.
Ex: ṭuro [ʈúːro]—mountain.

U u   Voiced close back rounded vowel.
        Ex: ṭuro [ṱúːro]—mountain.

2) *The school book*

In 1983, the first school book in the Turoyo language was compiled, tested by experts and then published by the Swedish National Board of Education. The book was called *Toxu Qorena!* ("Come Let's Read!"). The Turoyo-speaking children who were introduced to the book showed great interest in it and made distinctive progress in their reading and writing skills as compared to what they had achieved in written Syriac.

During the year 1984-85, the committee prepared a workbook to accompany the first textbook; this was called *Toxu Qorena! A* and published by the Swedish National Institute for Teaching Material Information (SIL); like the first book, it proved to be very useful.

In 1986-87 another workbook in this series of reading materials was composed by two members of the committee and myself and sent to the printing house under the title *Toxu Qorena! B.*

The committee has plans also for a second reading book, *Toxu Qorena! 2* and some additional materials, as well as children's books, short stories and a concise Turoyo grammar.

3) *The Swedish-Turoyo Dictionary*

Among the more interesting teaching materials in the Turoyo project is the *Swedish-Turoyo Dictionary*. This mini-dictionary is, in fact, one of a series of dictionaries especially composed to cover the demands of immigrant education. It offers the basic vocabulary necessary for primary education, which aims at laying a strong foundation for genuine bilingualism. It is comprised of about 4500 entries selected from the 17,000 words of the basic Swedish dictionary. The Swedish "vocabulary, compiled by the Department of Computational Linguistics at the University of Gothenburg, contains frequently used words as well as words which are related to conditions in Swedish society, important to immigrants trying to find their way in Swedish society" (from the introduction to the *Swedish-Turoyo Dictionary*).

The entries in this mini-dictionary are provided with the following linguistic information: pronunciation, full inflectional forms, explanation by phrases or synonyms, stylistic values and grammatical explanations and examples of usage in compound phrases, sentences and idioms.

The dictionary also has a picture supplement containing sixty-four pages of illustrations, mostly in four-color print. The illustrations and pictures are presented thematically under thirty-two headings such as the family, the human body, animals, birds, at the bank, etc.

The complete Swedish dictionary serves as a teaching tool in schools for pupils from the age of ten upward. The complete lexicon vocabulary has been used as the basis for at least three major dictionaries: Turkish, Serbo-Croat and Croat. The mini-version, of about 7600 entries, has been translated into Turoyo and several other languages of the immigrants in Sweden.

The dictionary project was initiated by the Swedish National Board of Education (SO) under the name *Språklexikon för invandrare* (LEXIN) and carried out in cooperation with the National Swedish Institute for Teaching Material Information (SIL), the National Immigration and Naturalization Board (SIV) and several university departments and consultants.

The development work on the dictionary project came to fruition in 1984. Later SIL carried the main responsibility for publishing the finished dictionaries in cooperation with both SO and SIV.

The translation into Turoyo was made by the author of this article and the above-mentioned committee. During that work we obviously faced many serious problems because Turoyo is a spoken language without any literary tradition. Thus, there existed no dictionaries for special fields, no teaching materials, no textbooks, except the first Turoyo school book compiled by the committee itself and a few other studies written on Turoyo or on one of its dialects by a number of well-known orientalists, among them the late Prof. Hellmut Ritter and our colleague Prof. Otto Jastrow of Erlangen University. We endeavored to find suitable names for birds, fish, animals, trees, flowers, besides a number of technical, political and social terms. Here are a few examples:

nënto d maye halye = perch
qundus kalbo dam maye = beaver
tëḥwiyo   = demonstration
safruno b ṣadro smoqo = bullfinch
taḥbarṭo   = trade union
maṣarto   = association
fasoqto   = comma

As soon as the translation was completed and checked thoroughly, the National Swedish Institute for Teaching Material Information invited a larger group from different occupations and walks of life to examine the finished translation and give their comments and recommendations. The group was as enthusiastic as the committee itself and, at the end of our long discussions, we received a number of useful suggestions which afterwards were incorporated into the text.

As a last step in the process of examining the dictionary the manuscript was forwarded to Prof. Otto Jastrow, who in turn was kind enough to read through the whole work and contribute many valuable suggestions.

The Swedish-Turoyo Dictionary has now found its way to the printing house after a long process of examination and re-examination, and there are now hundreds of Turoyo-speaking children and adults in Sweden waiting to make use of it.

4) *The Turoyo language used*

The authors of the series *Toxu Qorena!*, the *Swedish-Turoyo Dictionary* and several other reading materials have not chosen a specific dialect of the Turoyo language in composing the books mentioned. Rather, they have used a mixed (town-village) Turoyo which is now growing and developing among the emigrants in different countries, especially among children and young people.

This mixed dialect is in fact becoming very common among the people for the reason that the previously existing barriers between town and village in Tur Abdin are now completely removed in the countries of emigration. Children of different traditional dialects are now living in one and the same quarter of a Swedish city or town, attending the same school and having several teachers for home language instruction coming from various traditional dialects.

The spoken Turoyo has, however, been affected by written Syriac during the last two decades. The church schools in Qamishli and Aleppo (Syria), Mar Severios College in Beirut (Lebanon) and different schools in several municipalities in Sweden, who introduced written Syriac as a "mother tongue" about fifteen years ago, have indeed left a strong mark on what we call "mixed Turoyo." The trend of substituting Arabic, Turkish, and Kurdish loanwords with written Syriac equivalents is a direct result of this influence.

The authors of the above-mentioned books are convinced that this mixed, middle-of-the-road dialect of Turoyo is going to dominate gradually among the upcoming generation of emigrants. The young people have already started expressing themselves in the "mixed dialect" by composing songs and poems and writing short stories in it.

Works Cited

ISHAQ, Yusuf, *et al.: Toxu Qorena.* Stockholm: Skolöverstyrelsen, 1983.

ISHAQ, Yusuf, *et al.: Toxu Qorena A (Ktowo d cwodo A).* Stockholm: Statens Institut för Läromedelsinformation, 1985.

ISHAQ, Yusuf, *et al.: Toxu Qorena B (Ktowo d cwodo B).* Stockholm: Statens Institut för Läromedelsinformation, 1987.

ISHAQ, Yusuf, *et al.: Svensk-turabdinskt Lexikon. Leksiqon Swedoyo-Suryoyo.* Stockholm: Statens Institut för Läromedel 1988.

JASTROW, Otto: *Laut- und Formenlehre des neuaramäischen Dialekts von Midin im Tur 'Abdin.* 3rd edition. Wiesbaden: Otto Harrassowitz, 1985.

JASTROW, Otto: "The Turoyo Language Today," *Journal of the Assyrian Academic Society* 1 (1985-86).

KUIPERS, Florence: *A Comparative Lexicon of Three Modern Aramaic Dialects.* Thesis nr. 5325, Washington D.C., May 1983.

KUIPERS, Florence: *A Survey of Turkish Syriac.* Report submitted to the Department of Linguistics, Georgetown University, December 17, 1979.

NORDELL, Siv: *Behovsanalys angående undervisning av Assyriska- Syrianska elever inom Ungdomsskolan.* Stockholm: SO, Läromedelssektionen, 1982.

Sociologiska institutionen, Göteborgs Universitet: Assyrier-vilka är de. Nelhans (red.) Forskningsrapport nr. 45.

Skolöverstyrelsen: *Invandrarna och utbildningsväsendet.* Handlingsprogram för SO: s arbete med invandrarfrågor, 1979.

Skolöverstyrelsen: LGr. 80 "Home Language," 1 (5). (From the curriculum for the compulsory school 1980)

Skolöverstyrelsen: *Organization and Planning for Home Language Instruction and Auxilliary Swedish Lessons in Compulsory School.* A memorandum, May 1979.

Skolöverstyrelsen: *The Swedish School System.* Fact sheet published by the Swedish National Board of Education, Information section, S 106 42, Stockholm.

Utvandringen av Syrisk-Ortodoxa och andra kristna från Turkiet och Mellan-Ostern. Ett faktaunderlag sammanställt inom regeringskansliet.

Appendix

<table>
<tr><td>

٢.
</td><td>

١.
</td></tr>

<tr><td>

٤.
</td><td>

٣.
</td></tr>

<tr><td>

٩.
</td><td>

٨.
</td></tr>

<tr><td>

١١.
</td><td>

١٠.
</td></tr>

<tr><td>

١٣.
</td><td>

١٢.
</td></tr>
</table>

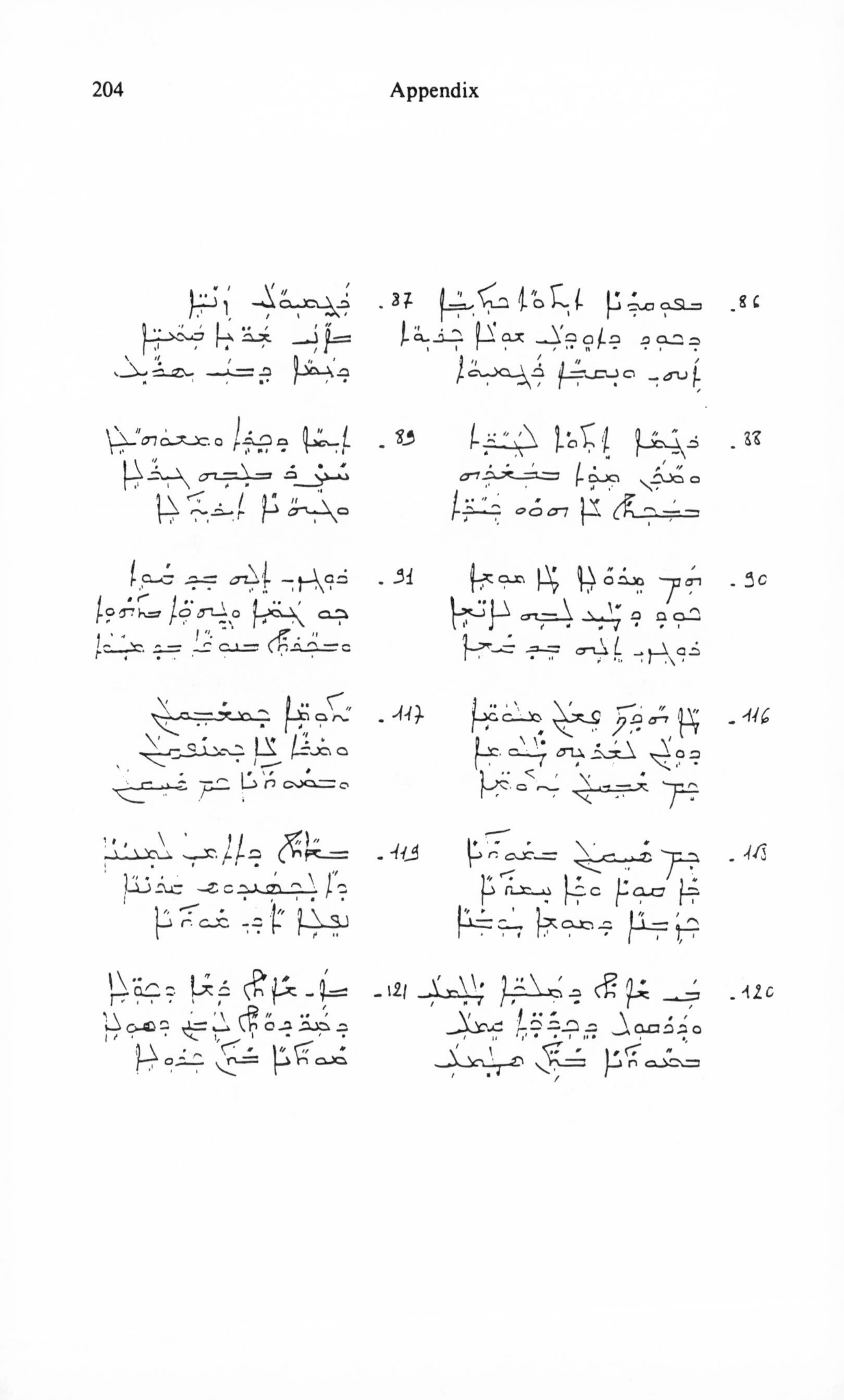

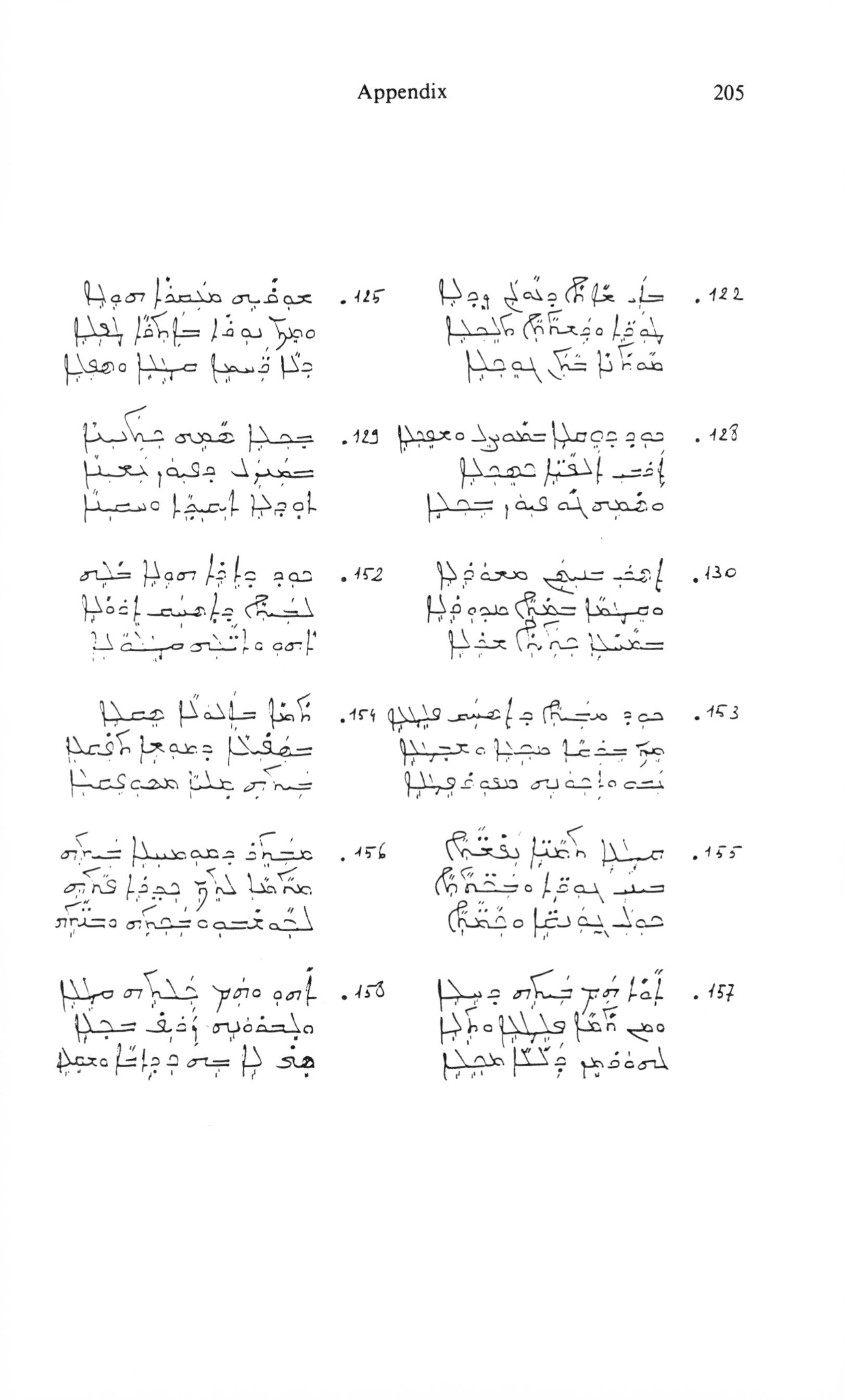

159.

160.

161.

162.

163.

164.

165.

166.

167.

168.

213.

214.

 226. | .225
 |
 |

 228. | .227
 |
 |

 233. | .235
 |
 |

 242. | .236
 |
 |

 244. | .243
 |
 |

 247. | .246
 |
 |